Starfish Publishing Company
5621 Delmar, Ste. 110
St. Louis, MO 63112-2660
(314) 367-9611

TAMING THE DRAGONS
Real Help for Real School Problems

by
Susan Setley, M.Sp.E.

Grateful acknowledgment is made for permission to reprint the following:

"Battle Cries" and "Taming the Dragon," written by Nancy Eggleston.

Material from *Diagnostic and Statistical Manual of Mental Disorders, Fourth Edition.* American Psychiatric Association, Washington, D.C., 1994.

Material from *How to Reach and Teach ADD/ADHD Children* by Sandra F. Rief. The Center for Applied Research in Education, West Nyack, NY, 1993.

Cover design by Lanny Chambers
Selected art by Diane W. Alcorn
Cover model: Jonathan Hummel

Publisher's Cataloging in Publication Data

Setley, Susan, M.Sp.E.
  Taming the Dragons: Real Help for Real School Problems / Susan Setley, M.Sp.E.—1st edition
      p.   cm.
      Illustrated
      Includes bibliographic references
      Includes index
      ISBN 1-886243-04-2

    Summary: A guide for parents of children who struggle with schoolwork, emphasizing grades K–8. Includes detailed information on the nature of learning disabilities and attentional disorders as they affect a child's school progress along with detailed instructions across multiple skills and subjects for parents who want help their child master their schoolwork.

    1. Learning disabled children—education.   2. Attention-deficit-disordered children—education.
    3. Education—parent participation.
    I. Setley, Susan, M.Sp.E., 1945–   II. Title
    LBxxxx.xxxxx   1995
    LCCN: 94-092425
    DDSCN: 371.9
    ISBN 1-886243-04-2

10 9 8 7 6 5 4 3 2

Printed in the United States of America

Dedication

This book is dedicated to Tina Fredericks, Mary Lou Bauer and all the participants at S.T.A.R.T., St. Louis, MO. Neither Mary Lou or Tina think or state the words "I give up!" Mary Lou, Tina and the participants at S.T.A.R.T. are living lessons in determination, perseverance and courage.

About the Author

Susan Setley, M.Sp.E., is an educator and a parent who has sat on both sides of the table—as a teacher telling parents about their child's difficulties; as a parent listening while the specialists told her about her children's learning and attentional problems.

Mrs. Setley has taught children and adults with behavior, learning and/or attentional problems since 1970. In 1973 she earned her master's degree in special education from Southern Illinois University. Since then she's continued her education with seminars and post-graduate courses.

Mrs. Setley began work on *Taming the Dragons* after writing out simple instructions for the parents of her learning disabled students to use at home. Those instructions eventually evolved into the book.

Her unique background both as an educator and as a parent of children who have faced difficulties has given her a special perspective of the problems parents face as they cop with their children's learning problems.She has been married since 1978 to Frank Clark, and they have two daughters.

In addition to *Taming the Dragons*, Mrs. Setley's writing has appeared in newspapers and magazines. Mrs. Setley can be contacted online through America On Line™ as SusanS29, and via the INTERNET at SusanS29@AOL.com.

Acknowledgments

It's not easy to say thank you, because the words seem so inadequate.

People rarely think about the technical skills that go into producing a book, but of course we had to. Diane Alcorn put heart and soul as well as extraordinary effort into the art work she did for us, and her dragon has become the company mascot.

Lanny Chambers did most of the present cover design. He gave generously and graciously of his considerable graphic design talents, and in fact there would have been no book without his guidance. For this he was paid a pittance and often gave of his time and knowledge out of friendship, accompanied by heavy doses of humor and wit. Where the page layout and typesetting look good, the credit goes to Lanny.

Linda Chambers, whom we nicknamed "Eagle Eyes," made an outstanding proof-reader. Any errors remaining are either because she was right but we didn't realize it, or because we made changes after the manuscript had passed under her microscope.

Dan Barger critiqued the first three chapters—and taught me more about writing in the process than I had learned in the previous ten years. I'll always be grateful for the encouragement he gave when I had just begun to write. Special thanks also go to Deb Morris, whose positive energy kept me going when it seemed there would be no way to finish this book.

My lifelong friend Barbara Arrowsmith, my sister Judy Wright and my husband Frank Clark, as well as newer but treasured friends Mary Bowman-Kruhm and Charlie Self, all gave the most precious gift anyone can give—their full and undivided time, day after day—by reading and commenting on the manuscript. They didn't let me get away with anything, and I thank them for it. Mary and Charlie deserve special mention because they have never met me except in the virtual writer's community of America-On-Line. To do so much for a person one has never met face-to-face requires exceptional heart.

Special mention also goes to Kenneth Shore, Psy. D., Judith Hummel, M.S., and Michael Foreman M.D. Their expertise improved the book. Leslie Glassberg, Psy.D. was always ready to look at the manuscript from the beginnings of the first idea to the final format. Her comments were always helpful and incisive, and the book is better for her suggestions.

There are some people whose support was so unending, so tireless, so unwavering, that words completely fail. My sister Judy and friend Barbara get another mention here, as well as Barbara's mother Bobbye Kelly, the project's self-appointed head cheerleader. Mary Daum, editor of ADD-ONS, should be mentioned, as well as Carroll Nahre and her husband John Nahre M.D., whose research assistance was invaluable.

Jim Salvas' on-line assistance has been persistent and invaluable. Nancy Eggleston, good friend now as well as talented poet, generously allowed me to print her moving poem for the book's introduction—and then wrote another, equally moving poem to close it. Ralph Copleman's expertise in the field of communication has been invaluable, but that's nothing compared to the overwhelming outpouring of support and friendship I have received from him.

Special thanks to Dr. John Jacob, wherever he is, who taught me to be an educational detective.

Finally, the only people more remarkable than my friends are my family. My husband Frank and my daughters Alison and Sharyn had plenty of reason to complain about the burdens my project placed on the family, but they never did. Words can't express my gratitude for having them in my life.

My heartfelt thanks to all; there would have been no book without you.

Starfish Publishing Company
gratefully acknowledges the assistance of the
St. Louis County Economic Council.

Warning—Disclaimer

This book is intended to be only one of many possible sources of information for the reader. It is not intended to substitute for appropriate medical, educational or psychological care, nor does it purport or claim to be the final and definitive word on any educational, psychological or medical matter.

It is not the purpose of this book to present all possible explanations or solutions for any problem addressed in the book. The reader is specifically advised to read all available information, learn as much as possible about the subjects covered and seek advice from those involved in your child's care and education before following any course of action, including ideas offered in this book.

Every effort has been made to make this book as accurate as possible, but the author does not intend to have this book used as the parent's only guide for information. She specifically encourages parents to seek professional help for any struggling child. *Any parents who choose to use this book in lieu of professional help and guidance for their child are advised that they may be doing their child a grave disservice.*

Therefore, parents who use these suggestions in spite of advice to the contrary from professionals do so at their own risk. The author cannot be held responsible for parents who either do not seek professional help for their child or who choose to disregard the advice they are given by those professionals.

Since the book represents only one of many approaches to solving educational problems, the author and Starfish Publishing shall have neither liability nor responsibility to any person or entity with respect to any loss or damage caused, or alleged to be caused, directly or indirectly by the information contained in this book.

> *If you do not wish to be bound by the above,*
> *you may return this book to the publisher for a refund.*

Table of Contents

Table of Contents

Battle Cries
by Nancy Eggleston

I'm sitting at my desk and I can hear the teacher say
that we'll be writing stories about dinosaurs today!
"Yes! I cry, "That's great!" and I begin to sort my thoughts
while Teacher gives directions
    about subjects, forms and plots.

But I'm already off in lands where dinosaurs roam free,
and birds I can't identify soar past the highest tree.
"Due tomorrow, pictures, and at least two pages long..."
I write it in my notebook,
    but somehow it will be wrong.

I climb inside my story and put up my daydream wall,
My dinosaur is green, and it has scales and stands up tall...
Together we fight battles, all mighty, fearless, brave—
the two of us together
    in a kingdom we must save!

I sit upon his back and my magic sword is drawn
In a world where my classmates suddenly... are gone.
The ground begins to shake as we run t'ward the enemy line...
Oh! My battle cries are horrid
    for a boy of only nine!

My teacher stands before me as I color on my page.
She wonders why she asked to teach a child of my age.
That's when I look around and see the kids all watching me.
I wonder when they started
    working on geography?

Then in an upset voice she says, "You'll have to start again.
"Your handwriting is terrible and do it all in pen."
It seems a hundred hours 'til the school bell rings at three.
I stuff my story in my bag and mutter,
    "Yay, I'm free!"

I ride my bike home dreaming about my dinosaur
And suddenly my watch says that it is twenty-five past four.
"I'm sorry, Mom," I say as I pour sand from in my shoe.
"And... I forgot my math book."
    Boy, mom is looking blue.

Later in the evening, when it's almost time for bed,
thoughts of Rex, my dinosaur, start filling up my head.
"Hey, Mom and Dad!" I holler, "Look at what I did today!
"I wrote a story, and colored it,
    but I won't get an A.

"My teacher says it's messy, and I guess it's pretty dumb."
I fold it back in half, and now I'm feeling pretty glum.
My Dad says, "Hey, let's see it..." and my Mom gives me a hug.
And soon she's typing while I color,
    sitting on the rug.

Rex, my dinosaur, takes life and runs a furious stride
through a little story in my heart that bursts with love and pride.
My parents give encouragement, and then I hear them say
"Perhaps you'll be a writer, or
    an artist, son, someday."

And...
The ground begins to shake as we run toward the enemy line.
Our battle cries are thunderous—
            my Mom's, my Dad's and mine.

Note to the Reader

It is widely believed that learning problems occur more commonly in boys than in girls. However, some recent research suggests that many girls who need help are being overlooked because learning problems reveal themselves differently in girls than in boys.

This research weighed on my mind as I considered whether to use traditional male pronouns to indicate both sexes. Other choices were awkward compromises such as *him or her* and *s/he*.

I dislike the artifice of *s/he*, but given the research mentioned above, was uncomfortable about using male pronouns exclusively. I didn't want to be responsible for perpetuating the notion that learning problems are in any way unusual in girls.

My decision has been to alternate pronoun usage with each chapter. Chapter One uses *he, him*, etc. to mean both sexes, and Chapter Two uses *she, her*, etc. Chapter Three returns to male pronouns, and they continue to alternate throughout the book.

Mystery
children

There was a child went forth every day,
And the first object he look'd upon, that object he became,
And that object became part of him for the day or a certain
part of the day,
      Or for many years or stretching cycles of years...

Walt Whitman

Max has a flair for science, which he often applies to everyday problem-solving—a remarkable feat for any first grader. Using these skills, he figured out why soda cans spray if they're opened right after they have been shaken up.

So when he dropped a soda can one day, he simply picked it up, turned it upside down, and tapped it firmly on the bottom. The bubbles rose, and when he turned it over and popped the top, the bubbles had spread evenly throughout the liquid. There was no explosion of soda in the Resource Room, where Max came every day for extensive help with his learning disabilities.

Max, despite his obvious intelligence and problem-solving skills, was at a pre-kindergarten reading level and could barely write his first name.

Betsy came to the Resource Room for different reasons. Although she had some of Max's difficulty with writing, she was reading at nearly a third grade level early in first grade. However, she didn't seem able to add or subtract the simplest facts, and sometimes wrote her name upside down and backwards. When she was shown the correct way to write her name compared to what she had written, she didn't always see any difference between the two.

Although Max and Betsy are very different types of students, they are both considered learning disabled, a difficulty which can show itself in many ways. You may think that you don't understand what's happening with Max, Betsy, and children like them. Most of us, though, have had experiences that show what it's like to have a learning disability.

For example, one common type of learning disability in children involves confusion in understanding, interpreting, and learning from visually presented lessons. No glasses of any type will help, because the problems stem from how their brains use what they see, not from anything wrong with their eyes. To get some sense of what this might be like, look at the following optical illusions. If you study the first picture, you may see either two faces looking at each other, or a goblet.

Although the picture can be viewed in two ways, you can choose which way to interpret the picture. You are in control of your perceptions and can force yourself to see either the faces or the goblet.

For comparison, study the drawing below. Stare at it without looking away or moving your head for a full minute, and focus on the center.

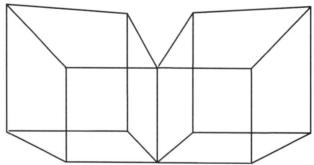

If you stared at it steadily, somewhere in that minute you experienced at least one involuntary perceptual shift. Parts of the figure which had appeared to recede suddenly jumped out at you. The four[1] possible appearances of the design are simply four different ways of perceiving the same thing. The longer you look at this figure, and the harder you try, the less control you may have over what you "see" when you look at it.

A child with visual-perceptual weaknesses seems to lack control over how he perceives what he sees, experiencing differences between common symbols (letters, numbers, shapes) from moment to moment or day to day—something like the perceptual shifts you just experienced. These perceptual difficulties interfere with ability to recognize, copy and remember the symbols used in school every day—letters, numbers, words.

They also will complicate many ordinary, everyday classroom experiences, such as learning from or copying from the blackboard and completing worksheets, which often are visually complex.

Similar difficulties in the auditory channel make it difficult for some children to learn by listening, even though there is nothing wrong with their hearing. Their ears send good, clear signals to their brains, but their brains do not make good use of them.

The shifting cubes are an imperfect example of what having one type of learning disability might be like. However, you probably have had other experiences that provide some insight into other types of learning problems.

For instance, someone's name might be "on the tip of your tongue," and yet you can't quite recall it. Students with difficulty retrieving information experience that frustration all the time. Their language is riddled with vague words like "things" and "stuff" instead of precise labels. They often have a hard time showing what they know in school because of their imprecise use of language.

Remembering phone numbers can be difficult and frustrating for most people when they're upset or angry. Some learning disabled children suffer the same sort of difficulty continually, forgetting things they need to remember or getting the sequence mixed up.

Perhaps one time when you were writing, you looked at a common word—for example, "people." You knew you had spelt it right, and yet, it didn't look right. You couldn't put your finger on anything that was wrong, but you checked a dictionary anyway. Most learning disabled students are terrible spellers. They're very familiar with your occasional confusion. It's common for learning disabled children to misspell the same word four different ways on the same page.

In high school or college you might have had a teacher who talked a mile a minute. She rambled and jumped from point to point. She was hard to follow, hard to keep up with, and you had trouble deciding what was important and what wasn't. When you tried to review your notes, you found that they didn't make any sense.

Some learning disabled individuals experience this type of confusion any time they have to write. They know what they want to say, but something breaks down when they pick up a pencil. They have more difficulty than they should putting their ideas into written word. Often, they begin adequately but the quality quickly deteriorates. Handwriting, spelling, content and grammar all worsen as they

---

[1]Largest rectangles toward the back, as if you were looking through square binoculars; largest rectangles toward the front, sort of like looking through the wrong end of the binoculars; left "lens" toward you and right one back; or right "lens" toward you and left one back.

continue to work. This leads to the assumption that they stopped trying, but lack of effort may not be the problem.

If you ever injured your writing hand, you had difficulty making your other hand direct the pencil and form letters. Try writing with your other hand now. This may give you an idea of the type of frustration some learning disabled children experience as they try to write neatly.

These examples are typical of some difficulties learning disabled people endure. It's not a complete list, and the difficulties can appear in infinite combinations and degrees of severity, making each learning disabled child unique. If you took one hundred students who don't have trouble in school, most of the time you could teach all of them using the same methods. However, take one hundred learning disabled students, and eventually, you will have to teach them in one hundred different ways.

Just what is a learning disability?

The federal definition of specific learning disability describes... "an imperfect ability [author's italics] to listen, think, speak, read, write, spell, or do mathematical calculations ...".[2] Imperfect is a strong word, but it does show what goes wrong for learning disabled children. Their learning skills are fine for some tasks, but in other areas, they function imperfectly. Because of this markedly uneven ability to learn, they can be very confusing to be around. So it shouldn't be too surprising when school personnel do not fully understand such children's problems, at least at first. Specialists have described these children as "puzzle children," "conundrum children," and "mystery children." All these descriptions have one thing in common: they reveal that the children baffle the adults around them by what they can and cannot do.

Starting in infancy, all children gradually develop the neurological organization necessary to grasp, walk and talk, and manipulate items. In learning disabled children, however, this development appears to progress unevenly. Some skills develop appropriately or even at an accelerated rate for the child's age, while other skills lag significantly behind what would be expected for his age. The result is a child with marked strengths and weaknesses.

For more understanding of how children develop learning skills, do what the famous educator, Maria Montessori, did: watch any young child as he explores his world. It is instinctive with a child to be constantly learning. The new and unique thing they have never seen before—a striped spider, or a rock sparkling in the sun, or tar soft and gooey in the summer heat—captures their utter attention. When a child is wholly immersed in discovering the world, he is deaf and blind to everything else. His attention is riveted intensely and completely to the thing he has found. If an adult interrupts the child, the child will be annoyed. He may appear willful or disobedient, but he instinctively resents having his basic need to learn about his world thwarted.

The same child could be quite bored by books—no matter how interesting the topic. Books on spiders, or rocks, or even how great animals like mastodons got caught in tar pits and died, may not hold his interest. Why is that? He was fascinated

---

[2]Weisenstein, Gregory R. and Pelz, Ruth. *Administrator's Desk Reference of Special Education.* Aspen Publishers, 1986, p. 129.

by the glittering rock outside. Shouldn't he be delighted to hear more about rocks from a book? Isn't that where we get most of our information, from books?

Dr. Montessori showed that the letters and words that form books are not real to a young, concrete child, who deals in the here and now, who delights in a world which can be touched, tasted, smelled, manipulated. To such a child the rock in his hand, with the fire inside it jumping from place to place as he wiggles it in the sunlight, the rough, tactile rock is real. The word "rock," whether read or heard, hangs in the air almost useless—an abstraction having little meaning to him.

And the child is right. The word "rock" alone says little. It could be the honey-combed chunk of lava he discovered under a tree at the gas station, or the smooth-as-satin pebble he found by the creek bed, or the flat chip with the imprint of part of a leaf on it he spotted at the base of that small cliff. He doesn't know the words to tell all this. He only knows that the word "rock" surely doesn't tell what he knows about rocks.

If the child is very young, none of this is any problem. It is the normal state of a four-year-old (no matter how bright) to be profoundly concrete. However, by the age of seven and a half or eight (usually second grade), most children can move comfortably into the world of books and words. By this time, the curriculum is moving past the concrete—things held, touched, manipulated—to the abstract (the spoken word and the printed page). The students who still have difficulty attaching meaning to symbols, such as spoken or written words, letters or numbers, will be frustrated. Their way of looking at the world is delightful, refreshing and creative, but it will inevitably interfere with their academic progress.

That's how it is for many learning disabled children. We expect them to set aside their concrete nature and deal with symbols as though the words were as real as the objects they represent. We ask them to learn symbolically before they are ready. We talk at length to a child with poor auditory memory, or we teach complex material from the blackboard to a child who learns much better by listening than by looking. These students will have a harder time in school than their intelligence would predict. Most of them will be easily frustrated by work they should be able to master.

Young children are rarely, if ever, lazy about learning, although a learning disability or other problem may be mistaken for laziness. Learning is a survival skill instinctive to the human being and is especially powerful in young children. Experts have noted the relative ease with which many children learn some things, such as foreign languages and computers. There's a window of opportunity in the mind of a child, so if the child is not learning, something is wrong. Even in older children (ten, eleven, twelve), if they have lost the motivation for learning, it is because something went very wrong when they were younger. Something has caused them to give up on learning despite their basic human nature.

So who are learning disabled children? They have average or above average intelligence (many are quite bright), and yet they don't learn easily or well. When examined by testers well-versed in learning disabilities, specific strengths and weaknesses are noted. All children have strengths and weaknesses, but in the learning disabled child a pattern of extremes is seen.

For instance, there is Alexis, the daughter of a learning disabilities teacher. She scored as high as a child her age could score on one test of general information, prompting the testers to ask if there was any way she might have read the test manual (there wasn't). However, on another test, she had difficulty copying the simplest block designs.

Had her potential been measured based solely on the blocks test, she would have appeared profoundly retarded. Based solely on the test of information, she would have appeared a genius. Obviously, the truth was somewhere in between. What was clear from the testing was that Alexis had a remarkable talent for learning verbally-presented information. She had learned to use her verbal skills to her advantage in reading, social studies and science, but she still performed quite poorly in math, spelling and writing.

Other learning disabled children might test quite differently than Alexis. Spencer had great difficulty with verbal skills, and yet he could solve the most complex non-verbal tasks. (Non-verbal skills include problem-solving tasks that do not need language to solve, such as completing puzzles and copying complex designs.) Although Spencer could barely read in fourth grade, he was good in math. He could also take a lawn mower engine apart and then put it back together.

Naturally, some learning disabilities are more of a hindrance than others. Other things being equal, Alexis has an advantage in school over Spencer, because verbal skills are more easily used in most schools than non-verbal skills are. It also makes sense that smaller differences will create fewer problems than larger ones. Sometimes, though, children whose difficulties do not seem severe according to the diagnostic tests do quite poorly in school. Someone else with more extreme test scores might be struggling less in school for a variety of reasons. Test scores have to be compared to how the child actually performs in school on a day-to-day basis.

Children with a language disability (difficulty acquiring, understanding or using spoken language) will have a harder time, and brighter students generally have an advantage. Unfortunately, a fair number of learning disabled youngsters also have significant behavior problems and/or difficulty maintaining their attention to their schoolwork. Those difficulties further complicate their education.

Although it's obvious by now that these children are more different than they are alike, three traits are typical of all properly identified learning disabled students, including:

- near average, average or above-average intelligence
- school achievement markedly below what their potential would predict (called a discrepancy) in specific academic areas: reading, math, and/or written expression. Difficulty in spelling or handwriting alone often is not enough to have a child diagnosed as learning disabled, but poor performance in those subjects is seen commonly.
  Many of these children will have language disabilities or coordination problems as well.
- a pattern of specific and marked differences among various intellectual processes which can explain most or all of the child's school difficulties.

A good learning disability diagnosis, made by a team of trained specialists, will use individual tests to measure the child's academic skills and mental strengths and weaknesses. Specific academic weaknesses will be clearly shown, and the probable cause of the learning problem will be identified. This is important, because identifying the nature of the learning disability and exactly how it affects the child's learning is the first step toward effective help for him.

Difficulties may be more obvious on some tasks than others. Visual or auditory learning may be more affected; verbal skills or non-verbal skills may be stronger. He may perform better, or worse, when required to work with pencil and paper. Ability to concentrate may vary from task to task. He may remember lessons one day but forget them the next. In the learning disabled student, a pattern will emerge that shows the child's problems.

The student's daily schoolwork will reflect his failure to learn well. His school performance will be as varied and unusual as the test results that identify his difficulties. When doing addition problems, for instance, he may start with the top row on one worksheet and the bottom row on the next; skip around on the page; sometimes count on fingers and sometimes make hash marks on the page to determine unknown answers; and sometimes just put anything down. To make things worse, the child, if he took a moment to think, might already have learned most of the facts and have needed to count only rarely.

By comparison, children who simply are slow learners usually will do the problems in a more orderly fashion. They will work their way down the page, completing each row before continuing to the next one. They will choose one method for unknown problems (ex: fingers, hash marks, number line, counting objects) and stick with it. They won't progress as fast as the average child, but unless teachers and parents set unrealistic expectations for them such children typically will be satisfied with their performance.

A learning disabled child, on the other hand, usually senses he is not working to his potential. He often becomes quite frustrated by his lack of progress, a state aggravated when he is admonished to "try harder." He is trying hard. He may be trying inefficiently, or ineffectively, but he is trying. In fact, he may already be trying too hard, but in ways unlikely to help himself.

An analogy may help. Your car probably does an adequate job of getting you around town. It handles traffic well and can accelerate when needed for passing on highways. If necessary, you could push your car to 110 mph, although you might never need to. You might even be able to accelerate up a mountainside at 100 mph for a short time. It would be unwise to try it on a mountainside for any length of time, though. You might burn up the engine. And you wouldn't do it repeatedly, day after day.

Learning disabled students often expend a great deal more effort than they are given credit for. A student will become very discouraged if he always has to work that hard, especially since his work won't always be right.

If that exceptional level of effort becomes the new minimum expectation for the student, he actually is being punished for trying. Now, on top of all his other difficulties, he has to deliver—all the time—at a level he isn't ready to sustain. Such children need immediate intervention before they become defeated and give up on school completely.

No one intends to inflict this type of distress on a child, so all adults (both teachers and parents) who know a struggling child need to be aware of one potentially destructive pitfall: most adults, including many educators, have a mistaken view of what "average" is.

We generally think of ourselves as average. If you take a moment to compare yourself to your friends, you probably will conclude that you and they have roughly equal talents and abilities.

As adults, though, we have special characteristics. We have finished more schooling: most of us have finished high school; some have finished college or even earned advanced degrees. Since we tend to choose our friends from people in similar circumstances to our own, even people with master's degrees and Ph.D.s tend to think of themselves as close to "average," because they surround themselves with people of like backgrounds.

As adults we have a special privilege not given to children: we choose how we spend our time. We have found our special talents and have developed them—perhaps skill with our hands, an ability to organize, or a flair for getting along with people. We capitalize on and are valued for our strengths, and our weaknesses become relatively unimportant.

Don't mistake your own outstanding strengths as being ordinary or average, or your child will have trouble meeting your expectations. Be cautious as you judge whether your child fits the descriptions found in this book of students with unusual learning styles. A clear view of what average really is for most children will help as we talk later on about whether your child might have an uneven learning pattern. As an adult your child also will develop strengths of his own. He doesn't have to show them all as a child.

What's going on with my child?

It is better to know some of the questions than all of the answers.

James Thurber

Sandra and Joel have had nagging concerns about their fourth grade son, Bobby, for some time. They debated about how early to enroll him in kindergarten, as he was one of the younger children. When he wasn't terribly successful, they willingly agreed to retention.

In fact, repeating kindergarten was Bobby's idea. He told his parents he was scared he wouldn't be able to do first grade work. The school agreed that it might be a good idea to repeat a year.

Sandra and her husband asked the school to test Bobby. The testers found that Bobby had an "uneven learning pattern," but that he did not have a learning disability and did not qualify for special help.

Classroom teachers now report that they are generally pleased with Bobby's work. They say his grades might be higher, given his general intelligence, but that he gets along well with his classmates and is rarely a behavior problem.

Sandra, however, sees a pattern of incomplete work and poor organizational skills. Bobby obviously finds writing reports frustrating. And yet he can tell her so clearly what he wants to say! She's beginning to think he just doesn't try in some subjects, like spelling.

Sandra has been told that anxiety causes his academic problems. But the question might well be raised: what has caused Bobby's anxiety? Is anxiety the cause of his school problems—or have subtle learning problems caused it?

Sandra wants to know what's going on with her child.

Does Bobby have a learning disability?
Maybe.
Clearly he has a problem learning, whatever it's called.

All classrooms, in all schools across the country, have children like Bobby in them. Something has gone awry with their education, but no one seems quite sure what, and no plans are in place to help the child function closer to his potential.

Students like Bobby are "shadow children," their difficulties not entirely disregarded but often postponed for another day. Their intellectual growth is a shadow of what it could be under optimal circumstances. Teachers would like to give them more of their precious time but are often overwhelmed already with problems they see as more urgent.

Most learning disabled children are "shadow children" also. Their teachers perform academic triage: for each subject helped, another will have to be given up. Choices must always be made. If we work on Mary's reading it will leave less time to help her in math or spelling, but reading is critical and gets most of the attention; math and other troublesome subjects are given inadequate amounts of time.

Many different factors work together to keep struggling students in the shadows, away from the specialized assistance which might help them.

Consider:

- **Regional differences.** Whether or not a child is diagnosed as having a learning disability (and receives help in school) will depend partly upon where she lives and how well she matches the community and state's definition. Federal guidelines exist, but each state interprets them differently and sets its own standards for diagnosis. The state guidelines are interpreted further by each individual school district. So a child who receives help in one school may not be considered eligible for extra help in a neighboring school district.
- **Gender differences.** Diagnosis of learning disabilities is strongly influenced by the sex of the child. Girls are underdiagnosed, although recent studies have suggested that nearly as many girls as boys have learning problems. In spite of this, in some communities more than four times as many boys receive help as girls. Girls' learning difficulties generally have to be more serious than boys' before they will be evaluated.
- **Focus on behavior instead of learning problems.** Classroom behavior often influences who receives help. Recent research shows that behavior

problems, not learning problems, trigger most referrals for academic help. Well-behaved boys with learning problems frequently are overlooked, and girls' behavior problems have to be more severe than boys' before they are evaluated.

- **Over-emphasis on low-functioning children.** Children with high intelligence often are overlooked, or if spotted, dismissed as not needing extra help. Low achievement often is discounted in a bright child, and average grades are considered acceptable, even if an intelligent child is struggling to earn them. Typically the brighter child will have to show more severe learning problems than other children before being noticed. The bright but learning disabled child probably won't be achieving to her potential, but if she isn't completely foundering (yet) she won't be diagnosed. She might not even be noticed.
- **Diagnosis by failure.** To receive help for learning disabilities, students have to be performing well below their grade level. Often by the time these children are spotted they are so far behind they have an extremely difficult time catching up, even with special help. For most, the gap becomes wider and wider over the years. It would make more sense to provide intensive help before they get so far behind, but that isn't how special education works.

  Remedial reading programs are offered in most schools, but classes reflect such a wide range of reading abilities that the lowest performing students may still receive ineffective or inadequate help. Remedial instruction in math, written language or spelling is available only rarely outside of special education.
- **Weaknesses given more emphasis than strengths.** Children considered "slow learners" (those who are not retarded, and have evenly developed learning abilities but are just not quite as bright as the average child) sometimes have some remarkable strengths or talents which could be developed. Often their special strengths are overlooked instead of explored.
- **Lack of funds.** Many other children, though not classified as learning disabled by their school district, still have significant weaknesses in their learning style. They would benefit from extra help if it were available, but it's unlikely the public schools ever will have enough money to truly individualize education for all children.

Students diagnosed with learning problems are noticed because they fail: they fail to understand, they fail to produce, they fail to progress, they fail socially or behaviorally, they fail subjects. Your child's learning style could be uneven enough to be highly frustrating to her, but not severe enough to cause her to fail, to be diagnosed, to be helped.

All people have strengths and weaknesses, of course, and just because some abilities are stronger than others does not mean the child has a problem learning. Having strengths and weaknesses is part of being human, and some of those strengths eventually will develop into strong talents and abilities. But when the pattern of strengths and weaknesses prevents a child from learning as well as possible (because the weaknesses are a hindrance to her school progress), we have a child who needs extra help. The weaknesses become personal dragons the child has to battle constantly. Even her strengths can get in her way if she relies on them too much and develops awkward or ineffective ways to cope.

Our educational system does not cope with individual differences in learning style as well as it has in the past, so your child may be caught in one of the following administrative or philosophical traps:

- **Dumbing down.** The children who are diagnosed and receive special services don't necessarily fare any better than those who are overlooked. Special classes often "dumb down" the curriculum. For every child who benefits from this strategy, there's another one who is capable of more but who isn't challenged.

- **Limited Resources.** For learning disabled children who are kept within regular schools and classes (called "mainstreaming"), supplemental help cannot always supply all they need to keep academic pace with the other children. Too often, the child is seen as little as once or twice a week by a resource teacher. The rest of the time the child, her classroom teacher and her parents are on their own to do the best they can.

- **Peas in a pod.** When educators place all children born in the same 12–month period in the same classroom, they suggest children of the same age are more alike than they really are. It's a pretty fiction that all second graders are ready to learn cursive writing, all third graders ready to learn multiplication facts and all fourth graders ready to write reports, but children's minds are not so neat and tidy. A second grader, for example, won't be taught her multiplication facts—even if she's ready to learn them—if it isn't part of that school's second grade curriculum. A fourth grader will be expected to master long division whether she's ready or not. Both children will suffer in different ways from such policies.

  In reading it's worse. Most schools cope inadequately with both accelerated and delayed readers. Virtually all first graders are placed in pre-primers, no matter how well they read, and many first grade teachers have great difficulty managing non-readers—even though it's well-known by educators that not all first graders are ready to read.

- **Who's in charge of this classroom?** Due to a tangled web of state, federal and administrative guidelines, teachers control neither the content of their instruction nor the methods by which they teach it.

  Textbooks often are selected by a state committee with little regard for the variability among students, schools or communities.

  Subjects taught have increased in number as topics such as sex education, values clarification, and drug awareness are added to the curriculum. For each new course, something must be sacrificed, and little room is left for the unique materials, skills and experiences individual teachers could bring to their job.

When curriculum is too strictly controlled, spontaneity is lost and content becomes superficial, lifeless and meaningless to young students.

- **"Our district's test scores are better than theirs!"** Other policies which have become popular in public education in recent years, such as standardized testing, sometimes take tremendous amounts of instructional time. In some school districts, achievement tests dictate what is taught.

  Overuse of achievement tests, combined with excessive reliance on textbook curriculum, are factors in the narrowing of our children's education. Achievement tests will be chosen by how well they reflect the content of the textbooks; texts will be chosen that reflect the tests; and little or no instructional time is left for enriching activities that cannot be measured on a multiple-choice test. If a fact or concept is not included on popular achievement tests, in some schools it is unlikely to be given much attention in either classroom or textbook.

- **Busywork makes busy hands.** Worksheets and workbooks have been shown to be the most inefficient way to teach, yet are the most commonly used teaching tool in the elementary grades. Textbooks aren't much better. Books, instead of hands-on materials, are typical even in subjects like science which lend themselves to more interesting and rewarding methods.

For these reasons plus others that will be explored in this book, many children with mild or moderate learning problems do not benefit fully from school, in spite of teachers' best efforts.

Sometimes children who struggle in silence learn to handle stress, pressure and frustration. Great personal strengths can grow from adversity. But for every child who pulls herself up by her bootstraps there's another going down for the third time, with no life preserver in sight. Learning disabled children are at high risk for drug abuse, dropping out of high school, teen pregnancy, juvenile delinquency, and for becoming one of the 27 million functionally illiterate adults in our country.

Special education, no matter how excellent, is an incomplete solution. Even daily help from specialists cannot fill in all the gaps. Again, the brightest learning disabled children are likely to receive the fewest services. C's are often acceptable to the special teacher even if the child has 'A' potential, simply because she has her hands full with children who struggle to earn D's.

Most teachers, administrators and specialists are doing the best they know how, but the question can be justifiably raised: would better and more varied techniques and materials reduce many children's school difficulties and help them tame the dragons they battle?

As a parent, you are in a unique position to help fill some of the gaps for your child when the school can't, and that's the purpose of this book: to give you tools, tips and techniques you can use efficiently and easily to help your child over her academic rough spots.

You may find options in this book which contradict textbooks, teachers, or school district philosophy. Parents frequently are told:

"The best help you can give your child is emotional support. Leave teaching to the teachers."

That is, of course, until your child comes home with homework she doesn't know how to do. Of course you're going to try to help your child. Helping with homework, however, isn't as simple as it sounds. It can be a minefield, with the parents' every step a potential explosion. Before you read any further, it's time for a little soul-searching.

Be sure what you want for your child is that she learns to accept complete responsibility for her homework. As the parent of a struggling child, you need to be available when help is genuinely needed. However, something is wrong if you find that night after night you sit next to your child, encouraging, praising, critiquing, correcting or commenting upon every bit of work done. Either the work is too hard, or you have allowed the child to make you responsible for her homework. Or both.

Make sure that your expectations are realistic. Out of any ten children, six will be solidly average in ability, and two will be brighter than typical. Two will be not quite as smart as the average child, and one of the ten stands a statistical chance of having a learning disability. Using methods from this book to try to push your child beyond her capabilities will only cause frustration and heartache for both of you.

If you can use the suggestions in this book to get a stalled child going again, then you're using the information well.

But if you're starting to feel more like a teacher than a parent, more aggravated than relieved, it's time to re-examine the situation. You should be available for short-term help, but not be your child's homework handservant. Ultimately, it's the school's job to teach your child, and your job to teach your child responsibility (such as completing homework to the best of her ability in a timely way). It's your child's job to get the homework done.

The danger with this book is that it will put new pressures on students who already are doing as well as they can. Have you been told that? That your child is already doing as well as she can? Then proceed cautiously and get professional advice as you go along. (Teachers and school counselors are good starting places.)

Disruptively uneven styles of learning are not the only cause of school difficulty, especially in older children and teenagers. If a child suddenly starts having difficulty after seventh grade or so, the possibility of some other problem (such as depression, motivation problems, drugs, or boredom) must be considered.

It's possible the child has an undiagnosed learning disability; there are many cases of students being diagnosed for the first time in high school or even college. But often with teenagers, something else is at work.

It's important in a case like this to go back deeply into the child's school history. Learning disabilities do not suddenly develop in a teenager where none was present before (although sometimes the evidence is missed until then). Did she have trouble learning to read? Did she struggle in math? Was she having consistent, borderline problems no one seemed to notice? In short, is this really a sudden problem?

It's never too late to find out what's happening. Good educational testers and psychologists can determine if the child has a learning disability or if some other problem is at work. Maybe the child is just not quite as bright as the parents had hoped, which makes high school and college more difficult than expected.

Most importantly, though, parents need to stay in charge of what happens to their children.

In the long run, parents are the only ones responsible for their child's well-being and upbringing—not school officials, nor the pediatrician, nor the special educator, nor the school counselor or the psychologist. This doesn't mean you shouldn't consult with the experts. Listen to them carefully and consider what they have to say. Believe in your perceptions as well, though, because no one person will have all the answers for your child.

Watch out especially for people with hidden agendas, who have a point to make and would make it at the expense of your child. Be cautious (including being cautious about following the suggestions given in this book). Before you follow someone else's advice, establish that it is focused on your child's needs and not the needs and biases of the advice-giver. The final decisions on what to do for your child must rest with you.

So get on your child's team. Be her biggest booster and stand behind her all the way. Successful learning disabled children have one trait in common. They aren't the smartest ones, nor the ones with the fewest problems; they're the ones whose parents are behind them 100 per cent.

Treat your child with respect. Believe your child. If she says an assignment is too hard, there's probably some truth to it.

Above all, don't assume all the other children have an advantage. Other families and other children have hidden burdens, too. Learning difficulties are only one facet of your child. Don't lose sight of her unique potential as you search for ways to ease her academic frustrations.

One last point should be made—about hope.

The theory of relativity was formulated by a man who struggled constantly in school and was not considered terribly bright. Einstein saw the world in ways never considered by people who were supposed to have more "potential." Perhaps his unique reasoning skills developed from his childhood struggles with school work. Thomas Edison, Woodrow Wilson, Hans Christian Anderson, Leonardo da Vinci, and Rodin also gave us new visions of a world the rest of us already thought we understood. As children, they exhibited many traits that today are considered typical of learning disabled individuals.

Out of the struggles learning disabled children face can come new and wonderful ways of thinking and combining information. Their creative problem-solving skills can lead to ideas that never would have occurred to the so-called "normal" person. Thinking of children with uneven learning patterns as both "learning disabled" and as having the capacity to learn in unique and wonderful ways is the first step. Their intense desire to learn will be at once their burden and their salvation—if we can make it work for them instead of against them.

For further reading:

Harrington, Diane and Laurette Young. *School Savvy: Everything You Need to Know to Guide Your Child Through Today's Schools.* Farrar, Strauss and Giroux, 1993.

Miller, Mary Susan. *Save Our Schools: 66 Things You Can Do to Improve Your School Without Spending an Extra Penny.* Harper, 1993.

> This book contains hundreds of ways you can get active and make a difference in your child's school district. It makes excellent reading if you want to know more about what is new and innovative in education.

Nehring, James: *The Schools We Want: An American Teacher on the Front Line.* 1992, Josey-Bass Publishers.

> Nehring presents a down-to-Earth and often funny account of teaching—what it's like and what it should be like. Although the author talks about high schools, many of the issues he grapples with exist throughout all grades.

Shore, Dr. Kenneth. *The Parents' Public School Handbook: How to Make the Most of Your Child's Education, from Kindergarten Through Middle School.* 1994, Simon & Schuster, ISBN 0–671–79498–1, $12.00.

> This book explains school operation simply but completely, and is an outstanding source for parents who seek an active role in their children's education. We recommend that parents purchase this book.

Naming the dragons

Only the mediocre are always at their best.

Jean Giraudoux

Note to the reader: turn to page 29 and photocopy the chart. You'll use it as you read this chapter.

Mrs. Jones' math class was learning long division. After several days of working on the basics, today's lesson was a review of what had been learned so far. Johnny, who sat in the front row where the teacher could keep an eye on him, was struggling to keep up. He found long division confusing.

"Take the divisor into the first two numerals of the dividend," Mrs. Jones was saying. "Write this quotient over the tens' place. It won't divide evenly—we'll get to that in a minute."

About then, Mrs. Jones noticed Johnny's attention had wandered (again). He was staring intently out the window.

"What are you doing, Johnny?" asked Mrs. Jones.

"I'm looking for the crow!"

When Mrs. Jones said "quotient," Johnny thought she had said "crow shin." He didn't know crows had shins, and he wanted a look at the crow she was talking about.

"You'd do better in math, Johnny, if you'd try to pay more attention," Mrs. Jones said dryly.

What's going on with Johnny?

Johnny wasn't a bad child, and he didn't mean to disrupt the classroom. He thought he was trying to be attentive.

Johnny was one of several undiagnosed learning disabled youngsters in fourth grade that year. When Mrs. Jones referred him for testing, he was found to have several learning problems which interfered with his ability to learn.

First, Johnny has poor auditory perceptual skills. Although there is nothing wrong with his hearing, his brain misinterprets what he hears. So when the teacher said "quotient," he perceived it as "crow shin."

Most people would have asked the teacher to repeat what she had said. But not Johnny. He made a quantum leap from mathematics to ornithology without even noticing, because he has the additional problem of attention deficit disorder. His thoughts jump quickly from place to place, so he isn't surprised when a teacher seems to. He has difficulty maintaining his attention to one topic, and tends to think (and talk) about things superficially. He is easily distracted by things the rest of us automatically ignore.

Johnny jumped from long division to crows because it's his nature to shift quickly and randomly from thought to thought. I don't have to tell you now that it takes great effort to keep Johnny on task: he is derailed by the slightest distractions.

Poor Johnny. Although his behavior supplied subtle clues about the nature of his problems, it looked like intentional misbehavior to his teacher.

But the worst thing about Johnny's predicament is that it is easily solved. His parents could have helped him tremendously with these difficulties. What Johnny needed was to be able to follow the teacher's explanations. In his case, this means hearing all the big new words accurately.

If Johnny's parents had understood his weaknesses and their effect on his math progress, here's what they could have done:

They could have taken his math book a day or two ahead of time, looked over the next section for new vocabulary, and drilled Johnny on it for just a minute or two. "Show me the quotient. Good. Show me the divisor. Oops, this is the divisor over here. Show me the divisor. Good! Show me the dividend. Excellent! Show me the divisor. Now say the three words back to me. Great! I think you've got it."

Rote drill? You bet! There was no need for his parents to actually teach him how to do long division, or even go into what the words mean. All Johnny needed was a little coaching on the sounds of the words so the teacher could teach him what they meant and how to do the problems. His parents would have explained to Johnny that these were new words the teacher would be using, and that he would need to listen for them in class.

He still would have had some difficulty; long division is hard. But he and the teacher would have been speaking the same language.

Johnny's parents could use the same strategy to help him stay up-to-date in math (and other subjects) all year, but final responsibility for paying attention in class and getting homework done would stay exactly where it belongs: with Johnny. His parents would be facilitators, supplying occasional guidance so that Johnny could function more independently.

It's completely possible for parents to help their child learn a variety of subjects and skills—once they know how he learns most effectively. That's what we'll do in this chapter: find out how to sift through the clues and determine the strengths and weaknesses of your child's learning style in an organized way.

As we work though the types of learning difficulties explained below, we'll develop a preliminary chart of your child's learning styles (found on page 29—photocopy it now if you didn't earlier). You will use this chart to pinpoint his particular strengths and weaknesses. You may not find all of them, but you'll find enough to help.

Then in the following chapter, we'll talk about the four specific stages a child progresses through when learning, because weaknesses interfere with children's progress differently at each stage of learning.

When we're done, you'll be able to look at nearly any assignment your child brings home, compare it with his individual strengths and weaknesses, and find at least one suggestion from the book likely to help. But first, we need to state in plain talk what all the fancy labels used in education mean (such as "auditory perception" in Johnny's case). Like Mrs. Jones and Johnny, we need to speak the same language before we proceed.

Learning styles

Learning specialists usually describe struggling students by emphasizing their weaknesses, but the weaknesses of one child may be the strengths of another. When looking for ways to help a student, strengths are just as important as weaknesses, but too often they are not given much attention.

We will not make that mistake, because effective learning is most likely to happen when both strengths and weaknesses are considered. It's also important to help each child recognize his strong points for the sake of his self-esteem. It is hard to over-estimate the value of acknowledging strengths: consider the number of times a struggling child's shortcomings will be pointed out to him.

Each strength and weakness has been given its own symbol.[1] You'll see them starting on the next page. These symbols will be used throughout the book to make references to each style of learning easier to locate.

Concrete vs. abstract

You know what a concrete learner is already from Chapter Two. It's the child who has difficulty making the shift from concrete learning to the symbolic world of formal education; the child who finds not only letters and printed words inadequate but sometimes spoken words as well; the child who always wants hands-on

---

[1]These symbols will appear in the margin whenever the problem they represent is discussed. You'll see them frequently in Chapters Nine through Sixteen. The larger symbols to the left stand for the trait when a strength. When they're smaller and on the right side of the margin they stand for the trait as a weakness. The exception is the symbol for Attention Deficit

| Strengths | Weaknesses |

experiences. All young children are by their nature concrete learners. Abstract learners, however, make the leap from the real to the symbolic world easily, and soon work comfortably with printed language. Abstract reasoning skills can be stronger or weaker either verbally or non-verbally.

These symbols represent strengths and weaknesses in abstract reasoning

Abstract reasoning

STRONG
verbal

weak
verbal

STRONG
nonverbal

weak
nonverbal

STRONG
verbal

weak
verbal

STRONG
nonverbal

Children weak in abstract reasoning will be concrete learners, children who learn best with hands-on activities.

Verbal strengths in abstract reasoning allow the child to understand idioms ("raining cats and dogs," "up a tree"). He may get the point of jokes at an early age. Weak verbal reasoning skills will lead to more difficulty than he should have with idiomatic language. He may have trouble arguing his point in disagreements and thus resort to name-calling or fighting.

Strong non-verbal reasoning skills are shown when a child excels at activities like puzzles, Legos® and Erector Sets®. Often such a child will be interested in tools at an early age. Some will take household items apart, like the two-year-old boy who removed all the lower kitchen cabinet doors from their hinges. (After that, he took his crib apart.) Sometimes these junior mechanics can put the dismantled items back together as well, but don't count on it! Children who show a weakness in non-verbal reasoning may have difficulty with some hands-on learning activities.

weak
nonverbal

This is why it's important for parents and teachers to know why they choose the techniques they use. No one approach is right for everyone, and not choosing carefully is just a shot in the dark.

Global vs. sequential

STRONG
global learner

weak
global

STRONG
sequential

weak
sequential

STRONG
global learner

Global learners learn in layers. They prefer an overview of where they are going first before learning a complex process. They

Disorder, placed in the center because that trait can sometimes be a strength as well as a weakness.

like having a map, knowing where they are headed and what they are working toward. For example, global learners learn phonics quicker if they are shown the result first—that they will be able to figure out unknown words. They enjoy having examples shown to them even if they aren't capable of imitating the skill yet.

Sequential learners find introductory overviews distracting and confusing. They expect to learn whatever they are shown immediately or they become frustrated because they don't have the ability of the global learner to see "the big picture." They prefer to proceed step-by-step, in an orderly way, to the end result. Sequential learners are in the majority, and most educational materials are laid out in a sequential rather than a global way.

STRONG
sequential

These learning styles—concrete vs. abstract and global vs. sequential—are ways of thinking and learning that can affect a child across a variety of skills. Most people can be divided according to their tendency to be more concrete or abstract; more global or more sequential. Just because your child prefers one style over another does not mean he has a serious learning problem or a learning disability. Sometimes he may have difficulties with schoolwork, however, if his learning strengths don't match up with the teaching methods being used in his school. These learning styles are important to your child even when they don't reveal a serious learning problem. Any learner has an advantage when he knows what his strengths are and how to use them to his benefit.

The exception is that having weak sequential reasoning skills can be a significant barrier to learning and is dealt with in more depth in the next section. However, weak global reasoning skills usually means only that the individual is a sequential learner. The solution is typically as simple as choosing a sequential instructional method, something done in education already.

weak
sequential

The skills listed next affect learning more profoundly. Their symbols are given next:

STRONG   *weak*   **STRONG**   *weak*   *weak*
visual   visual   auditory   auditory   basic skills

Children with strengths in these areas are unlikely to be noticed because of them; but children with weaknesses in these areas often are diagnosed as learning disabled. These skills, when weak, often are far more serious stumbling blocks to school success than the general learning styles we mentioned earlier.

Strengths   Weaknesses

STRONG   *weak*   **STRONG**   *weak*   Attention
grapho-motor   grapho-motor   memory   memory   Deficit

STRONG
visual

weak
visual

Children with visual-perceptual strengths learn best by looking. Demonstrations from the blackboard, diagrams, graphs and charts are all valuable tools for them.

Students with weak visual perception skills, by contrast, have difficulty interpreting what they see consistently and without distortion, like the optical illusions in Chapter Two. Because they perceive differently, they won't learn well by studying visual examples. The farther away an example is, such as teacher demonstrations given at the blackboard, the more difficulty they probably will have.

As youngsters, they may recognize letters in one form but not another (ex: [a] vs. [ɑ]). They may have difficulty memorizing sight words because of their inconsistent perceptions.

Older students will have difficulty with diagrams in textbooks and get confused when looking at workbook pages, such as not knowing which answers go with which questions. Even when visual examples are explained clearly, the child may not connect the meaning of the words with the illustrations. Often, they will put their answers in the wrong places on answer sheets or skip lines when reading.

Such students will have difficulty organizing their work on paper. Their work will have uneven margins and irregular spaces between words. In math, they will have a hard time keeping numbers lined up neatly in columns, thus causing errors. They may have difficulty recalling how to do simple problems, especially if the problem looks "different" to them in any way. Just a change in type style (ex: 7 vs. **7**), or writing a problem horizontally instead of vertically (see below) can throw them completely.

$$7 \times 3 = 21 \qquad \begin{array}{r} 7 \\ \times\ 3 \\ \hline 21 \end{array}$$

Often, children with visual-perceptual weaknesses have difficulty as well with directionality: left-right, and sometimes even up-down. Directional confusion causes errors such as starting on the wrong side of math problems, and it makes reading maps and using globes difficult. Sometimes they get confused about which way to run in athletic games, and even learning one's way around a new school can be hard.

STRONG
auditory

weak
auditory

A child with an auditory-perceptual strength will have better than average ability to learn by listening. He'll remember details from class discussions, and will be able to ignore the distracting sounds that might keep others from concentrating, such as a conversation out in the hall. This skill is an even greater strength when the student has strong verbal skills as well.

Difficulties with auditory perception cause students to garble what they hear (as in "crow shin" for "quotient"; "this" for "fish"). The result is that although they listen, the words don't always make sense to them. The problem is aggravated by long, involved sets of directions or new, complex vocabulary.

Often, a child with auditory-perceptual weaknesses can follow verbal directions adequately one-on-one. In a group, though, all sounds receive equal parts of his listening attention—the teacher's voice, the child next to him thumbing through a book, a person walking down the hall, and a lawn mower in the distance. If the child is also attention-deficient (see page 25), he may start listening to the conversation or even the lawn mower exclusively and completely ignore the teacher.

STRONG
grapho-motor

Children with a strength in grapho-motor skills stand out early in their schooling because of their neat printing. They will not have difficulty learning either printing or cursive writing (so long as they have no visual-perceptual or memory deficit to obstruct their talents).

Weak grapho-motor skills make it hard for students to produce written work. They have difficulty learning to form letters. Their writing is awkwardly and unevenly formed, and tends to deteriorate on longer assignments.

In math, these children have difficulty keeping numbers lined up—their numerals are unevenly sized, making straight columns nearly impossible. Such children perform pencil/paper, coloring and cut-and-paste tasks slowly, further reducing the amount of work they can do. Sometimes, however, these problems are caused not by a grapho-motor deficit but by attention deficit disorder—see page 25. Grapho-motor problems can be a serious complication if the child also has difficulty with memory (see below) and needs extra practice to master his work.

weak
grapho-motor

Memory is a complex skill and can be divided into three types. First is active working memory. This is what we use immediately after we see or hear something. We can think of it as a temporary storage facility until our brain can put the information into what we call short-term memory.

STRONG
memory

weak
memory

Short-term memory is adequate for short periods of time, but the child may forget what he's learned by the next day. Or the child may remember new information for a few days, but have

| Strengths | Weaknesses |

STRONG
memory

oral

weak
memory

weak
sequential

difficulty retaining it over a longer period of time (long-term memory). In some cases the child has difficulty holding on to information long enough in his active working memory to get it into his short-term memory. When memory works well, material learned gets placed into long-term memory without too much trouble.

Children with memory strengths are easy to spot because they know tremendous amounts of information. They can retain information from a variety of sources easily. They may participate well in class discussion and yet struggle on tests if they have difficulty reading the test or writing the answers down, but when the teacher quizzes them orally she might be amazed to find how much they have learned.

A child with memory weaknesses initially will appear to understand something, yet need to study it again and again. If the difficulty occurs mostly when listening, he may need to have directions explained several times. If it's more of a visual problem, though, he may quickly forget what he's read. Sometimes memory difficulties cause problems in all areas.

Some children have adequate memory until they are required to write an answer. For these children, any sort of pencil activity seems to interfere with organizing their thoughts. Ideas they can state clearly out loud contain poor sequencing, missing words and inadequate grammar when they write them down.

A child's memory may be stronger, or weaker, in visual or auditory channels, or you may find it is stronger in verbal or non-verbal areas. Children who have poor memory skills need repeated review, even on things they appear to have learned well. They are described as "inconsistent" by their teachers.

Sequencing difficulties are mentioned here again because they often aggravate any difficulties with memory. Sequential problems will cause children to garble the order of almost anything: the letters in their name, simple spelling words, steps to completing an assignment.

Confusion when sequencing is involved may be the result of overload: the child is trying to do more than he can handle. For instance, if he has a grapho-motor weakness, sequential errors might be switched letters or words out of order in a sentence. The possibility of an attentional problem also must be considered.

The combination of sequential difficulties and memory problems interfere especially with the child's progress in math, spelling and written expression.

Weaknesses in sequencing may be less apparent in children with good reasoning skills (see icons on the next page). These students often can compensate by reasoning through a task, thus

STRONG
verbal

STRONG
nonverbal

redetermining the right order—often more than once. Sometimes the strategy backfires. If they do it in math, they will probably come up with a new, "creative" but erroneous way to do the problems. However, since they thought it up, they will take pride in their new "method" and tend to remember it instead of the correct way. Errors in spelling can become stubbornly imbedded in a child's mind in the same way.

When such self-defeating thought processes take place, a new problem occurs. This is an obvious case of a child working overtime to do what other children do easily. It is counter-productive and calls for a level of effort the child will have difficulty sustaining over time.

Parents should keep in mind that the way children—all children—learn changes over time. As a child grows and matures his or her brain grows, develops and matures. A child's brain makes some quite dramatic changes over time. One result of this growth and development can be that a child will appear to have a strength at one time, but if tested three or four years later that same skill may be judged a weakness. The reasons are complex. The important thing to know is that a child's strengths and weaknesses aren't carved in stone. As time passes the way your child learns best may change significantly.

Attention Deficit Disorders

Attention
Deficit

Attention deficit/hyperactivity disorder[2] (AD/HD, often called ADD) is an insidious and often devastating stumbling block to learning. The name of the difficulty is misleading; these children actually seem to have too much attention. They pay attention to more than they should, unable to screen out what is important from what is unimportant. A more accurate name would be "Attention Focusing Disorders." Although many events may initially grab the attention of children with ADD, few have the power to hold their attention, leading to the second characteristic: they don't focus on any one thing for very long. These traits show up in their school work in specific ways:

- They concentrate on what they are doing for only short spurts—sometimes as little as three to five seconds. They drift between "tuning in" to the teacher and "tuning out," often unaware their attention is wandering. Hence, they have a hard time learning complex tasks that call for sustained concentration.
- The quality of their concentration, or attention, is poor. Even when they try to do their work, they give it minimal thought and complete it inaccurately.

[2]In ADD, it's the attentional problems that interfere with learning, not the hyperactivity. Although hyperactivity can cause serious problems for both the child and the people around him, it is the learning problems associated with attentional weaknesses that will be covered in this book. See the reading list at the end of the chapter for other books on ADD.

Strengths   Weaknesses

For example, they might put down the wrong answer to multiplication facts they know well; do each problem differently; scatter their efforts all over the page; and absent-mindedly put answers in the wrong place. One student with ADD finished an addition facts test with lightning speed, but missed items because she added some problems and multiplied others. Although she knew her facts well, she wasn't fully focused on the task at hand.

A student may feel he is trying hard to do his work well. What he's probably doing, though, is trying hard but inefficiently and in short spurts, with long stretches of scattered effort in between. These are the children who aren't aware the teacher assigned homework yesterday, who rarely remember to put their names on their (incomplete) papers before they turn them in.

One of the most serious consequences of ADD is that with the child's on-again-off-again approach to learning, he will miss one of school's essential lessons: that working hard leads to success.

Until recently, many school districts excluded students with ADD from special education services despite its tremendous effect on learning. Only students with both attentional difficulties and other diagnoses as well were considered eligible. Various rules and laws have recently been changed to make it easier to serve children with attentional problems, but many schools have not decided yet how best to serve these students.

Because of the particular learning problems ADD presents and the frequent lack of academic help available for children with the problem, Chapter Seven will cover ADD in more detail.

weak
basic skills

Often, as a result of the accumulated effects of learning difficulties, struggling students lack basic skills for instruction in several or all subjects. Their knowledge is full of large gaps (symbolized by the holes in the cheese) that complicate their efforts to learn. The pieces of missing knowledge are of unpredictable size, frequency and importance. The problem is aggravated when the child has memory deficits as well as other learning problems.

For example, a child will have difficulty learning a weekly spelling list if he does not yet know the sounds of most of the consonants, but formal spelling lessons usually start in first grade. A new problem is created when the parent sees the spelling list and believes this to be one way they can help their foundering child: they can make sure he studies his spelling words each night. Nightly battles over homework can begin in this way before a child is out of first grade.

Another example is math calculation. A child who does not know his subtraction facts will have a hard time with long division, where subtraction is a basic component. A child who has a poor fund of general knowledge will find such subjects as social studies and science difficult and confusing, because new information builds on old knowledge the student didn't master in the first place.

The older a child is, the more serious the problem is likely to be, as the deficits accumulate. The gleeful cry of children playing hide-and-seek, "Ready or not, here I come!" takes on chilling significance for some students as they are repeatedly presented new materials and skills for which they are not yet ready.

Using what you've read

Now that you've read the descriptions, think about your child and whether he shows each skill as a strength or as a weakness. As you re-read the descriptions of the learning styles, you may want to use the checklist on page 29 that you photocopied to help you get focused on your child's current strengths and weaknesses.

Here's how to use the checklist. If you see a particular learning style as a strength for your child, put a check in the left box. If it seems a weakness to you, mark a check in the right box. Average skills should be marked in the middle.

If you're not sure, don't mark it for now. The unmarked ones may be areas where your child has average abilities. Often they will be strong enough to be used on occasion to help him cope with his more difficult areas. Don't worry too much about getting the checklist marked perfectly. You will probably continue to modify your opinions for weeks or even months after you have marked it for the first time.

Besides your own perceptions of how your child learns, you have many other sources of information. You would be wise to use those other sources as well as this book, and people who have taught your child or worked with him personally are the best place to get the information you need. If your child has been individually tested, look through the report of his test results.

However, remember that sometimes things mentioned on test results are not hugely significant. Also, new strengths sometimes emerge as a child grows, so the younger the child when he was tested and the older his report, the more cautiously the results must be used. Use the most current information available to you. You'll find many learning styles we talked about listed as strengths or weaknesses in those reports.

Also, you can talk to his teachers about what they see as his strengths and weaknesses. If your child has had a teacher in the past year or so with whom he enjoyed a particularly good relationship, you have another good source for information. Any special teachers, speech therapists or other specialists who work with your child should have good insights, and don't forget the school counselor. Be sure you get feedback on both weaknesses and strengths from these people. You should call ahead for conference times to give these people a little time to consider your questions.

Lastly, depending on the child's age, you can ask him what type of things he feels helps or gets in the way of his learning.

Don't be too alarmed if you feel you are finding a pattern of extreme strengths and weaknesses; even children who have no apparent school difficulty often show quite strong preferences in learning style. And if your child does struggle, even sporadically, this information can be used as his path to further successes.

Simple strategies will be supplied later in the book to help your child master a variety of skills—from printing neatly, to learning multiplication facts, to studying for tests. Each strategy will have one or more symbols by it (like bunny ears or a globe, for example) to show what type of learner is likeliest to find it useful. Then you can easily compare your child's chart to the suggestions.

For further reading:

Farnham-Diggory, Sylvia. *The Learning Disabled Child.* Harvard University Press, 1992. ISBN 0-674-51924-8.

> People who read professional journals easily will be most comfortable with this book. However, for those with the determination to work through the technical information, the book contains valuable insights about how we learn.

Hamaguchi, Patricia McAller, Ma, CCC/SLP. *Childhood Speech, Language & Listening Problems: What Every Parent Should Know.* John Wiley & Sons, 1995. ISBN 0-471-03413-4.

> Speech and language problems are explained in detail but in layman's language. This is a "must-have" book for any parent of a child any kind of speech or language problem. It's also an excellent resource for teachers and other related professionals.

Recommended videotape:

How Difficult Can it Be?

> Rick Lavoie demonstrates to teachers what it's like to have a learning disability, using methods you'll understand even though you weren't present for his demonstration.

Rent this videotape and others related to learning problems from:
> WASHINGTON PAVE
> 6316 South 12th Street
> Tacoma, WA 98465
> (206) 565-2266

Organizations:

Learning Disabilities Association
> National Headquarters:
> 4156 Library Road
> Pittsburgh, PA 15234
> (412) 341-1515

CHECKLIST FOR STRENGTHS AND WEAKNESSES

	VERY STRONG	STRONG	average	weak	very weak
Verbal reasoning	☐	☐	☐	☐	☐
Non-verbal reasoning	☐	☐	☐	☐	☐
Global learner	☐	☐	☐	☐	☐
Sequential learner	☐	☐	☐	☐	☐
Visual perception	☐	☐	☐	☐	☐
Auditory perception	☐	☐	☐	☐	☐
Memory	☐	☐	☐	☐	☐
Grapho-motor skills	☐	☐	☐	☐	☐
Attention Deficit Disorders	☐	☐	☐	☐	☐
Basic skills	☐	☐	☐	☐	☐

Feel free to photocopy this page from *Taming the Dragons: Real Help for Real School Problems.*

The real scoop on how children learn

The object of teaching a child is to enable him to get along <u>without</u> his teachers.

Elbert Hubbard

Children who struggle with their schoolwork show three patterns in their learning: they learn inefficiently, inconsistently, and incompletely. In Chapter Three we talked about the difficulties that cause inefficient or inconsistent learning. Now it's time to talk about the third problem, incomplete learning.

Recent research on how primitive lifeforms learn suggests that physical changes may occur during learning. In his book, *The Naked Neuron*, Dr. R. Joseph describes what some of these changes might be. The neurons, or cells in our brain, are long, thin structures with finger-like extensions on the end called axons and dendrites. Magnified many times, two neurons might look somewhat like this:

As you can see, the axons and neurons reach out toward each other but don't actually touch. How, then, does information travel from neuron to neuron?

To carry the information—in the form of electrical impulses—from the end of one dendrite to the beginning of the next, we have chemicals in our brain called "neuro-transmitters." These chemicals, carrying electrical impulses with them, travel back and forth across the neural gap between the two cells. You might imagine chemical "ferries" carrying messages across from one riverbank to the other.

The researchers have discovered that some simple life forms build bridges connecting one nerve cell to the next, sort of like this:

These researchers suspect that the human brain also builds such bridges between brain cells. As more and more cells join the chain, researchers of learning theorize that a *neural pathway* may form, something like this:

Observing children as they learn suggests that the more we use what we learn, the more permanent the neural pathway, and the knowledge, becomes.

This preliminary research barely scratches the surface, and we can't say with confidence that the human brain really works precisely this way. Still, imagining a path through the brain that becomes more permanent in time is a useful way to visualize how we learn.

However memories are formed, we know that repeated, successful use strengthens them. The completion of these supposed paths through the brain would be what we think of as learning. The more solidly we establish learning, the more easily we'll do the task or recall the knowledge. Anyone who has learned to play a musical instrument is familiar with this experience: repeated and diligent practice of a scale makes it easier and easier to play until finally we can play it automatically.

Children who learn inconsistently or inefficiently seem to build inadequate or fragile pathways to the information they need, and thus perform unevenly.

The brain contains 100 billion inter-connecting nerve cells—that's more stars than are found in the Milky Way! So it's not surprising that we would need some method to find our way around it. It stands to reason that inefficient learners will have a harder time finding their way through this huge mass of nerve cells than people with no learning problems would have.

Struggling students don't seem to "find their way through" their brain as quickly or as well as efficient learners do. It's possible that one time their brain takes one route and another time chooses a different route. They use several partly-built paths to the information, but none of them consistently enough to be able to get to the information quickly, easily and confidently. Or, they may fragment the information, and store it incompletely in several places instead of establishing one reliable site.

The four stages of learning

Sooner or later, most of us have to work hard to learn something. We don't always realize it, but instant learning rarely takes place. If we "cram" for a test, for example, we may squeak through on the exam only to find that we have forgotten the material within a few weeks. That's because we didn't learn it solidly to begin with. Complete learning, learning that stays with us for long periods of time, takes place in steps, or stages. At each of these steps, which we'll call the Four Stages of Learning, we master a task a little more thoroughly, until we finally know it extremely well. For this book those stages have been named "Exposure Stage," Guided Learning Stage," "Independence Stage" and "Mastery Stage."

We all go through these stages as we learn, but some of us move through them faster than others, and we all learn some kinds of knowledge more easily than others. When we're learning something we're good at we may not be aware of these four stages, but we still move through them, perhaps very rapidly. To explain these four stages, we're going to use a skill nearly everyone struggled to learn: long division.

Stage one is the *Exposure Stage* and is encountered any time a concept is completely new to us. Using our example, when our teacher first explained long division to us, most of us got confused. If we could examine the pathway for this information, we might (if the preliminary research is right) find that at the beginning, in the Exposure Stage, the nerves are completely unconnected, with visible gaps between cells:

We call stage two the *Guided Learning Stage* because we still can't do the problems without help and guidance from our teacher. We are beginning to catch on though, and with support, encouragement and clues from the teacher, we can attempt the problems. But it's hard work, and since we make a variety of mistakes we still need the teacher's help often. We are still dependent on the teacher for success, so complete learning hasn't taken place yet.

During the Guided Learning Stage the connection between the dendrites might look something like this, not yet strong or dependable:

Knowledge "learned" only to the Guided Learning Stage is learned inadequately and incompletely. If a student stops at this level and doesn't progress to the Independence Stage she hasn't really learned anything useful.

With review, guidance and hard work we reach stage three, called the *Independence Stage*. At this stage we can do most of the problems on our own, most of the time. This is when we begin to think of the task as "easy," and we gain confidence in our abilities.

Examination of the neural pathway might now look more solid:

However, we would need occasional review or eventually we might forget (perhaps only partially) how to do the problems. If that happened, the connections might weaken, something like this:

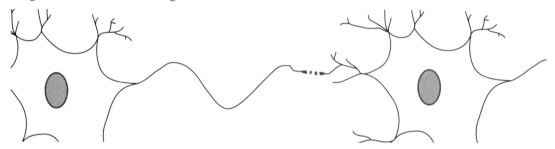

If the pathway for a skill weakens we may drop back to the Guided Learning Stage, once again unable to do the work independently.

This is why elementary school math textbooks begin the school year with a thorough review of the last year's skills. The review maintains independent skills and prevents students from slipping back to stage two, Guided Learning.

The final, fourth level, *Mastery Stage*, comes with still more practice. At Mastery Stage we have learned to do long division so thoroughly and completely we can perform it for the rest of our lives with no clues, no help, no review. Our understanding of it is automatic, and we can do the steps without stopping to think what to do next.

Using our model, communication between cells is rapid and consistent; we literally know the information without thinking. The path might look something like this now:

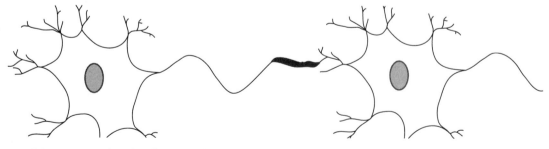

Mastery is the final goal of education. We rarely forget anything we've learned this well.

The struggling student's bumpy ride through the four stages of learning

The learning disabled student's problem is that her uneven learning style interferes with her progress through the stages described above. Struggling students move more slowly, often stalling and getting stuck at the second stage (Guided Learning). Remaining dependent on teacher clues and help, these students rarely have the powerful and liberating experience of considering any of their schoolwork "easy."

Not surprisingly, they feel frustrated and irritated by schoolwork. They may be inefficient learners, but they're not stupid, and they know they haven't yet come close to mastering their work.

Getting to the Independence Stage is a heady experience for a struggling student. Working efficiently feels terrific, and most people don't believe they have learned a skill until they can do it easily. When students can't do their schoolwork easily, they don't feel smart. That's why the "tips and tricks" offered in Chapters Nine through Sixteen are designed to blast students past the wall they face at the Guided Learning Stage to Independence, and eventually, Mastery.

Learned helplessness

The uneven learning styles we talked about in Chapter Three interfere in a variety of ways with the four stages we've just mapped out. Whether the child doesn't "get" what the teacher says, is confused by its appearance, finds her attention wandering in and out, or has difficulty remembering what to do, the result is the same: she builds an inadequate neural path for that skill.

Since progress comes slowly for struggling students, at least in their troublesome areas, many never develop mastery of a task before the teacher moves on to the next skill. Teachers want their students to master their work, but they need to move their classes along. Too often, a teacher accepts the incomplete learning of the second stage (Guided Learning) as satisfactory for her struggling students. That is, she stops teaching the child one skill (leaving her adrift for that task), and moves on to the next task—which, likely, the student will learn badly and incompletely also.

This incomplete instruction happens all the time, both in regular classrooms and in remedial programs such as resource rooms and special education classrooms. Often as a result the child develops something educators call learned helplessness. In this state, the student doesn't try to function independently within the classroom because she has had little success at taking responsibility for doing her work on her own. When she tried to work independently she failed miserably but was pushed on to new skills anyway. Making things worse, the teacher accepted her incomplete learning as adequate—and may have even praised her for it.[1]

Students who routinely have been moved on to new tasks before old ones have been learned develop large gaps in their knowledge and skills. This problem builds upon itself: the student hasn't learned to subtract well, but the teacher moves her on to multiplication facts anyway, and then to long division before she's learned the multiplication facts. She is now wholly unprepared for long division, which requires her to use those math facts, as well as other poorly-mastered math skills, in new and complex ways.

---

[1] Please note that this is not in any way an endorsement for the educational practice known as "retention." Retention means the child repeats the grade and implies that although children vary widely, they should all be at the same place academically at the same time. It is possible to cope with individual differences without resorting to retention.

This pattern of incomplete mastery, repeated over months and years, leads the student to the conclusion that she will never do her work well. Unfamiliar with the experience of doing her work easily, she concludes that the struggle that comes with stage two (Guided Learning) is success—for her, at least. She knows others may come to a skill easily, but she believes, perhaps without being able to say it aloud, that she will never do her work easily.

Soon such a student will mistake the struggle of the second stage for real learning instead of what it really is: informed exposure. Once the student has made this view of herself part of her personality she may resist efforts to move her past Guided Learning to Independence and Mastery Stages. Having rarely or never experienced anything but struggle, she doesn't see the point of the extra effort. She may think she has already learned the skill as well as she should be expected to and that the teacher is badgering her. Although her conclusions are understandable, they constitute yet another barrier to learning. Worse, teachers often misinterpret these self-defeating attitudes and label the student "stubborn," "lazy," or "unmotivated."

We cannot persuade such a student that she's smart under these circumstances. Threatened by the fear of failure, she is likely to insist "I can't!" rather than attempt to get to a level of functioning she believes to be unattainable. Soon the struggling student convinces herself that she can't do any work without help.

In fact, because of their lack of solid progress (of which they are painfully aware), many struggling students secretly live with either the fear or the firm belief that they are remarkably stupid or even retarded. They know quite well that although others can complete tasks easily, they continue to struggle.

Bringing it all together

There's a two-fold approach to avoiding or ending this miserable state of affairs. First, we have to tame the dragon that tells her she is stupid, and allow her to re-discover her strengths. We must pick ways to teach and review skills that use her strengths while by-passing her weaknesses. Meanwhile, we provide as much review as needed to build a solid memory path through the brain for the skill being learned (Chapters Nine through Sixteen will detail specific ways to do this). We don't short-circuit all this work by ending the instruction and review too soon. Educators call this sort of plan "over-learning," but the term doesn't accurately describe the practice when it's what the student needs.

To accomplish these goals the student must develop confidence in what she can do and allow herself to learn that she can do it easily. This is why moving at a slower pace at first may result in more progress in the long run: the extra time allows her to master a skill thoroughly, working through all the stages. It gives her a chance to find out that she is capable of mastering her work.

Research tells us how we learn complex tasks best: instruction followed by guided practice, then a time delay followed later by more review. Again, anyone who plays a musical instrument will recognize this pattern: our playing improves more rapidly if we practice for shorter daily periods than if we practice for one long session just before our lesson. It appears that the brain consolidates what it's learning during the delays between practice sessions. Those gaps between practice sessions or review may be when the brain does most of its work building those pathways for the skill.

Since students do their homework some time after initial instruction (providing the valuable time delay), this makes homework a potentially powerful learning tool. The student is taught, works some problems herself, goes on to another subject (the delay) and then does more of the problems that night as homework.

Praise: the double-edged sword

Do you praise your child for doing her homework? Does she believe the good things you say? Is it possible to praise badly, or too much?

Most struggling students handle badly the praise they receive. On the one hand, they rarely hear it. When they do hear praise, they find many reasons to disbelieve it. What does "You're a good girl" really mean? Is she good all the time? (Not likely.) Did she do well on the math test? (No.) Did she try hard? (No one seems to think so except her.)

To be effective, praise has to be honest, precise and frequent. To help you get this kind of effective praise placed at the tip of your tongue, this chapter includes a long list of "praise phrases." You shouldn't copy this list slavishly. Instead, use it as a guide to create your own personalized list of things you can genuinely praise about your son or daughter. Make your own list, make it as specific as you can, and study it frequently so the positive words will come to mind immediately when you need them.

A caution about praise, however: most people believe that any praise improves a child's self-esteem, but this isn't true. Research shows that children with poor self-esteem see most praise as thinly-disguised criticism. Before such a child believes praise, she must see the truth of it herself. Effective praise is specific and exact ("You did that problem well.") Ineffective praise tends to be vague and not associated with any specific thing the child did ("You're smart"). Children who have experienced repeated failure only believe non-specific comments when they're negative. They'll believe "You're stupid," but not "You're smart." They think, "I'm not smart. Sure I got that one problem right, but I've flunked math for three years. Big deal: one problem right and I'm smart? Right..."

Specific praise is easy to remember and hard to deny. When you specifically say "You did that problem well," the child is likely to think, "Yes. I did do that problem well!" This way she hears the praise twice—once from you and once from herself. When she hears it from herself it's extremely convincing.

Make sure you know your child's strengths, so you can praise with conviction and credibility. In addition, make sure your child knows her strengths. It is not possible to point out real, specific accomplishments to a struggling child too often. Knowledge of her strengths will help her keep a sense of balance about the things she finds difficult.

But be careful. If you only bring out the praise when you have a complaint as well, she will soon pair the praise with the criticism and in her mind remember only the criticism. Worse, she will stop believing the positive things you say and begin to take all your praise as implied criticism. You have to search out and seize the positive moments whenever they occur. If you offer praise only when you criticize as well, the praise will soon sound hollow to her.

Sample praise phrases

Adjust these to meet your needs. Remember to use them about a specific thing your child has done and not in a general or vague way. Also, notice the complete lack of the word "I"—all these comments are strictly about the child.

You did that well!
Look...you have (insert number) done already!
You're working hard on this.
You did a good job on that problem.
You listened well, didn't you?
This work is neat.
Way to go!
You caught on to that quickly!
You've got that one knocked.
You're on your way.
That's super!
That was hard, but you did it.
You didn't give up easily.
You've been a hard worker.
You completed (...) well.
Your teacher told me (something good!)
Terrific!
You got that right.
You're concentrating well.
Nice printing.
Outstanding!
Good job.
You did that carefully.
You can be proud of this work.
Your teacher will be pleased.
You worked accurately.
You've followed the instructions well.
Correct!
Good thinking!
You solved that problem well.
Good margins.
You remembered to indent.
It's obvious you care about doing a good job on this.
You really stuck to it.
You must be pleased with this.

You used your time well.
Excellent.
Well done.
Super-duper!
That's fine (work, or something else specific) you've done.
This is well-organized.
Nice cursive.
You took the time to get it right.
That wasn't easy, but you got it.
You didn't give up just because it got a little hard. You're no quitter!
You must be proud of yourself.
Good work!
Keep up the good work!
That's first class!
Perfect!
You've got this mastered!
You've learned to do that well.
Clever girl to work that out!
You've got a real ability to ... (fill in the blank).
That's (number) in a row!
You're on a roll now!
(Applause)
What you did there (be specific) shows a good imagination!
Remarkably good work.
Wonderful!
You did a whopping good job on that!
You were resourceful.
Superb!
You've got that shipshape now!
Fine job!
Peachy!
Terrific!
That's top-drawer stuff!
Top-notch!

Absolutely right!
Fine work!
Your hard effort paid off.
Marvelous!
Quality work there!
That's the best you've ever done on
     that!

Use the praise words listed next carefully, because they're strong words and easily disbelieved. However, sometimes you may feel they're just right. One young man named Bryan, about whom you'll hear more later, has learned a tremendous amount about survival skills. The word "tremendous" only begins to cover what Bryan accomplished. He enrolled in a survival program, left a relatively warm Southern state in December and walked into the Idaho wilderness. For the next three weeks, often hip-deep in snow, he depended only upon himself and his survival knowledge to find his food, cook it and eat it. He kept himself warm, dry and safe. Although he accomplished these feats within a structured program and could have been rescued, it wasn't necessary. "Clever" or "good job" doesn't begin to cover what Bryan accomplished.

If these very strong words are accurate, go ahead and use them, but the level of the praise must match both the level of the effort and the quality of the work.

Use these words with great caution:

Phenomenal	Colossal
Magnificent	Overwhelming
Tremendous	Astonishing
Extraordinary	Sensational
Brilliant	Astounding
Stunning	Fabulous
Stupendous	Awesome
Monumental	Fantastic

These last words masquerade as compliments but often feel like "backdoor praise," appearing to build up self-esteem while actually undermining it. They all imply that you really don't believe your child is capable of what she has done. Although you wouldn't intend it that way, she might take it that way, so I don't recommend using these words:

Incredible
Amazing
Unbelievable

Once you have your customized list of "praise phrases" for your child, make a list of her strengths and weaknesses. Again, this is a time to be positive. You should list four strengths for every weakness. What will this accomplish? It will force you to concentrate only on the most important weaknesses while recognizing that her strengths are more numerous.

For example, when we asked Bryan's mother to make such a list for her son, she came up with the list you see below:

Bryan's strengths:	*Where Bryan needs help:*
• Athletic: high scorer on his soccer and basketball teams; black belt in karate when he was only ten	• Has trouble finishing his homework; forgets to study for tests
• Natural leader	
• Excellent finger dexterity	
• Has outstanding outdoor survival skills (he survived on his own in a winter wilderness program for three weeks!)	
• He asks for help when he needs it	• Has trouble remembering what he's read
• Good creative writing skills—superb imagination	
• Composes his own music; plays the guitar very well by ear	
• A kind and loving person	

You should make your list as well. Stick to the rule of four positive traits for every negative one. Train yourself to see her strengths. You may even find ways to turn negatives into positives. Highly distractible children, for instance, also notice fascinating details the rest of us tend to overlook.

Put the positive items on the left side of the page, and the negative items on the right. We read from left to right, so any time you look at the list you'll start with the strengths. If this list does its job, any time you think about your child—even momentarily—her strengths will pop into your head as well as her weaknesses.

Some parents have discovered a remarkable secret. Sometimes children doubt compliments given to them directly. However, they almost always believe praise (and criticism) they overhear. Knowing this, some parents plan times when their children can "accidentally" overhear them saying good things about them to someone else. If she overhears you telling her grandmother or a family friend that she's a hard worker, or that she's making good progress in math, or that she did an excellent job of raking the leaves for you, she will believe it.

Keeping your perspective

Keeping an eagle eye out for your child's strengths will also help you keep her difficulties in perspective. If you can't accept it when your child struggles with schoolwork, she won't feel comfortable coming to you with the hurts, frustrations and disappointments that will surely occur. Your child will accept who she is to the extent that you do.

Some children, especially older ones who understand their learning problems, enjoy making lists of their strengths as well, but use your best judgment about this. Although she will come up with strengths you would never have thought of, if she's feeling terribly defeated making the list could turn into a painful and negative experience for her.

Finally, talk honestly to your child about yourself and your strengths and weaknesses. Share with your child how you learn best and what you find hard. Admit it when you make mistakes. Doing these things makes it OK to the child to have weaknesses as well as strengths and to make mistakes.

Every Person's Bill of Rights[2]

The Right to make mistakes
The Right to do less than you are humanly capable of doing
The Right to change your mind
The Right to take the time you need to respond
The Right to ask for help
The Right to disagree
The Right to feel and express anger
The Right to ask why
The Right to say "no" and not feel guilty
The Right to be treated with respect

[2]*Education...A Family Affair,* Nov./Dec. 1989, p. 3.

Variations are to be expected, and are in no way to be considered a defect.

Hang tag from Madras shirt

What do those experts know, anyway? How in the world can they tell if your child has a learning disability or not? Maybe he's just lazy. Maybe math just isn't his thing. Don't boys learn to read later than girls? Maybe he'll catch up on his own... .

Figuring out whether or not a child has a learning problem takes skill, practice and judgment, and the professionals who make these decisions disagree on many diagnostic issues. These differences of opinion don't always affect whether or not a child will get help, but often cause much confusion in parents' minds.

How common are learning disabilities?

The standards by which children are diagnosed vary from year to year, from state to state and sometimes from even town to town. Statistics reflect this confusion. Depending on who you read, some experts say we have about eight hundred-thousand learning disabled children in the country. Others put the figure as high as eight million.

How do we explain such a wide range of numbers?

Many times extremely high or extremely low numbers come from biased sources. For instance, the expert who places the number very low may sincerely believe that many children are diagnosed who should not be. Such a person would interpret statistics based on a personal bias.

Others view learning difficulties through lenses colored by their professional biases. A psychiatrist may blame emotional problems for the child's difficulty and prescribe some psychological or psychiatric intervention. A family counselor may lay the blame at the feet of family conflict and assume that family therapy will lead to improved school performance.

Among educators, some over-zealous specialists see learning disabilities in the normal strengths and weaknesses we all possess. Others disregard overall ability and diagnose a learning disability any time a child performs below grade level. Most specialists in learning disabilities wouldn't agree with that standard. Or an organization may over-estimate the numbers to make a point. One outspoken critic believes our schools over-diagnose out of extreme, rigid need for conformity among their students. He reflects this bias when he talks about how many children he thinks have learning disabilities.

The real number lies somewhere among all the opinions, with each view containing at least a kernel of truth. The debate shows that diagnosis is often open to interpretation and isn't a simple matter.

We do know we've seen a steady increase in the number of children diagnosed. Several legitimate reasons explain this:

- **Teacher accountability.** When we hold teachers accountable for the progress of their students, it's in their best interest to find those who are struggling and to find out why they aren't learning as well as they should.
- **The "Back to Basics" movement.** In some areas, teachers have dropped back to more rigid ways of teaching than they previously used. Rigid teaching styles cause unnecessary difficulties for many students, because when teachers can present information in a variety of formats the number of students who learn well increases.
- **Stiff competency requirements for promotion.** Some schools, in an effort to improve education—or at least test scores—have set tough requirements for promotion to the next grade. Well-run schools combine retention with efforts to discover what the child's problem is, and often they find that the child has a learning disability. Unfortunately a great many schools view retention as a solution instead of a warning sign, so this response isn't universal by any means.
- **Increased parental expectations.** The number of parents who expect their children to be good students who will graduate from college has steadily risen in this century. These parents seek answers and solutions when their children struggle to learn.
- **Harder school work.** For example, the author learned the parts of speech in eighth grade, but today's textbooks begin teaching them in first grade. The

author studied the parts of a cell in tenth grade, but her children learned it in sixth. While some children can handle the faster pace, by making ever-more difficult demands of students we doom some children to struggle. Some of them would have been just fine had the curriculum not been rushed. Does that make them learning disabled?

- **Graded classrooms.** What? Graded classrooms? How else can you teach? When we taught our children in one-room schoolhouses, students studied what they needed to learn next, not what was in the textbooks for their grade. The child who needed extra time to master his multiplication facts or paragraph-writing created no problem because the teacher never expected all the students to be in the same place.

  Most of today's teachers, however, hold firm views about what children should know at each grade. Grade level expectations encourage us to examine each child's progress closely, allowing us to spot potentially learning disabled students more easily than in the past.

- **We know what we're looking for.** In 1963, when "learning disabilities" were first described, we found very few students with the problem and thought the problem was rare. As we worked with these students, however, we developed clearer and clearer pictures of just what learning disabilities are and how to spot it in children.

Some critics maintain that many diagnoses are made simply so the school district can get the extra federal money. The author's experience doesn't support such a notion. Special education programs are expensive to run. The author's experience has been that the intentions of the people doing the diagnoses have been to help the children, not to raise funds or increase the size of their department.

Why would anyone lash out against efforts to help struggling children achieve? Some people feel that too much money is spent on special education. They suspect the money (or at least some of it) could be better spent on the other children, whom they believe are neglected by comparison.

Other critics have their own personal axes to grind. For some specialists, a diagnosis of "learning disability" doesn't fit their diagnostic model well. This is an example of the old saying, "When your only tool is a hammer, all your problems will look like nails." Since these people know their particular field very well, they can argue quite persuasively.

It's important to listen to the critics, though. We can find an element of truth in their comments. Just because a student is behind academically doesn't make him learning disabled, but sometimes psychologists will call him "learning disabled" anyway because they like the child and want to see him get some help. They aren't treating the child fairly. If he's doing the best he can and just isn't quite as bright as the average child, giving him extra help won't change that and may put too much pressure on him. We also run the risk of allowing our learning disabilities programs to become a dumping ground for anyone who can't keep up for whatever reason.

For the child's sake as well as to promote good education for everyone, the diagnosis given needs to be the right one.

What do the testers look for?

The typical student learns adequately no matter how the information is presented. A learning disabled child by comparison will show pronounced strengths and weaknesses in his learning style. Usually the weaknesses interfere with school progress, and his unusual learning style makes it especially hard for him to learn as he should.

The child's schoolwork reflects a checkerboard of "can's" and "can't's." He is bright, but his brain works unpredictably, interfering with his progress in spite of his intelligence. Sometimes it seems as if the information gets garbled during transit from ear or eye to brain. Sometimes it doesn't get scrambled until he tries to think about it or when he tries to get the information back out again.

In most classrooms, most of the time, we expect children to learn by listening and looking. If they have serious difficulty learning in these traditional ways they're automatically in trouble. In a more enlightened class where the teacher used a wider variety of approaches, the same child might be able to "make it" without special help. Sometimes good teaching makes the difference between a child with problems and a child needing help, but poor teaching explains few cases of suspected learning problems.

A vocal minority believe that students have the right to be different and that schools should welcome diverse ways of learning. The reality is that if the child attends a public school, he must cope with the methods being used.

How different is "different?"

Learning problems exist on a continuum from very slight to completely incapacitating. Severity depends partly on what strengths the child brings to counterbalance his weaknesses, and partly on how useful those strengths are for formal learning.

All other things being equal (which they never are), the brighter learning disabled child will master his school work better than one who doesn't have that edge. Often this works against him in the diagnostic process; some states and some teams won't diagnose a very bright or gifted child if he's managing to keep his head above the water, even if he performs well below his real potential.

To complicate things still further, the younger the child is, the trickier the process of diagnosis becomes. That's because there's a very wide range of "normal" in young children. Many beginning kindergartners don't know the alphabet yet, and many leave kindergarten without reading. At the same time some children come to kindergarten knowing the letters, knowing the sounds they make and even reading. Some leave kindergarten fluent readers.

Typically, we spot learning disabled children when they have trouble learning what they're being taught. For instance, by the end of first grade the students without any difficulties are learning rapidly on their own, and first grade teachers know who is struggling with basic skills and who is not by the end of the first semester. Although occasionally a child isn't diagnosed until high school or college, generally the further the child progresses in school the more likely it becomes that his problems will be spotted.

Who best to diagnose?

Your pediatrician may provide excellent care for your child's medical needs and yet not be up to the task of helping you find out why your child struggles with schoolwork.

There are several reasons for this. First, doctors rarely see definitive medical signs. When medical clues are present, by themselves they aren't enough to make a diagnosis. Second, your pediatrician knows medicine far better than he or she knows education. Learning disabilities are educational, not medical, problems: an intelligent child fails to learn as expected based on his overall intelligence. So learning disabilities aren't a problem that can be identified by physical exam or medical tests.

In spite of this, the first place you should go is your pediatrician—who will check for medical problems such as anemia, ear infections, or neurological or thyroid problems that can mimic or complicate learning problems. The doctor can do a cursory check of vision and hearing and refer you to specialists in those fields if necessary.

Some parents choose to go to a private practitioner, such as a psychologist who specializes in learning problems, for their child's first evaluation. However, except in unusual circumstances you'll pay for this service yourself. Since the school district can choose to disregard this evaluation in favor of its own, private evaluation can be an expensive first choice.

Most parents choose to have their child's school do the evaluation for learning problems. By law, school districts must provide this service when needed.

Diagnosis: how it's done[1]

When school teams test, or assess a child, they look at four things: 1) the overall learning ability of the child; 2) what skills he possesses to help him learn; 3) what skills, if any, he seems to be weak in, and 4) whether or not the school can help with any problems they find. For instance, if the testers discover the child needs long-term counseling to cope with the death of a sibling, they can tell the parent their opinion but aren't obligated to provide the counseling, because the difficulty isn't school-related.

This process is called *assessment*. The team assesses, or evaluates, how the child learns, what skills he brings to the tasks he's presented with and what skills he seems to be weak in. When they're done, both staff and parents have a much clearer view of the child as a student. School districts vary in how they move through the steps listed below, but each step leads to the next, and by the time they're done the diagnostic team will understand how the child learns.

---

[1]Public schools must conform to various state and federal requirements when deciding which children have learning problems. As a result the kinds of tests they choose are somewhat predictable. Evaluations done by private practitioners may vary considerably.

Step 1: Someone states a concern

Sometimes it's the parent; more often it's the classroom teacher who first suspects a problem. If the teacher raises the concern, she takes her questions to her school's evaluation team[2] who looks informally at the child. They may decide to watch the child for the time being, begin the evaluation process, or call the parents in for a preliminary meeting.

Step 2: In-school evaluation

The evaluation team will study information in the child's cumulative file (his year-to-year record). This record usually contains group test scores, report cards and comments from previous teachers. They'll include results of individual testing previously done with the child. They're searching for some reason to explain the child's apparent difficulties. Sometimes they conclude that the child is all right just as he is, in which case, unless the parents express some continuing concern, action is likely to stop.

Step 3: Referral to diagnostic team

Schools count on specialists to assist them in the diagnostic process. If they don't have enough information to draw solid conclusions, they obtain parent permission and contact their formal diagnostic team.

Step 4: Initial diagnostic team meeting

A child may need help and yet need only small amounts of support. So at this point the evaluation team may make specific recommendations such as reducing the child's work load, providing tutors or short-term counseling, trying behavior modification, or a host of other possibilities. Ideally the committee custom-designs this list for each child, with the child's apparent, unique difficulties in mind.

Step 5: Diagnostic team meets

After those recommendations have been tried, the team meets again to see if the simpler solutions have eased the child's problem. If so, the team usually ends the evaluation process, although someone can start it again if needed. If, however, significant problems remain, the evaluation team enlarges to include people with expertise in various areas: psychological testing (by an psychological examiner or psychologist), individual educational testing (by a educational examiner), classroom observations (often done by a learning disabilities and behavioral specialist), and screening (and more detailed testing if warranted) by a speech/language pathologist.

Step 6: The evaluation team gathers more information

Parents describe their child as they know him to a team member and often fill out a questionnaire. Team members discuss the child with his teacher, observe him in the classroom several times and have the teacher fill out a questionnaire as well. They combine all this information with the information gathered earlier from school records. Sometimes a social worker gathers more detailed family information.

---

[2]Terms used may vary from state to state.

The school nurse includes medical information to make sure the child's vision and hearing are adequate for schoolwork and that there are no other medical concerns that might affect his ability to learn.

Step 7: Testing

The testing team must accomplish two things now. First, they must establish that a learning disability may be causing the child's difficulty. Second, they must rule out other possible causes.

Good testers choose tests individually for each child beginning with a good test of intellectual potential. Often some form of the Weschler intelligence scales are used because the ten sub-tests that make them up can provide useful extra information about the child's way of learning. Such tests were designed to predict school success. Although some controversy surrounds them they give skilled testers an effective way to measure what the child should be able to do.

The testers also use individualized achievement tests in the three main educational areas: reading, math, and written expression. Group achievement and IQ tests are often inaccurate for children with special educational needs. While group achievement test scores may be referred to during evaluation, a good diagnosis doesn't use them as its basis.

After the student completes the first few tests, examiners choose additional tests to confirm or rule out problems (including a diagnosis of "no educational problem"). They evaluate the child's learning style to determine if it includes any unusual weaknesses. For example, the speech and language therapist judges the child's ability to communicate. If she suspects any difficulty using language, she then does a more in-depth language evaluation to confirm or rule out a language disorder. If the child seems clumsy or shows difficulty using pencil, paper and scissors, an occupational therapy evaluation may be ordered to determine if the child has serious coordination problems that might be interfering with his school performance. (See Chapter Three for a summary of some common learning styles.)

In addition, the testing team must rule out other causes for the child's difficulty. All sorts of things from lack of native intelligence to emotional problems to an unstable home life can interfere with learning. Some possible labels besides learning disabled or "non-handicapped" (the phrase used in special education law) are language impaired, behaviorally disordered, or retarded.

These three factors—potential, achievement, and learning style—are used to determine whether the child has a learning disability. A diagnosis of learning disabilities uses those three things named above to determine:

- normal or near normal academic potential (usually stated as I.Q.)
- school achievement well below what the child's potential would predict
- identification of some weakness in the child's learning style likely to explain the poor achievement.

How big the difference, or discrepancy, must be before a diagnosis is made varies wildly from state to state and sometimes from community to community. Some states require that testers identify a specific difficulty receiving, using or producing information (the classic definition of a learning disability), but some do not. This means that a child could be accepted for help in one state but rejected in a neighboring one. Some states decide whether a discrepancy exists based on intellectual potential; others simply compare grade level with the child's achievement. In the second example, slower learners without any learning disability will be diagnosed while brighter children with a problem will be overlooked.

Step 8: Evaluation conference

When the team has gathered their information and completed their testing, the parents attend a meeting to discuss the results. At this meeting the team decides if the child meets any diagnostic criteria. Each member of the multi-disciplinary team presents his or her findings. If the team concludes (and parents agree) that the child is not eligible for services, the whole process has been completed. However, if the team concludes that the child has a significant educational problem, they decide which diagnosis is most appropriate. At this meeting or shortly thereafter, the special education teacher and parent choose a date to write the Individualized Education Plan (widely known as an "IEP").

Step 9: Writing the IEP

Until now, the team has studied the child but not helped him much. That situation changes when parents and staff (which may include the child's classroom teacher and other school personnel such as counselor or principal as well as the new special education teacher) sit down to write the IEP. The IEP details what the child's difficulties are and what the school intends to do to help the child become more successful.

Federal law requires schools and parents to write IEPs together, and parents need to be an active part of the IEP team. They need to be present when it's written and to monitor the child's education to make sure teachers follow his plan. The team must re-write the IEP once a year, but it can be amended at any time. Either the school or the parents can request that it be rewritten or amended, and both school and parents need to participate.

Sorting out what is and isn't "normal"

Unfortunately for parents and teachers, it's not always obvious what is "normal" learning and what isn't. Younger children quite naturally vary widely in what they have learned. Other factors, such as overall academic potential, affect how quickly a child learns. So a tester may find no significant problem even though the child doesn't learn rapidly. Or, the testers could find a problem and the parent's reaction might be "So what? I was just like that when I was young." At the same time the parents might be quite concerned about something that was quite within normal range.

To give examples, the author has known parents who weren't concerned that their third grader couldn't seem to print or write legibly. She heard things such as "Neither could I, and I'm fine now," or "So he'll have a secretary." These parents didn't realize that the difficulty causing the writing problem also caused other problems as well. The parents were focusing on the clue—the pencil/paper problem—instead of what the clue revealed.

In another case the parents believed their daughter had a reading problem based on reading they'd tried to do with her at home. They didn't realize that the books they had given her were too hard and that their expectations were unrealistic. That's why diagnostic teams rely on standardized tests of academic achievement when determining whether or not a child has a learning disability.

Some teachers struggle with the issue in a different way. They hope that if only they can find the right instructional method, all the students they teach will perform at grade level.

Children's abilities vary greatly, and just as some excel, some will struggle. Just because a child learns slowly does not mean the child has a true learning disability. Good teaching can help a child to cope with his weaknesses better or to work around them, but no amount of extra or specialized instruction can make a real learning disability go away.

After the diagnosis: then what?

Once the testing team has diagnosed your child with some learning problem, you, the parent, have a few things to do.

First, you decide if you agree with the diagnosis or not. If you don't agree with it, read the section in the next chapter about contesting the diagnosis.

If the testing team found your child ineligible for services and you disagree, you have the same rights. Just as it's unfair to diagnose a learning disability in a child who has no serious problem, it's also unfair to deny services to a child who should be receiving them. However, parental opinion alone won't be strong enough evidence to overturn a decision. See the next chapter for information on how to assert your child's rights.

Finally, if you and the testing team agree that your child has a learning disability, don't panic. Your child hasn't arrived at a dead end; it's the beginning of a new path. Each child will follow a different path, one carved by his individual strengths and weaknesses, enhanced by his personality and support from his parents.

The path
through the
maze

Nobody's family can hang out the sign "Nothing the matter here."

Chinese proverb

If your child has received a diagnosis as described in Chapter Five, you know that you and the school must write an *Individualized Education Plan*, or IEP, for her. Before your child receives any kind of special education you need to understand IEPs completely.

Written well, an IEP contains an excellent educational summary of your child's strengths and weaknesses as well as what she needs to get her education back on track. Done poorly it's nothing more than an ineffective waste of time. Which way your child's IEP goes depends on two things: how involved *you* are when it is written, and how well *you* monitor its use.

Each word in the phrase "Individualized Education Plan" carries great meaning.

The first word, ***Individualized***, revolutionized special education. In 1972, when the author started teaching special education, few guidelines existed. Parents assumed the school personnel knew how to meet each child's special needs, but lesson plans were typically written for groups, not individuals.

That changed in 1975 when Congress passed Public Law 94-142 (often called HB 94-142 or just 94-142), a law requiring educators to plan carefully for each child receiving special education. For the first time, a law mandated that all learning disabled children receive education customized to their particular needs. (Congress has amended this law several times and now we call it the "Individuals with Disabilities Education Act," or "IDEA.")

The second word, **Education**, reflects the fact that the schools do not take charge of every aspect of a child's life. The school accepts responsibility only for those things that directly affect the child's ability to learn, but does not guarantee that the school will meet non-educational needs.

The final word, **Plan**, suggests an orderly, step-by-step approach to achieve specific goals and objectives, one based on careful thought.

Twenty years after the passage of 94-142, individualization remains the most difficult aspect of writing and using IEPs. Since individualization, or making sure the IEP meets the precise educational needs of the child for whom it is being written, is so important, we'll discuss how to customize a child's education by using an IEP throughout the next section.

Who writes the IEP?

Typically the teacher who will provide the specialized education chairs the IEP meeting, but an IEP is supposed to be written jointly by a group of people including the special education teacher, a representative from the school who made the referral and the *parents*. Others can attend as well; often the psychologist who guided the testing team attends, frequently the school counselor comes along with the child's classroom teacher, and parents are entitled to invite anyone they choose. Some parents invite another friend or relative for moral support, and sometimes parents include an outside professional already working with the child, such as a child psychologist.

Rules, rules, rules!

The law gives specific instructions about how the IEP must be written. The school must make every effort to involve you, the parents, in the process so it can be written in your presence.

This law also states what information to include in the IEP. Some of this information either requires no special knowledge (ex: name and date of birth of the student) or is best filled out by the teacher. In the interest of saving everyone's time, teachers usually come to the meeting with these parts of the IEP already completed: do you really want to sit there and watch her write your child's name and birthdate on each page? Don't blindly accept a wholly pre-written IEP, however. You may have additions or comments to make about many of the sections, as you will see as we discuss each part of the IEP.

The school must tell you who will be attending the meeting. People you might not expect could include the special education teacher's supervisor, or in small school districts, the superintendent. If you spot extra people on the list you may call the teacher and find out why all the people will be there.

During the IEP meeting, the Chairperson must tell you all of your rights should you disagree with the recommendations made. You should also receive this information in printed form. If you don't receive it from the IEP Chairperson, ask for it.

The law also says that the student's placement must reflect her unique needs. The school may only place your child in the most suitable program they have if it is also the most suitable for your child. For example, they can't say "Your child needs a special class, but she can't go into a special class because we don't have any."

Likewise, goals and objectives (explained further below) must reflect your child's educational needs and may not be dictated by the program she will be attending. This sounds obvious, but the author has seen IEPs with reading goals written for strong readers because the resource teacher already had a reading program set up and could fit the child into her schedule more easily that way.

The law states clearly that the child must be placed in what is the "least restrictive environment" for her. That really means "least restrictive *appropriate* environment." They may not automatically place all students with learning disabilities into a special class. We know that many such children can do well while remaining in their present class and school if they receive good support teaching (which may be provided in a resource room or within his regular classroom). Likewise, a school district cannot deny special class placement for a child if that is truly what the child needs. However, they can try less restrictive environments first, since no one can predict with 100% accuracy who will need special placement all day and who will not.

By law, your child's IEP must be evaluated once a year and a new one written. IEPs can be amended at any time (but not without your knowledge and participation). Your child's IEP Committee can rewrite the entire IEP before the year is over if it will help your child.

What's included in an IEP?

A good IEP provides a road map of the child's strengths and weaknesses and indicates the things the school can do that are most likely to help her.

The *cover sheet*[1] lists the child's name, birth date and other identifying information and her diagnosis (the diagnosis will include the specific subject affected by the learning disability). It includes a place for each person to sign, and states the child's educational placement. Often the parts that directly relate to the child's special services are filled in little by little as the IEP meeting progresses. Parents need to be alarmed only when someone has filled in the sections dealing with decisions (such as educational placement and amount of special help) before the meeting. These decisions are supposed to be made during the IEP meeting and in the parents' presence, not prior to it.

A Resource Room is a reasonable first placement for all but the most severely learning disabled students. When a child receives Resource Room help, she leaves her regular classroom for a specified length of time to get specialized help from the Resource Teacher. The Chairperson will write in the amount of time the child will

---

[1]There probably aren't two school districts in the country that use the same names for all the forms making up an IEP. However, all IEPs must include the information listed in these sections no matter what they're called, and any well-written IEP will contain all the information described.

spend there after discussion with the rest of the IEP Committee.[2] If the child will attend a special class, this part of the IEP will say how much time she will spend "integrated" in a regular classroom.

Finally, the cover sheet is the most likely place to list secondary diagnoses (such as speech, language, occupational therapy, or severe behavioral problems).

Unless this is your child's first IEP, the next section contains some sort of summary (often called *Goals Evaluation Page*) of her progress during the last year. Look at this summary carefully, and ask exactly how the teacher judged your child's progress. If your child didn't meet her goals perhaps the Committee aimed too high, or perhaps the methods used should be changed for the next year.

Next, the Committee considers your child's *Present Levels of Performance*. This section should include all her significant strengths and weaknesses. Present levels in your child's first IEP should be based on tests and observations completed during diagnosis, and can include both academic and behavioral traits.

The Chairperson writes this section based on her special knowledge of education and test interpretation, and may write it ahead of time to save time during the actual meeting. You should come prepared to discuss your child's present levels from your own perspective, to challenge erroneous assumptions, to ask for documentation of weaknesses, and to request that strengths be added as well.

Don't accept an IEP that lists only weaknesses and no strengths in the Present Levels. Parents can contribute by naming special abilities the child possesses. All children have strengths, or at least relative strengths, in some areas. These strengths should be listed as positively as possible but not dishonestly. Your child may have several different teachers, and they should have an accurate but balanced view of your child. Your child's strengths can be used sometimes to help her cope with her weaknesses—but only if her teachers know about them.

Parents need to pay particular attention to the Present Levels, as that section dictates the areas in which your child will receive help.

The next section lists *Goals and Objectives*, the first place where the Committee has a real opportunity to customize and personalize your child's education. In this section the Committee writes exactly how they intend to help your child. Goals and objectives must match up with weaknesses listed in the Present Levels section.

Goals are more general, and objectives break each goal down into more manageable pieces. Good objectives state how the child's progress will be measured. Together, the Goals and Objectives should reflect the child's most urgent needs as listed in the Present Levels.

During the Evaluation Conference (covered in Chapter Five), the diagnostic team may have made recommendations about how to teach your child. Although the diagnostic team is knowledgeable, that part of their report is not an IEP, and often the person writing the Evaluation Report is not a teacher. Be ready to listen if the teacher who will be teaching your child feels some other approach would be more appropriate. If the Chairperson of the IEP Committee will teach your child, she should be given some leeway in setting goals, especially if she can explain her reasoning clearly.

---

[2]Remember, you are an active member of that IEP Committee.

However, remember that the teacher has a potential conflict of interest here. If she can fit your child in with another child or group, and use the same approach and materials, it will simplify her job. A balance always has to be struck (it simply isn't possible for all children to receive exclusively one-on-one tutoring, for instance). The teacher who has a hand in planning is more likely to follow through well. There is no danger in these necessary compromises so long as the child progresses well.

In rare and isolated incidents, teachers have sometimes written goals based on what they wanted to teach rather than what the child needed to learn. Make certain the goals and objectives set for your child match her educational needs.

The *Adaptations and Modifications* page specializes your child's education still further. Some of the things that might be listed here are special testing arrangements, such as having tests read to her or eliminating time limits on tests. These adaptations can be both good and bad for your child; although they can help they can also coddle her too much. Your child's education shouldn't be fine-tuned to this degree merely to raise her grades. Other adjustments listed here might be:

- shortening her spelling list
- shortening the number of math problems she must do
- reducing the amount of written work required

These modifications often mean the child is working below grade level. If instructional level is lowered, the child's report card should reflect this. One option is to grade the child on work completed, and then mark the child "below grade level" if such an option exists on the report card—if not, add a note that the child is working below grade level and that grades are not based on grade-level work. An Adaptations and Modifications page is now required as part of all IEPs.

As you read Chapters Nine through Sixteen, look for the symbol shown to the right. It will alert you to effective IEP modifications.

Good IEP idea!

Differences of opinion

What do you do if you don't agree with the direction in which your child's IEP is developing?

Keep in mind that you are an expert also. The teacher may have had lots of education and years of experience, but no one on that committee knows your child better than you do. Try to remember, however, that the others on the committee intend only the best for your child, even if they don't agree with you about the methods to use. Try to hang on to a sense of perspective. If you keep hearing other experts say similar things about your child, over and over, it might be time to listen and consider what they're saying.

How long does it take to write an IEP?

Your child's first IEP will probably take longer to write than the ones that follow. The first one may take an hour. In following years they may take a half hour or less.

IEPs take longer to write when the parties involved can't agree on what is best for the student involved.

Those danged computers!

IEPs take a long time for teachers to develop and write, especially when they're writing one for a new student. Teachers would prefer to spend more of their time teaching, so to speed the process along some districts now use computers to help produce IEPs. This allows teachers to do much of the tedious IEP work automatically: the child's name, birthdate and identifying number only have to be entered once, and then the computer places the information every place it's needed. Other sections can be completed by choosing options from a menu. Often the teachers can choose from a large database of pre-written goals and objectives as well and save still more writing time. A printer produces the IEP, saving much laborious writing by hand. By comparison, the old way of writing in everything by hand was time-consuming.

School districts started using computers when they noticed they kept writing the same goals and objectives over and over.

The motive—to save teachers' time for teaching—is admirable, but parents need to read any computer-generated IEPs carefully. Often choosing from a large set of pre-written goals and objectives works well, but sometimes those objectives must be modified to fine-tune them for a specific child's needs.

In addition, computer-generated or not, the Chairperson of your child's IEP Committee should not arrive at the meeting with the IEP already completely written. This happens often enough that you need to be aware of the possibility.

Again, balance is the key. Most of the time your child's teacher will have solid knowledge about what your child should work on next, and it saves a lot of time for everyone when the teacher writes these in ahead of time, so long as everyone fully understands that the goals and objectives entered are tentative until everyone, including parents, agree that they are appropriate. Don't hesitate to assert yourself if the goals and objectives selected from the data base don't seem to meet your child's need, and don't hesitate to insist that the IEP be modified and reprinted or rewritten if necessary. Details about your child's placement should never be written in ahead of time.

We've got an IEP. Now what do we do?

First, get smart. Be thoroughly familiar with the IEP and what it says will be done. Knowing how much time will be spent in the Resource Room isn't enough. You also have to know some details about how that time will be used.

Second, get organized. Many parents keep all papers involving their child's special help in a large three-ringed notebook. This notebook contains copies of every IEP, every report card, every psychological report, all appropriate medical records, any correspondence, group achievement test scores, and anything else useful. It's tremendously helpful to have the information literally at your fingertips.

Third, follow your child's progress carefully. If your child will receive reading instruction or support, in most cases she should come to the Resource Room during reading time. If she will receive math support, the time should come from math. It isn't OK for your child's schedule to remove her from math (or science or social studies or music) to work on reading. Music, art and physical education contribute to all children's education and are crucial to your child, who may discover and develop previously unnoticed talents and strengths in these areas.

The important thing to remember is that scheduling should minimize the impact your child's extra help has on the rest of her education.

Your child should not miss special events, such as guest speakers, just to be in the Resource Room at her regularly scheduled time. This is sometimes the only time classroom teaching includes new, novel or concrete instructional methods. Often a child with a learning disability can connect to this information even when she struggles with lectures, textbooks and worksheets.

Any time an IEP results in a schedule that requires your child to give up some other school-sponsored activity, such as a sports team, band, orchestra, chorus, drama club, etc., the scheduling must be challenged. Do not let your child's special needs interfere with opportunities for her to develop her talents.

Fourth, understand the nuts and bolts of how services are delivered.

Tremendous variety exists in how schools provide special education. Here's a list of options. As in everything else we've discussed in this chapter the terms used where you live may vary.

- The specialist advises the teacher but never works with the child.
- The specialist works with the child (and others) within the regular classroom, sometimes in the back of the room and sometimes team-teaching with the classroom teacher.
- The child is removed from the regular classroom for a part of the day (for varying lengths of time, usually less than half the day) for instruction in a resource room. The child may be worked with individually, or more typically, in a small group.
- The child is placed in a special class housed within a regular public school. The child participates in a regular class and other school activities as he or she is able to. (Time in regular classes is considered "mainstreaming;" time in the special class is called "self-contained.")
- The child is placed in a publicly-funded special school which teaches only exceptional children.
- Rarely, if they have no suitable setting for the child within their school district, the school district pays for private tuition at a special school serving learning disabled students.

Most resource rooms are multi-categorical, meaning that although your child may be diagnosed learning disabled, other students with different problems may be instructed with her at the same time.

Some states go further and use a non-specific label such as *educationally handicapped*. The more vague your child's label is, the more important it becomes that your child's IEP reflects her needs and that you monitor her progress carefully. More than ever you need to be familiar with her IEP so you can judge how well it's being followed.

Multi-category Resource Rooms provide some real educational benefits. They allow the teacher to group her students by instructional need rather than by label or other arbitrary standards.

For example, reading is a language-based skill. For students who have severe difficulty learning to read, effective teaching could include scheduling them with language disordered students for that skill.

Children with behavioral problems frequently have difficulty with math. A learning disability in the area of math is relatively rare; grouping children together for math even if their labels differ sometimes results in opportunities to teach all of them better.

I'm no teacher. How do I monitor my child's progress?

Call or visit the Resource Room frequently. Ask to see textbooks and work samples. If you have any doubts about whether your child's IEP is being implemented, make an appointment with the teacher and ask specific questions. If you don't understand the methods the teacher is using, ask her to demonstrate. Good teachers welcome these questions and may give you more information than you were prepared for.

Before each annual IEP, the special teacher will test your child's academic progress. Don't be afraid to ask hard questions about her progress during that IEP meeting.

Ask the teacher to compare your child's test scores from year to year, but understand that if different tests are used the scores may not really be very comparable. You're entitled to request that the same tests be used each year as much as possible.

There is no guarantee your child will make a year's progress; even with excellent help some learning problems remain quite stubborn. But some progress should be made, and if progress isn't being made the reasons should be examined.

Checklist for a good IEP:

Initial IEP
- Do my child's goals and objectives match her "Present Levels" as listed in the IEP?
- Are the goals and objectives reasonable, or do they start significantly below or above my child's current level of performance?
- How much time will my child spend in special education, and how much time in the regular classroom?
- What will my child miss while she's in the Resource Room, and how will that be handled?
- How many other children will be in the room with my child? Will they be grouped so they can work together or will they all be working independently? (One isn't necessarily better than the other, but you should know how your child is being taught.)

Repeat IEP

(Sometimes called "Continuation IEP" or "IEPC")

- How much progress has she made since last year? Ask the teacher to compare last year's test results with this year's.
- Is she working up to her potential?
- Where specifically is she doing well, and where is she having the most problems?
- How is her self-esteem?
- Does she have friends?
- Does she try hard to complete her work?
- Does she seem to feel she's being generally successful?
- What methods work best with her, and which don't seem to work?
- If she receives support help, such as from a Resource Room, how much of her progress in the Resource Room translates into success for her in the regular classroom?
- Is she falling further and further behind, or is she catching up?

Conclusions

When the experts have finished talking, the parents' job of educating themselves has just begun. "I think a [parent] has a very good instinct about what works best, for herself and for her child," says Elizabeth Weiss in her book, *Mothers Talk About Learning Disabilities.* "While it is helpful to be aware of pervasive professional wisdom, I think she should follow that instinct."[3]

If you find you have difficulty expressing your views, or feel uncomfortable doing it, the greatest favor you do for your child might be to take a class in assertiveness training, so you can be her advocate if you need to be. Check junior colleges and community education programs in your area for inexpensive but effective classes.

The most important thing for a parent to know about special education is that it cannot and will not solve all problems, and it cannot make a learning disability go away. Even if that could be done, it would require such a heavy dose of special education that it would do more harm than good.

To illustrate, a physician told the author about a woman who broke her arm shortly before Thanksgiving. He told her the cast would be on her arm for a month, and made her an appointment to have it removed just before Christmas.

"Oh, good!" she said. "I can still go on my ski trip over the holidays!"

"I'm sorry, but you can't," the doctor said. He explained that as the cast allowed the bone to heal it would also injure her immobilized wrist in the process. Striking a balance between the serious injury to the arm and the guaranteed injury to the wrist, her cast would be removed before the break was completely healed. The slightest fall would re-break it.

Like a cast on a broken bone, special education can be helpful and harmful at the same time, so a balance must be sought. The right amount of help for your child is the amount that allows her to progress as fast as possible while doing as little damage as possible.

---

[3]Weiss, Elizabeth. *Mothers Talk About Learning Disabilities: Personal Feelings, Practical Advice.* 1989, Prentice-Hall.

For further reading:

Shore, Kenneth, Psy.D. *The Special Education Handbook: How to Get the Best Education Possible for Your Learning Disabled Child*. 1988, Warner Books.

Weiss, Elizabeth. *Mothers Talk About Learning Disabilities: Personal Feelings, Practical Advice*. 1989, Prentice-Hall.

Lost in the crowd: attention deficit disorders

"I tried so very hard. Don't say I didn't try hard enough. Harder never would have been enough."

Chris G., an adult diagnosed with ADD when he was 49, talking about his school experiences

IMPORTANT NOTE TO READERS:

This book does not provide a complete overview of Attention Deficit Disorder; it emphasizes educational issues. For more complete information on ADD see the list of books at the end of the chapter.

Comments about therapeutic approaches and medications reflect the author's bias. In no way should parents substitute these views for medical guidance. Parents are urged to seek professional help if they suspect their child has a significant attentional or hyperactivity problem.

This chapter can supplement but cannot substitute for medical treatment, educational interventions, family or individual counseling, psychotherapy, or other appropriate treatment plans for the problems discussed. Parents should look to their

child's physician for medical guidance, not to this book. The purpose of this chapter is to provide enough background information that parents can intelligently evaluate the educational advice offered in this book.

Carla's mother, Lucy, found this note on her pillow one day in 1981.

```
Dere Mom
I LorE You
you ARe my mome
i lov you
love
Carla
```

Although the contents made her smile, she sighed with discouragement. Carla was in third grade and should have been able to write much better than that. Lucy thought the note was more like what a young first-grader would write.

"Why can't Carla write any better than that?" she asked Carla's resource teacher.

Carla's special teacher was baffled. Carla could write better than that, but unless prodded, would do all her work in just such a superficial and apparently careless manner. When supervised, Carla wrote longer sentences and expressed more complex thoughts. The teacher knew Carla could spell every word in the note.

In 1981 Carla's resource teacher had never heard of Attention Deficit Disorder, often shortened to ADD.[1] The problem was called "hyperactivity" then, and since Carla wasn't hyperactive the label didn't seem to suit her.

We've learned a lot about diagnosis of children with ADD (AD/HD when the child shows hyperactivity) since Carla wrote her mother that note. In 1981 ADD was under-diagnosed, especially when the clue of hyperactivity was absent. Hyperactivity was considered a behavioral problem, not an educational one; all discussion focused on behavior; and we didn't expect to see the problem in girls.

---

[1]ADD is also called AD/HD (Attention Deficit/Hyperactivity Disorder). Occasionally we see ADDH used. Experts have used many labels over the years, and in all likelihood the name used by experts will change again. Readers should realize that the traits and difficulties discussed are also common in children diagnosed as "hyperactive." The author will use Attention Deficit

Many experts believe that ADD still goes undiagnosed quite frequently today and that the same diagnostic mistakes persist: ADD without hyperactivity, and in girls, gets overlooked. By contrast some other specialists are convinced that too many children have been diagnosed already. That view is understandable when we see claims that up to 20% of our student population has ADD. One wonders if anything found in 20% of the population can fairly be called a disorder. Some of these critics believe the whole problem of ADD is overblown out of excessive need to have students conform to rigid behavioral expectations.

Somewhere among all the views lies the truth, and most reasonable estimates suggest that between 3% and 5% of all children show the signs of ADD. This range allows for children who haven't been diagnosed—most often girls[2] but also boys whose attentional difficulties don't trigger behavior problems as well. ADD can cause tremendous amounts of frustration and even grief for the people who have to cope with it. The problem goes well beyond "normal variation," and if left untreated ADD can be a devastating educational problem.

The name of the disorder doesn't describe the difficulty accurately, however. A child with ADD shows too much attention. He notices too many things but often on a superficial level. His attention jumps from place to place and from idea to idea, accompanied by diminished ability to focus selectively or to sustain concentration when needed. Better titles for the problem might be Attention Focusing Disorder, Attention Fluctuation Disorder or even Attention Surplus Disorder, since these children seem to attend to everything around them instead of pulling out important features from all the surrounding clutter.

Children with ADD typically have difficulty choosing what to focus on, and they have difficulty maintaining that focus. The level of difficulty people with attention deficits experience ranges from mild to incapacitating. In addition, an individual's difficulty may vary from hour to hour, day to day, or week to week. The only thing consistent about ADD is its inconsistency.

This inconsistency leads some teachers to assume a child really can perform better than he typically does. The teacher has seen the child at his best and mistakenly believes he can deliver top performance all the time.

Many factors affect how severely an attentional problem interferes. A student with ADD will be able to concentrate better in subjects he's stronger in than subjects he's weaker in. If his mind wanders while working through his strengths he'll return to task and get re-focused more efficiently and reliably. This is true of all of us, but attentional problems magnify the tendency to the point that it stands out.

This explains how some children with attentional problems can learn the words to hit songs and yet struggle over math facts. Remembering words to songs takes place in a different area of the brain than learning math facts does, and a child really could be much better at the one function than the other.

Lack of sleep aggravates attentional difficulties for most people with ADD, as does any kind of strong emotion or stress.

Recent research on attention problems points to a biochemical disorder of the brain as its root cause. To understand how this disorder interferes with ability to focus and sustain attention, we need to review how the brain manages information.

Disorder, shortened to ADD, throughout the book, because it's the attentional problems that interfere with learning. For a selected list of books talking about the behavior difficulties of students with ADD or AD/HD, see the end of the chapter.

You'll recall from Chapter Four that each brain cell has one axon, the part that sends messages to other cells, and many dendrites, the part that receives messages from other cells.

We call the space between the end of the axon and the end of the neuron a neural gap.

Since the nerve endings don't actually touch, special chemicals called neuro-transmitters carry the message from the end of an axon to the dendrite that will receive it. With Attention Deficit Disorder we suspect two problems with the neuro-transmitters implicated. Perhaps the person's brain doesn't produce enough of them, or maybe the levels swing wildly from adequate to low. Either problem would prevent the person's brain from functioning in a predictable, organized way.

ADD and education

Most children with ADD have a remarkably hard time focusing and sustaining their attention on their schoolwork. Although perhaps not hyperactive in the usual sense, they may fidget a lot, act impulsively and have a hard time controlling where their attention roams.

About 60% of children with attentional problems show hyperactivity as well—either by marked physical impulsivity or by talking a great deal (often not saying much of anything). With or without hyperactivity, most if not all have difficulty maintaining impulse control and with considering the consequences of actions before acting. Their impulsiveness also shows in their schoolwork, where they are likely to put down any answer—even though they really know the right answer. They just don't stop to think first.

[2]Bain, Lisa J. *A Parent's Guide to Attention Deficit Disorders.* 1991, Doubleday Dell, p. 48.

Students with ADD frequently show difficulty using their memory well. They don't separate out the important details from the unimportant details, and remember both equally well. The renowned specialist in childhood learning problems Dr. Mel Levine calls the tendency to remember trivial or unimportant facts "impaired forgetting." The things they should forget clutter up their minds while important facts remain unlearned.

Since these students typically focus only superficially on their work, they don't concentrate well enough to get information into permanent memory with any consistency. Many students with ADD perform poorly in subjects that rely heavily on memory skills, such as foreign languages. Often in "content area" subjects such as biology and history they will grasp the basic concepts but fail to retain names, dates, or technical terminology well.

Finally, their scattered and disorganized approach leads to forgotten textbooks, papers, assignments and other routine school expectations.

A significant number of these students have serious problems getting along with other children. Some, but not all, have behavior problems as well.

Trigger points

Some circumstances strongly affect the school work of a child with attentional problems. These factors affect all students, but they affect children with ADD much more than they do the typical child.

- **The difficulty of the task for that child.** The more difficult the task, the more likely he is to have trouble concentrating on it.
- **How well the task matches the child's emotional needs of the moment.** If he urgently wants to talk with his friends, it won't take much to derail him from what he's supposed to be doing. If, on the other hand, the assigned work is a subject he enjoys, uses a method he finds engaging or involves a project that has captured his imagination, his attention may be much better.
- **Who's in charge.** If he likes and respects the adult in charge, and if he feels he is getting positive attention from this person, he'll work harder. A positive bond with the teacher enhances a child's ability to pay attention.
- **How interesting he finds the task.** Children with ADD are easily bored and cope quite badly with boredom. This does not mean such a child is being willful, defiant or controlling, however. If the task is not too hard for him, innate interest in the task helps him marshal his unpredictable focusing abilities to get the most out of the lesson.
- **Whether the setting encourages him to stay focused.** In a noisy classroom where the teacher possesses few skills for maintaining control of her students a child with ADD will display many more problems than he would in an orderly, predictable classroom. We also know that children with ADD learn new, complex material better when working one-on-one or in small groups than in large group settings.

The effects of these factors vary widely from child to child and lead to the need for carefully chosen work—work truly on his instructional level. It shouldn't be too easy, which leads to boredom, or too hard, which results in quick frustration.

No one description fits all students with attentional problems. There isn't any one way to describe children with ADD except that all have the same internal communication disorder: a brain that doesn't communicate within itself reliably, efficiently, or consistently.

Diagnosis

The purpose of an educational diagnosis is to turn a child who struggles into a child who learns. Many kinds of practitioners possess the legal right to diagnose (or rule out) attentional problems in children. The difficulty parents face is that these professionals, although they all mean well, vary greatly in their skills and knowledge of the problem. Specialists who diagnose ADD or AD/HD include pediatricians, pediatric neurologists, child psychologists, child psychiatrists, and school diagnostic teams. Some diagnosticians do excellent jobs, but some aren't really up to the task. Inexperienced or inadequately trained diagnosticians frequently confuse ADD or AD/HD with other childhood problems. They may mistake ADD for some other difficulty, or they may diagnose ADD when some other, serious problem actually accounted for the child's difficulties.

The people who diagnose childhood problems take on a complex task. No one test exists that will prove with 100% confidence that your child does or does not have ADD. Inattentiveness, hyperactivity and distractibility—the benchmarks of ADD and AD/HD—are superficial signs of several other childhood problems as well. These problems include temporary anxiety from family upheaval—such as recent divorce or long-term chaotic home life.

Severe family dysfunction, such as when the parents are severely alcoholic or when the child suffers physical, psychological or sexual abuse, can mimic ADD at first look. Furthermore, significant family dysfunction of all kinds occurs more frequently when one or both parents have attentional problems. So, because ADD tends to be passed genetically from one generation to the next, many children in troubled families also have ADD. Finding serious problems within the family doesn't rule out ADD but makes it more difficult for the specialists to make a good diagnosis. In addition some medications can aggravate ADD or mimic its symptoms as a side effect, especially some medications for asthma, some cold/allergy medications and some anti-convulsants.

Another diagnostic complication has its basis in the nature of children with ADD. They behave differently in different settings. Sometimes, captivated by all the intriguing sights, sounds and smells of a medical office, they appear fully in control. They ask what the equipment is used for and engage the doctor in interesting conversation. The doctor gets the impression of a bright, curious child, not a flighty and unfocused one.

That doctor might get a wholly different impression if he ignored the child's questions, took control of the conversation and asked the child to do some math problems.

Parents' best protection from diagnosticians who aren't "up to speed" on ADD is to read everything they can get their hands on about the problem before taking their child to be tested. Then they can ask intelligent questions, and they'll be more likely to know whether they're getting accurate and detailed answers or not.

Some questions to ask might be:

- How many children have ADD?
- How many of the children who come to you end up diagnosed with the problem?
- What criteria do you use for diagnosis?
- What else looks like ADD on the surface, and how do you make sure the child has ADD and not some other problem?
- What treatments do you feel are most effective?
- How would you describe your success rate?

Another problem in diagnosis turns on issues mentioned earlier in this chapter. Some diagnosticians see ADD under every rock; others think the problem quite rare. Neither view is accurate. One way to sort this problem out is to ask the examiner how many children, in his or her opinion, have ADD or AD/HD. If the examiner reports that 10% or even 20% of children have ADD, this person may have a too-strong bias toward diagnosis.

But you must also avoid bias against diagnosis as well. Whether the specialist sees ADD where it doesn't exist or overlooks the problem when it's present, it's your child who runs the risk of an inaccurate diagnosis. If the specialist says something like "3%–5%, but we're not absolutely certain because we know some children go undiagnosed..." this person has a good perspective on how common the problem is.

Diagnostic criteria for Attention-Deficit/Hyperactivity Disorder[3]

According to new guidelines contained in the *Diagnostic and Statistical Manual (DSM-IV)*, the child must meet the criteria under either (1) or (2) below:

(1) Six (or more) of the following symptoms of inattention have persisted for at least 6 months to a degree that is maladaptive and inconsistent with developmental level:
Inattention
   (a) often fails to give close attention to details or makes careless mistakes in schoolwork, work, or other activities
   (b) often has difficulty sustaining attention in tasks or play activities
   (c) often does not seem to listen when spoken to directly
   (d) often does not follow through on instructions and fails to finish schoolwork, chores, or duties in the workplace (not due to oppositional behavior or failure to understand instructions)
   (e) often has difficulty organizing tasks and activities
   (f) often avoids, dislikes, or is reluctant to engage in tasks that require sustained mental effort (such as schoolwork or homework)

---

[3]American Psychiatric Association: *Diagnostic and Statistical Manual of Mental Disorders, Fourth Edition*, pp. 89-90. American Psychiatric Association, Washington, D.C., 1994.

(g) often loses things necessary for tasks or activities (e.g., toys, school assignments, pencils, books, or tools)

(h) is often easily distracted by extraneous stimuli

(i) is often forgetful in daily activities

(2) Six (or more) of the following symptoms of hyperactivity-impulsivity have persisted for at least 6 months to a degree that is maladaptive and inconsistent with developmental level:

Hyperactivity

(a) often fidgets with hands or feet or squirms in seat

(b) often leaves seat in classroom or in other situations in which remaining seated is expected

(c) often runs about or climbs excessively in situations in which it is in appropriate (in adolescents and adults, may be limited to subjective feelings of restlessness)

(d) often has difficulty engaging in leisure activities quietly

(e) often is "on the go" or often acts as if "driven by a motor"

(f) often talks excessively

Impulsivity

(g) often blurts out answers before questions have been completed

(h) often has difficulty awaiting turn

(i) often interrupts or intrudes on others (e.g., butts into conversations or games)

Some of the symptoms that caused the difficulties must have been present before the age of 7 years. In addition the impairment must be observed in more than one setting, such as home and school. There must also be clear evidence that the child is actually impaired significantly either socially or academically (in people old enough to hold a job impairment at work would be considered significant as well). Finally, for a valid diagnosis of Attention Deficit Disorder the difficulties cannot be caused exclusively by a Pervasive Developmental Disorder, Schizophrenia, or other Psychotic Disorder. The person's difficulties can't be explained better by some other mental disorder, such as Mood Disorder, Anxiety Disorder, Dissociative Disorder, or a Personality Disorder.

Getting to yes or no

In Chapter Five we saw that diagnosis is the process of confirming some hunches while ruling out others. This is as true of ADD as it is for learning disabilities. Just as we do when looking for learning disabilities, we gather information from a variety of sources. Teachers and parents fill out questionnaires about the child's behavior and characteristics. A physician rules out medical causes for the child's difficulties, such as seizure disorders, side-effects of other medication the child has to take, or other physical conditions that can affect attention span.

The examiner interviews child and parents, and a really good evaluation includes observations of the child in school. Individual testing determines overall intellectual potential and detects any other learning problems that might be present. Other specialists may be called in if needed. The author prefers to see the child's learning style as well as attentional abilities explored. Diagnosis is made by combining information from all these sources.

Myths about ADD

Diagnostic myths:

Myth: Your child's teacher can tell if he has ADD or not.

Reality: Teachers spot struggling children very well. They aren't as good at judging what the cause of the problem is. For this reason, teachers should not advise parents to place their child on medication. However, encouraging them to seek an evaluation is entirely appropriate.

Myth: Your pediatrician is always the best person to determine whether your child has ADD or not.

Reality: Some pediatricians have made a point to learn all they can about ADD, but others have not. If you follow the advice given earlier to educate yourself about ADD, you'll be in a better position to judge what your child's doctor knows about it. ADD is more than a medical problem and often brings educational and social problems with it as well. The doctor may be able to treat ADD medically, but you will probably need help and guidance from other specialists.

Myth: Highly intelligent children cannot have ADD.

Reality: Attentional problems have nothing to do with a person's intelligence. Extremely bright children—even those we might call true geniuses—can have severe attentional problems. Retarded children can have ADD as well, although their difficulties have to be compared to their mental age and not their chronological age.

Myths parents often believe:

Myth: This child can't have ADD. He can concentrate for 30 minutes at a time—or more—when he wants to. He watches TV for hours if we let him.

Reality: Many people believe that if a child has attentional problems it means he can *never* concentrate. A child's ability to sustain his focus depends on several things, including how interesting he finds the task and whether it taps into his strengths.

TV-watching makes a particularly poor indicator of attention span. The content of a TV show changes every few seconds and sometimes even faster. In addition, all we really know is that the child's body is pointed at the TV. We don't know what's going on in his mind.

Myth: He doesn't have ADD. He's just spontaneous (bright, imaginative, creative...).

Reality: Children with ADD are typically described as bright, imaginative, spontaneous or creative. In fact, ADD may enhance those characteristics. However, there's an important difference between "spontaneous" and "impulsive." When we say "impulsive" we mean the person shows diminished ability to act in a planned and controlled way. Impulsive people have lessened control over their spontaneity.

Myth: A lot of so-called ADD is nothing more than a clash of personalities between child and teacher. Put him with a different (or better) teacher and his problems will evaporate.
Reality: Matching the personality of the child to the teacher may help tremendously, but it won't make true ADD go away.

School-related myths:

Myth: He's just lazy. He could do it if he tried.
Reality: Children innately want to learn. If a child doesn't learn, or doesn't learn as well as he should be able to, there has to be a reason, and we owe it to the child to find out what that reason is. Calling a child names ("lazy," "unmotivated," "underachiever") solves nothing and stops the search for a real explanation of his difficulties.
Myth: He can't have ADD. He isn't hyperactive. He's not a behavior problem.
Reality: Not all children with ADD are hyperactive; not all show behavior problems; and those without hyperactivity can still have quite serious educational and social problems. Those problems must be dealt with if the child is to grow up healthy and whole.

Myths about outcome:

Myth: ADD never goes away.
Reality: About 20% - 35% of all children with ADD will either outgrow it after puberty or see their symptoms lessen so much that it's not much of a problem for them anymore. Some people with ADD, however, don't get diagnosed until middle/junior high, senior high, or college, and some struggle through school but are diagnosed during adulthood.
Myth: ADD is all bad.
Reality: People with attentional problems show some remarkable strengths that non-ADD people often don't have. They may include:
- a refreshingly new view of the world;
- the ability to make connections between facts or events that non-ADD people might have overlooked;
- an ability to focus on the present without worrying too much about the past or the future (a tremendous asset in a sales career);
- the ability to make the person they are talking to feel like the only other important person in the world.

When adults with ADD learn to capitalize on their strengths and compensate for their weaknesses they can make the ADD work for them instead of against them.

Treatment

The goal of treatment is to increase the child's level of success in all things important to him: learning, behavior, socialization, and development of recreational skills. The interventions most likely to meet this goal are medication combined with these others as necessary: behavior modification, individual and/or family counseling, group counseling, educational support, and training the parents in behavior management skills. Not every child will need every kind of help.

Medication

We've listed medication first because so many children with ADD benefit from its intelligent and careful use. The other interventions mentioned all work better when combined with medication.

What does medication do?

Drugs used to treat ADD act at the chemical level in the brain. Evidence strongly suggests that low or fluctuating levels of neuro-transmitters are at the heart[4] of ADD, and medications partly correct this problem. Increased levels of neuro-transmitters (and we know of no way to do this except with medication) allow people with ADD to focus their attention better on one thing rather than jumping from thing to thing to thing to thing. A favorite story among parents of children with ADD is that they think like this: "Ready... fire!!! OOPS!—Aim!" Medication increases the likelihood that they will "aim"—that is, think—first, before "firing" off an answer or an action.

What medication for ADD actually does is improve communication between nerve cells within the child's brain, allowing the child to distinguish the important features of what he is doing and hold his focus on them.

Why are some people so opposed to medication?

There are several reasons. First, for many years medication, particularly Ritalin, was presented erroneously as a "magic bullet," a total cure. Some schools got extremely aggressive with parents, sometimes pushing hard for a child to take medication even when no diagnosis had been made.[5]

This situation was aggravated when a prominent newspaper got its facts wrong and reported that up to 10% of all students in one community took medication "to control their behavior." Actually the school had said that 10% of their students had *learning disabilities*. The school wasn't even talking about either hyperactivity (as it was called then) or medication.

One special interest group in particular latched on to this report and began a campaign of disinformation. They succeeded because the diagnostic process for ADD hadn't been refined to the level it is at today, and Ritalin was used inappropriately sometimes. The media was already full of suggestions that Ritalin was being over-used. It has been remarkably easy for this special-interest group to keep the disinformation going to suit their own purposes.

It's crucial for parents to check the sources of information they read, especially when the claims are alarmist in nature. It's fairly easy to spot inaccurate but scary claims: through distortions and outright fabrications the reports grossly exaggerate the occasional mild side effects, especially targeting Ritalin. Almost always these wild claims include the wholly erroneous notion that medications used for ADD

---

[4]For detailed information about current thought on the biology of ADD, see Hallowell and Ratey's book listed at the end of the chapter.
[5]Teachers should not recommend medication. They also should avoid discouraging its use when it's needed (although as trained observers of children they should report any problems

somehow "drug the child into submission" (the words used to say it may vary) and that the children will be more likely to experiment with drugs later. Neither claim has any merit.

Why do so many people seem to believe these inaccurate claims?

Two reasons. First, doctors invite criticism any time they recommend medication casually or in the absence of the other interventions so often necessary.

Second, the most commonly used medication—Ritalin—works quickly and leaves the child's body quickly. Often doctors prescribe it during the school day only, with the result that the parents don't observe their child while the medication is active.

Parents should ask the doctor to let the child take it during a couple of weekends if their child takes medication only during school hours. That way they can see exactly how the medication does and does not affect their child. A parent's best protection against overlooking other equally necessary therapies and relying too heavily on medication is to get a multidisciplinary evaluation, one involving doctor, child psychologist, learning specialist and others.

We've mentioned Ritalin (methylphenidate). Although highly effective for many children, other medications also help achieve the goal of a child more able to control himself. They include Dexedrine (dextroamphetamine), Cylert (pemoline), some antidepressants, such as forms of desipramine, and even some medications originally designed to treat high blood pressure, such as Catapress (Clonidine). Sometimes a variety of medications must be tried before the right one is found for any one individual, and occasionally a combination is used.

Once in a while doctors prescribe a "double-blind" study[6] to make absolutely certain the medication is working as everyone thinks it is. In a double-blind study, the child takes capsules for four weeks. For two of those weeks he actually takes the medication, but for the other two weeks he takes a placebo, or fake pill with no medication in it. Only the pharmacist knows which weeks the child is really taking medication. Then the doctor compares behavior reports from home and school to see if the reported improvements, if any, occurred when the child was actually getting the medication. This may be a good option for parents who have reservations about medication and want to be certain it's really helping.

Common questions

What can medication do for my child?
— Enable him to benefit more from other interventions, such as academic support and behavior modification;
— enable him to stay on task more;
— decrease purposeless physical activity (what we call "hyperactivity");
— enhance his ability to get along with classmates and teachers (and family, if he takes it at home as well);
— increase his tendency to cooperate with others;
— decrease tendencies toward aggressive behavior (unless the aggression was purposeful, not impulsive);

they observe to the child's parents and doctor). Educators do not have the background needed to evaluate medical treatment.

[6]Double-blind studies don't work with all medications, only fast-acting ones such as Ritalin. Other medications, such as Cylert and Tofranil, build up effectiveness in the child's body over

— may enhance academic performance, but that will depend on what else interferes with learning.

These improvements may not be immediate, and they aren't guaranteed. They happen often enough to make medication a powerful tool in the management of ADD.

What can't medication do by itself?
— By itself, fix any accompanying learning problems;
— guarantee long-term academic success;
— solve all behavior problems;
— solve all social problems.

Medication increases the odds that the additional methods used to solve those problems will be successful, however.

Medication myths

Myth: Medication is given for the convenience of parents or teachers.
Reality: Although parents and teachers may benefit from a child who is easier to deal with, that happens because the child functions better. The real benefit, and the important one, is to the child.

Myth: Medication "drugs children into submission."
Reality: Medications for ADD, with rare exceptions, stimulate. They don't sedate, and they don't mask symptoms. They can't force a child to meet someone's arbitrary behavior standards. Medications that help ADD allow the child to make better choices about his actions.

Myth: Medication makes the child more "manageable," but does not address the cause of the problem.
Reality: The cause of the problem does seem to be decreased brain activity[7], so increasing brain activity with medication works directly at the cause of the problem.

Myth: Ritalin is prescribed casually.
Reality: This was a valid criticism twenty years ago and may still be valid in some isolated areas. Parents should not accept a prescription to treat ADD unless they're convinced the child has the problem. When that is the case, medication is not being prescribed casually. The parents' best protection against frivolous drug therapy is to get the best evaluation for their child they can find.

Myth: Ritalin is dangerous because it is highly addictive.
Reality: The author did extensive research prepared to accept any findings. She didn't find a single case of youth with ADD addicted to Ritalin. The concern is theoretical. In reality Ritalin isn't prescribed in addictive doses.

Myth: Medication can make attentional problems go away.
Reality: Medication often eases symptoms but rarely eliminates them.

Myth: Medication always works.
Reality: Ritalin helps about 70 - 85% of the children with ADD. For the remaining children, other medications can be tried, but there is a small

time. Double-blind studies won't work well with those medications.
[7]Zametkin, A. J. et al., "Cerebral Glucose Metabolism in Adults with Hyperactivity of Childhood Onset," *New England Journal of Medicine,*323 (1990): 1361–66.

group of children who do seem to have ADD but for whom the doctor can find no suitable and effective medication.

Myth: Ritalin is always the medication to use.

Reality: Some children should not take Ritalin for medical reasons. If your child has some secondary difficulty, such as anxiety or depression, your doctor may choose a different medication. Your doctor may also choose a different medication for reasons not listed here. If you don't understand your doctor's recommendations, ask questions.

Myth: Stimulant medication works differently in children with ADD than in other children.

Reality: This is the so-called "paradoxical effect." People noticed that stimulants appeared to calm over-active children, the opposite of what stimulants were supposed to do. They reasoned that stimulants must work in these children in some unusual, or paradoxical, way.

We now know Ritalin affects all people in the same way, whether young or old, with or without ADD. We see the dramatic improvement in children with ADD because there's so much space for improvement. Some children with ADD reveal the disorganization in their brain by disorganized, impulsive and purposeless movements, which we see as "hyperactivity." Improved brain function translates into more organized movement.

Myth: Good alternatives to medication exist but are not commonly known for some reason.

Reality: Everyone would love to find an alternative to medication, but research presently doesn't support most non-traditional therapies. The things we know help—learning compensating strategies, academic support, counseling to aid specific difficulties (not to counsel the ADD away), and behavior modification—all work better when combined with the skilled use of medication.

Drug therapy may require many adjustments in both medication and dosage. Your child is an individual unlike any other child on Earth with or without attentional problems. ADD traits show themselves within the personality of the child and the world (home and school) he lives in. Just as each child is unique, each solution will be unique as well. Attention-focusing problems have a strong medical component. Medication can be an important part of the overall plan but cannot and should not be viewed as the whole solution, and will not be suitable for all children with ADD.

What else works?

Behavior modification

Behavior modification is a collection of techniques used to increase desired behaviors and decrease undesired behaviors. It works on the principle that if we're rewarded for doing something we're more likely to do it again, and if we're not rewarded for doing something we're less likely to do it again. Although that sounds simple, designing a behavior modification program that works for your child can be a complicated matter.

To keep a behavior modification system going requires a considerable investment of time by the parents. To use it effectively, everyone involved with the child must agree to focus on one or two target behaviors. The rewards should be ones chosen by the child, not just things the adults assume the child will welcome. It's best to involve the child when planning the behavior modification. That way he is less likely to feel "bossed around."

Well done, behavior modification can, and often does, improve a child's ability to get along in the world. Badly done it can, and often does, blow up in the parent's or teacher's face.

The most common mistake made with behavior modification is that people end it too soon. The temptation is to stop the program before the child has internalized the behavior changes—that is, has made it a part of his personality so completely that rewards are no longer necessary. In addition, the parents must respond to inappropriate behavior in a truly neutral way, because positive and neutral responses work much better than negative or punishing ones. One of the toughest things for parents to learn how to do is how to remain neutral in the face of repeated provocative behavior by their child.

Sometimes the behavior improvements wear off rapidly in spite of the most careful efforts, and some children don't seem to respond well to behavior modification no matter how skillfully it is used.

In spite of this, behavior modification can be a powerful tool, especially when part of an overall treatment plan. Because it is such a complex technique, most parents will be better off to use it under the guidance of a therapist or counselor. That way, when they have difficulties with the technique—and they will—they'll be able to call someone for advice. All behavior modification systems have to be fine-tuned occasionally to keep them working well.

Those opposed to use of medication often trot out behavior modification as an example of an easily-used alternative. In reality behavior modification by itself is unlikely to solve all the problems that come with ADD. The only effective way to use behavior modification is to target one or two behaviors at a time. While the parents might be able to keep such a long-term plan in mind, it might not be best for the child, who might need more rapid help than that.

For excellent descriptions of behavior modification, see the bibliography at the end of the chapter.

Academic support

Many children with ADD struggle with one or more school subjects. By the time they are diagnosed they may be seriously behind. Or, they may fall behind later on. As they advance through school and expectations increase, most have considerable difficulty keeping homework, textbooks, materials and assignments organized. Parents should monitor their child's school progress carefully and be ready to step in sooner rather than later. Sometimes the only help needed is an occasional tutor, but any child who has difficulty with schoolwork because of ADD is entitled to support and help to convert frustration into success. For a list of interventions known to work with attention-deficient children, see the Chapter Seven Appendix starting on page 227.

Forty percent or more of all children with ADD also have learning disabilities. If your child struggles with his schoolwork, get him an educational evaluation (see Chapter Five).

Family counseling

Raising a child with ADD requires turbo-charged parenting skills, so many families find short-term family counseling invaluable. The parents learn it's not their fault their child has this problem. They master specialized techniques for dealing with what can be a difficult child, and they have an expert they can call on for advice when new problems emerge. The brothers and sisters of children with problems often harbor resentment and frustration, and family counseling can get these feelings out into the open where they can be dealt with.

Short-term family counseling can provide new tools to solve many problems. When your child is grown, you'll know you did everything you could to help him cope with the problem. Don't be afraid to try several therapists until you find one you're all comfortable with.

Individual and group counseling

Traditional psychotherapy concentrates on working through the presumed underlying psychological causes of problems. Since ADD has a biochemical cause, talk therapy won't make the ADD go away. However, a therapist who understands ADD can help a child cope with numerous frustrations or secondary problems. Psychological support can also help the child understand himself and accept his weaknesses while recognizing and taking pride in his strengths. Group therapy targeted at social skills often helps children who have difficulty making and keeping friends.

Researchers make remarkable discoveries every day that affect the treatment of children with ADD. By the time most books (including this one) have gone to print, some of their information will be out of date. Specifically, the areas of diagnosis, drug therapy and other effective treatments continue to be researched aggressively. However, it can be difficult to get accurate and up-to-date information.

Parents need to know: except for people doing scientific research, people write because they hold an opinion. Whether you read it in a book or magazine the possibility of bias exists. The first thing publishers (book or magazine) want to know from an author is "What's your slant?" Newspapers try to avoid bias but because of their short deadlines, don't always get all their facts right, and frequently cover issues incompletely.

The way to handle this dilemma is to read everything you can find, but always remain alert for potential bias. Was the publication put out by a drug company? If so, was their purpose to promote the use of their medication, or conversely, to protect themselves from liability? Either slant will affect the contents profoundly. If it's a magazine article, examine the magazine. Does it have a clear bias? Many magazines do. If you're reading the newspaper, consider the source the paper got its information from. Think about whether the article really covered the issue in depth or not.

Ask your child's doctor to do a search of the medical literature once a year for any new information, but allow your doctor to interpret the results. Details such as the number of participants in a study and how they were selected can have tremendous effect on whether decisions should be based on the results or not.

But most of all, take to heart Elizabeth Weiss' statement when she says to "...hold in suspicion the idea that all children must excel in the same way."[8] Help your child find his strengths, and then rejoice in them with him. There's no such thing as a child without strengths.

For further reading:

Bain, Lisa J. *A Parent's Guide to Attention Deficit Disorder.* 1991, Bantam Doubleday Dell Publishing Group, Inc.
> See this book in particular for an excellent explanation of behavior modification and other support therapies for ADD.

Fowler, Mary, in collaboration with others. *CH.A.D.D. Educators Manual: An In-Depth Look at Attention Deficit Disorders from an Educational Perspective.* 1992, CH.A.D.D: 499 N.W. 70th Ave., Plantation, FL 33317.

> This booklet explains everything you—and your child's school—need to know about the educational needs and rights of children with ADD. Buy two copies of this manual. Read yours carefully, and then make a gift of the second one for your child's teacher.

Garber, Stephen, Marianne Garber, and Robin Spizman. *If Your Child is Hyperactive, Inattentive, Impulsive, Distractible... .* 1990, Villard.
> This book may be out of print by the time *Taming the Dragons* has gone to press. However, its excellence makes it worth the trouble to find it at a library if bookstores no longer carry it.

Hallowell, Edward M., M.D. and John J. Ratey, M.D. *Driven to Distraction: Recognizing and Coping with Attention Deficit Disorder from Childhood through Adulthood.* 1994, Pantheon. Paperback ISBN: 0-684-8012-80.
> *Driven to Distraction* provides a broad and detailed discussion of ADD and may give parents some insight into the question they're sometimes afraid to ask: "What about when he's grown?" We strongly recommend this book.

---

[8]Weiss, Elizabeth. *Mothers Talk About Learning Disabilities: Personal Feelings, Practical Advice.* 1989, Prentice-Hall.

Hallowell, Edward M., M.D. and John J. Ratey, M.D. *Answers to Distraction*. 1994, Pantheon. ISBN: 0-679-43973-0.

> *Answers to Distraction* provides additional information in an easily read question-and-answer format. Contains outstanding information for classroom teachers, including proven classroom management tips. Parents should share this book with their child's teachers.

Ingersoll, Barbara. *Your Hyperactive Child*. 1991, Doubleday.

> This book provides an excellent overview of attentional problems in childhood and a particularly good explanation of the strengths and weaknesses of behavior modification.

Ingersoll, Barbara, and Sam Goldstein. *Attention Deficit Disorder and Learning Disabilities: Realities, Myths and Controversial Treatments*. 1993, Doubleday. ISBN 0-385-46931-4.

> We recommend that any parent read this book before considering a nontraditional treatment for either attentional or learning problems.

Organizations

ADDA
(Attention Deficit Disorder Association)
P.O. Box 972
Mentor, OH 44061
800-487-2282

CH.A.D.D.
(Children and Adults with Attention Deficit Disorders)
499 NW 70th Avenue, Suite 308
Plantation, FL 33317
305-587-3700
Fax: 305-587-4599

Newsletters

ADD-ONS: A Paper "Support Group" for Those Living with ADD.
ADD-ONS, Ltd.
P.O. Box 675
Frankfurt, IL 60423

CH.A.D.D.ER
CH.A.D.D.
499 NW 70th Avenue, Suite 308
Plantation, FL 33317
305-587-3700

> (This newsletter is included with membership in CH.A.D.D.)

How to use the "tips and tricks"

I hear and I forget,
I see and I remember,
I do and I understand.

Chinese proverb

If your child learns in an atypical way you can't do much to change that fact, but you can help her learn to capitalize on her strengths as well as cope with her weaknesses. Carefully chosen strategies can sometimes transform those apparent weaknesses into strengths. You, the parent, can play an important part in the work to convert failure into success.

This chapter will give you a little review combined with a little more information that you'll find useful. At that point you'll be fully ready to use the "tips and tricks" that make up Chapters Nine through Sixteen. As you read this information keep in mind that a child's brain is continually developing. The strengths and

Strengths   Weakesses

weaknesses your child shows when she's five may be quite different than her strengths and weaknesses when she's ten or fourteen.

Many ways to get there

Although we have been encouraging you to explore in what ways your child learns best, effective teaching usually combines several approaches, or *multi-sensory* instruction, so the child uses more than one sense at a time while learning.

Multi-sensory approaches work well because of the way our brain is organized. When we learn, information takes one path into our brain when we use our eyes, another when we use our ears, and a yet a third when we use our hands. By using more than one sense we bombard our brain with the new information in multiple ways. As a result we learn better.

According to the noted educator Sandra Rief,[1] students retain

- 10% of what they read
- 20% of what they hear
- 30% of what they see
- 50% of what they see and hear
- 70% of what they say
- 90% of what they say and do.

So—in spite of everything you've read in this book about the various learning styles—avoid thinking about them too rigidly. We tend to talk about learning styles as if they're all one thing or another. By focusing too closely on the child's current strengths we may overlook her ability to benefit from methods using combined approaches.

More about learning styles

STRONG
nonverbal

Concrete learners like a hands-on approach. They don't want just to read about an experiment; they want to do it. Concrete learners advertise their nature to observant parents as they touch everything. Children with ADD usually learn better by concrete methods.

- *Effect on learning*: The concrete learner will remember best what has been made real to her through hands-on instruction.
- *Strategies:* Any time you need to make materials, such as flash cards, have the child help you. She'll understand the materials better and work harder with them just because she's helped make them.

[1]Rief, Sandra F. *How to Reach and Teach ADD/ADHD Children: Practical Techniques, Strategies, and Interventions for Helping Children with Attention Problems and Hyperactivity.* The Center for Applied Research in Education, 1993, p. 53.

Strengths	Weaknesses

- *Example:* If you're making flash cards for math facts, guide the child as she makes them instead of making them yourself. Don't tell her the answer to the facts; give her a calculator and let her find the answer.

Global learners sometimes get confused by step-by-step instructions, especially if the steps are numerous and complex.

STRONG
global learner

- *Effect on learning:* These students get confused easily and lose sight of the point of the lesson during step-by-step instruction. When these students grow older, however, they will grasp important underlying concepts and theories more quickly than strongly sequential learners.
- *Strategies:* Provide an overview, a clue of where the lesson is headed, before beginning instruction or review.
- *Examples:* Global learners have an easier time with multi-step processes if they first understand what all the steps do. For example, they'll better grasp the purpose and uses of the imaginary lines on maps and globes such as longitude and latitude if they understand that those lines gave the first explorers a way to tell where they were in the ocean when they couldn't see land.

Visual-perceptual weaknesses: Children with visual-perceptual difficulties get confused easily when using their eyes to learn.

*weak
visual*

- *Effect on learning:* These students can be good readers (reading is a language-based skill, not a perceptually-based one). However, poor perception can cause them to lose their place or misinterpret the organization of worksheets. Copying from a distance, such as from a blackboard, often makes their problem more severe.
- *Strategies:* To work with visual perception problems efficiently, simplify or organize what the student looks at. Sometimes this is called "simplifying the visual field."
- *Example:* Make sure worksheets are reproduced clearly and are easy to read. Use highlighters to separate the assignment into distinct sections. See suggestions in Chapters Nine through Sixteen for specific suggestions across many subjects and skills.

Auditory-perceptual weaknesses: This is really more than one kind of problem. The child may have difficulty remembering what she hears, in which case her auditory problems are involved

*weak
auditory*

with memory difficulties. She may confuse sounds, as in Chapter Three's example, where the teacher said "quotient" and the child thought she had said "crow shin."

- *Effect on learning:* Teachers often wrongly accuse these children of not paying attention, especially when the students must listen for long periods of time.
- *Strategies:* Support the child's ability to learn through listening by adding visual clues—key words, illustrations, etc.
- *Example:* As you discuss a problem or task with your child, you could write down key words that would help her retain what you're saying.

weak
grapho-motor

Weak grapho-motor skills: The hallmark sign is that the child has difficulty learning to write both in print and in cursive. Sometimes they can draw well, because while one part of the brain controls writing, another part controls drawing. However, if the child also has visual perceptual difficulties, both skills will be affected.

- *Effect on learning:* This child will perform paper/pencil tasks slowly. She'll copy from the board with difficulty and have trouble organizing her work on paper. When older, she's likely to have difficulty taking notes. Writing takes extra brain power for these children, so when writing they learn inefficiently.
- *Strategies:* Provide one-on-one instruction for cursive and printing before the child learns to write incorrectly. Limit the amount of copying required. Teach the child to use brief note cards to organize thoughts.

  Allow her to dictate longer writing assignments while encouraging her to write smaller ones so she can develop her written expression skills.

  Encourage computer use (but don't rush touch-typing at an early age).
- *Example:* The child can copy the first three math problems from the board and then be given a photocopy of the teacher's worksheets for the rest of the problems.

weak
memory

Memory problems: Children with *short-term memory problems* will seem to know something one moment but not be able to recall it a few minutes later. If the child has difficulty with *long-term memory*, however, she's more likely to know it one week but not recall it the next. The functional difference between short-and long-term memory is in the length of time before the child forgets.

One other kind of memory problem involves *active working memory*. With memory problems of this type, the child doesn't focus fully enough or intensely enough to get the information into short- or long-term memory.

Methods you see in Chapters Nine through Sixteen that work well with children who have Attention Deficit Disorder will also help children who have difficulty with active working memory.

- *Effect on learning:* Effects will vary from child to child, partly depending on the other strengths and weaknesses present. A child might have more difficulty remembering details from some subjects than others. Some students can recall complex words when reading but fail to spell even simple ones correctly. Others will remember how to do math problems but not the facts needed to complete them.

- *Strategies:* Two things work to help build memory: frequent practice and short sessions—five minutes or less. Mix skills during one work session: work on sight words for a few minutes, then switch to times facts. Variety is the spice of life; using multiple ways to study enhances learning for many children.

  Review frequently. Keep lists or samples of what's been initially learned to make sure your child hangs on to her new knowledge. Back up and review any time retention drops below 90%.

  Children with memory problems sometimes develop peculiar habits they display while trying to recall information. The child may talk about how she's "almost got it," wrinkle her forehead or even strike her head with her hand. This buys her more time to think, but the actions interfere with recall and are counter-productive. Try to discourage such gestures and chatter.

Sequential problems: These children have difficulty with any information where order is an important part. Sequencing weaknesses cause the most trouble when a child has to rearrange things "in her head."

weak
sequential

- *Effect on learning:* Often such a child has trouble sounding out words and will resist reading phonetically even if she's learned the basic phonics sounds. Such a student also may struggle with math. Difficulty with sequencing can be one cause of slow work rate.

Strengths   Weaknesses

**Attention
Deficit**

- *Strategies:* Allow the child to work visually and with her hands. For instance, if she's supposed to alphabetize a list of words, give her the words on 3 x 5 cards she can spread out on a table.

Attention deficit disorders: Recall that children with ADD pay attention in very shorts spurts and that they often apply minimal thought to their work.

- *Effect on learning:* Children with ADD pay attention to the teacher's instructions only for short periods of time before their mind starts wandering. This leaves gaps in their information. When they do pay attention they tend to do so superficially, which causes them to miss important points.
- *Strategies and examples for school:* See suggestions in Chapters Nine through Sixteen for specific suggestions across many subjects and skills. See also the Chapter Seven Appendix starting on page 227 for a list of classroom interventions known to help children with ADD cope.
- *Strategies for home:* Try to keep a neat environment. Don't let books, papers, etc. accumulate around the house. A tidy home will make it easier for your child to locate the inevitable misplaced items.

  Help your child organize her life. Teach her to use a wall calendar and an assignment notebook.

  Help your child get everything she needs for school together the night before.

  Help her plan her time. Children with ADD judge time badly and will poorly estimate how long assignments take to complete.

Lacks basic skills: After years of struggle, some children will have developed significant gaps in their knowledge. They may know the names of most of the states in the U.S., for instance, but not know the names of continents. Or they may know some math facts but not all of them, and not well enough to use them with ease.

*weak
basic skills*

- *Effect on learning:* When a student has serious gaps in her foundation knowledge, the struggle to learn new material takes up too much of her thought. That leaves less brain power to learn the new information with.
- *Strategies:* The obvious solution is to teach the child on her instructional level. Teachers should be alert and watch for

gaps in her knowledge, and fill in those gaps instead of plowing on to work the child isn't ready for. Good tutors can help these children tremendously.

- *Example:* The child who doesn't know that the Earth consists of continents and oceans with specific names will have trouble following lessons about explorers such as Magellan and Columbus. A quick lesson on the major features of the geography of the Earth will help this child tremendously with her history class.

Brighter students: Students with strong potential but an uneven learning style face a double whammy. They're more likely to be labeled (called names) such as "lazy" or "unmotivated." Slapping such nonproductive terms on children stops efforts to help them.

Bright students are less likely to receive the intensive kind of help that would allow them to reach their potential: resources tend to be concentrated on children who will fail completely without support.

- *Effect on learning:* Too often, teachers assume that a bright child can overcome her learning difficulties without much help. As a result the child gets less review in her weaker areas than other students might get.
- *Strategies:* Monitor your child's progress closely in the subjects she finds difficult.
- *Example:* If she finds math hard, review with her once a week the new skills she's been taught (even if her teachers report that she's learned it). See if she really can do the work independently or if she needs clues and support (the "Guided Learning" stage from Chapter Four—incomplete learning, instead of "Independence" or "Mastery.") Alert her teachers immediately if she struggles with things they say she's mastered, and push for better academic support at school for her.

General tips for working with your child

Keep portfolios. Collect samples of your child's work over time by photocopying work samples once a month or so. Include work she brings home from school as well as samples of her homework. Date each item. This is your easiest measure of your child's progress.

Understanding is power. Your child needs to know about her strengths and weaknesses. If you don't feel you can explain them well to her, talk to her resource teacher, counselor or other specialist until you can. Your child will develop a positive view of herself and her abilities only if you do also.

Make checklists. Even the youngest child can help develop them. Checklists can include morning routines, bedtime routines, getting the following day's materials together—whatever areas she needs help in. Checklists help your child begin to take responsibility for herself while providing a safety net.

Consider where your child should do her homework. Contrary to what most adults believe, some people really do learn better with some sort of noise in the background, including music. The test of their preferences should be how well they stay on task and how accurately they do their work. Some children much prefer to lie on the floor; others prefer the structure of a desk or the kitchen table.

Have a regular time to do homework. There are a couple of reasons for this. First, doing homework at the same time every day gives a rhythm and predictability to your child's life that diminishes arguments. Second, monitoring just how long she's spending on her homework will be easier. You need to know how much time she spends on homework so you have some measure of whether she's working inefficiently, if she finds the quantity overwhelming, or if she finds the work too hard.

Think about who should help her with her homework. It's not easy to help your child with her homework. Sometimes children know just how to push their parents' buttons, and creating uproar is one highly effective way to get out of homework. Occasionally parents bring their own unresolved school frustrations from when they were a child to their child's homework sessions.

Try to stay calm if your child shows angry outbursts over homework. Some children avoid homework because it's easier for them to believe that they *didn't* do their homework than that they *couldn't* do it. Arguments over homework are extremely unpleasant, but your child sends an important message about her level of frustration when they occur.

Choose a designated tutor when homework sessions turn your home into a battlefield—a person in the family she can always turn to for help and support. It should be a person she can work with congenially, but the person has to be available dependably and regularly.

If no one in the family seems suitable, try paying a teenaged helper—a girl for girls and a boy for boys often works best. You may need to go to the expense of a professional tutor. If none of these suggestions work, counseling may be needed.

Encourage independence. Be near your child while she does her homework, but have something to do yourself as well. Choose letter-writing, hobbies, reading or some other activity that can be interrupted if your child needs help. You'll provide a role model as you demonstrate that we sit down to work and we finish what we start. Your proximity will also encourage sustained effort.

Stall for time sometimes if you think your child asks for help too quickly instead of thinking just a little longer herself: "Let me think about that for a moment..."."That's a good question...".

Homework Trouble-Shooting Checklist

Problem: Your child has trouble memorizing new material.
Solutions:
- Your child may be faced with too much new information at once. See suggestions in the next chapters with the "weak memory" symbol by them. Adapt those methods to the assignment she's having trouble with.
- Keep old study materials handy for frequent review.
- For spelling and sight vocabulary, use the Word List Form at the end of Chapter Nine and Chapter Ten. Use that form to increase the amount of organized, systematic review your child gets.

Problem: Your child forgets previously learned information.
Solutions:
- She hasn't reviewed the material enough. Slow the pace down, don't include quite so much new material at each session, and review more often what she's worked on previously.
- Consider picking an alternative method from this book.

Problem: The method you chose doesn't seem to be working.
Solutions:
- First, make sure you didn't skip any steps. There are no shortcuts; these methods have already been made as simple as they can be made and still work.
- Try another method. Maybe this one just doesn't appeal to your child.

Problem: Your child seems to have the skill mastered, but then she can't do it on her own.
Solutions:
- Perhaps you've been giving subtle clues which helped your child more than you realized. Busy yourself with something while she works to make sure she can to it himself.
- Re-read the section on "The Four Stages of Learning" in Chapter Four. Make sure your child is in "Stage Three" of learning before moving on, and provide frequent review.

Problem: Your child knows the skill well enough to do it in a quiet place, one-on-one, but can't seem to do it in a classroom with all its distractions.
Solutions:
- Be sure your child really can do it independently (maybe you are giving subtle clues).

- Try overlearning—that is, continued review for some time after you think she has mastered the material. Overlearning may help her compensate for the factors that interfere with her classroom performance.
- Make sure the classroom teacher is making simple accommodations where appropriate. See Chapter Seven and the Chapter Seven Appendix.
- Consider getting a professional evaluation if you think your child might have Attention Deficit Disorder, one common cause of this problem.

Problem: Your child resists help with her homework.
Solutions:
- *Make sure she really needs help.*
- Be certain the work is not too hard for her.
- Make sure the quantity is within her ability to complete.
- Pick a "designated tutor." Sometimes children work much better with one individual than another.
- If the problem persists and is serious, talk to the school counselor.
- Ask the school to provide after-school tutoring. If the school cannot do this, hire a tutor for your child.
- Some short-term counseling may help.

Problem: The child simply can't do her homework. It's too hard for her.
Solution:
- Talk to her teacher about why the work is so hard for your child. Find out what skills your child lacks, and work with her teacher to make a plan that will help her catch up.

Problem: Your child starts out doing the homework diligently, but eventually her attention wanders.
Solution:
- Estimate how long she can work well. If it's 20 minutes, build in a short break, say for a snack, after 18 minutes. Gradually (over a period of weeks, not days) lengthen the time between breaks. Always let your child be the guide of how long she can work; don't set arbitrary standards. She will progress at her own pace. When in doubt, believe your child is doing the best she can.

Problem: Your child complains that she has so much homework she'll never get it done.
Solutions:
- Examine the amount of her homework in light of her strengths and weaknesses. Talk to the teacher about the problem if you think your child often has more homework than she can handle.
- If she has a lot of homework because she isn't completing her class work in the time the teacher gives at school, you need to find out why. She should not bring home uncompleted class work to finish at home. That's a school problem and needs a school-based solution.

– Perhaps the work only appears overwhelming to your child. In that case, help her break it into manageable chunks. For instance, divide a math assignment into two sections. She can do the first part (and check it), work on another subject—spelling, perhaps—and then complete the math. You can help her learn to do this herself. Sometimes the structure of a checklist where she can check the first half of the math off as done will help her see her progress.

Problem: She doesn't get her homework assignments straight.
Solutions:
– She should use an assignment book and have a "study buddy" for each subject. After she's written down each homework assignment she should double-check with her study buddy to make sure she wrote it down accurately. If there's no assignment, she should write "no homework" by that subject for the day and double-check that this is true with the study buddy.
– If she fails to write the assignment down she can call her study buddy to get it.

Problem: She frequently forgets she has an assignment until bedtime.
Solutions:
– She should use her "study buddies" at school to check her assignment book at the end of each period.
– She should look over her assignment book and check with her study buddy for each subject not filled in as soon as she gets home from school. She mustn't delay: friends go out to eat with their families, or shopping, or to dance class or baseball practice. They aren't always available to double-check assignments.
– Set her homework time early enough in the evening that she has time to borrow textbooks or get other needed materials.

Problem: She has the assignment written down but doesn't have the needed supplies.
Solution:
– Children with severe organizational problems should have a duplicate set of textbooks and supplies at home.

Problem: She finishes her homework but doesn't get it back in her backpack, so she frequently fails to turn it in on time.
Solution:
– Use a homework checklist that includes a place for her to check off when her homework is in her backpack. Children with ADD particularly have difficulty with this kind of closure. If necessary have show you that all books and papers are in the backpack.

Problem: She forgets to give you important papers, such as permission forms for field trips and orders for school photos.

Solution:
- Add a place on her daily assignment sheet for things requiring money or parent signature. Her study buddy can double-check to make sure she has these items.

Problem: She resists doing homework, asking to postpone it.
Solution:
- First, make sure her homework schedule suits her needs. Children need some time to relax after school, and the afternoon may be the only time she has to play with neighborhood friends. School can be a real pressure cooker for struggling students. Second, make sure her homework isn't chronically either too hard or of overwhelming quantity. If you have examined these issues and see no problem, stick to your guns.

When you need more help...

Some parents find a carefully-chosen support group a good place to share experiences and learn from each other. The participants work well together, share information positively and provide valuable emotional reassurance for its members.

Choose your group carefully, however. Some groups seem to draw only resentful and frustrated members who don't cope well with their children's difficulties. Those groups spend too much energy venting their anger unproductively and not enough time looking for workable solutions. Visit several groups before choosing one for yourself.

If you notice a pattern in your family of ongoing frustration, repeatedly raised voices, ineffective discipline or out-of-control behavior, consider short-term family counseling. It can work miracles. Shop around, get references from others such as support group members and school counselors, and interview any therapist you consider. You want a non-judgmental person who knows a lot about learning and attentional problems and who won't casually blame you for your child's difficulties. Assigning blame solves nothing and stops progress toward finding workable solutions.

About the "tips and tricks"

When you get to the "tips and tricks" that start in the next chapter, you'll see the symbols from Chapter Three in the margins. These symbols show what type of learner is most likely to benefit from the strategy. Symbols for strengths sit on the left side of the margin, and symbols for weaknesses are to the right.

Sometimes you'll see only strengths shown, and sometimes only weaknesses, but usually you'll find some combination. A star (shown to the left) means the method works with most children.

Works with
most

Each strategy is organized as follows:

PROBLEM: What the child is having difficulty learning.

INFORMATION: While not always included, this section gives details that help the parent understand the problem.

MATERIALS: Lists any special materials, such as 3 x 5 cards, needed to try the suggestion.

TIP: Information that might make you and your child's work just a little easier. Indicated by a light bulb in the margin.

SOLUTION: Gives the specific things you and the child should do to solve the problem. More than one solution may be given.

COMMENTS: Provides extra information about the difficulty under discussion.

WARNING: Explains special problems you have to watch out for when trying the solution.

IEP IDEA: The letters "I.E.P." stand for "Individualized Education Plan," discussed in Chapter Six. This symbol alerts you to modifications you can write into your child's IEP to help guide her teachers.

Finding supplies

Some of these suggestions, or "tips and tricks," recommend books or materials you aren't likely to have around your house. Most will be available at teacher supply stores, so check your local Yellow Pages.

TIPS AND TRICKS

CHAPTERS NINE
THROUGH
SIXTEEN

"Nothing in the world can take the place of persistence. Talent will not; nothing is more common than unsuccessful men with talent. Genius will not; the world is full of educated derelicts. Persistence and determination alone are omnipotent."

Calvin Coolidge

Tips and tricks:
reading

Make the work interesting and the discipline will take care of itself.

E. B. White

Reading takes place when the mind converts symbols—letters which have been presented in an organized way—into a meaningful message. A child can, unfortunately, come to school already in possession of problems that will make learning to read quite difficult. He may develop more difficulties along the way as well.

One of the most frustrating tasks parents can undertake is to try to help their child learn to read well. As a learning specialist, the author realizes that most parents aren't willing to take on the task of being their child's main reading teacher. With that in mind, this chapter will give ways parents can support the efforts of their child and his various teachers.

To do that we should talk briefly about the main components of reading instruction.

- *Word attack skills* include phonics plus other approaches based on word structure.
- *Sight vocabulary* consists of those words we know instantly without using any word attack skills.
- *Comprehension*, or understanding what we've read, is the goal of reading. Without comprehension, the rest is a waste of time.

Good readers don't use these skills in isolation. For example, read this paragraph:

"Billy watched the elequardests parade around the circus ring. The elequardest in front held his trunk high in the air, as if he were proud to be the leader. The next one wrapped his trunk around the leader's tail. All the other elequardests did the same, forming a procession of huge animals working together flawlessly. Billy realized that these elequardests were extremely intelligent animals, and he wanted to know more about them."

When you read that paragraph, you knew most of the words on sight. However, there was one you hadn't seen before.

You probably figured out by the second sentence that an **elequardest** was actually an elephant. Using simple word attack skills you may have recognized **"ele"** from a word you already knew—perhaps "elevator;" **"quar"** from a word like "quarter;" and **"dest"** was easy because you have seen the word ending, or suffix, "est," many times. By the end of the paragraph you had learned that **"elequardest"** meant "elephant." Determining what a word must be by considering what the rest of the section says is called using *context clues*.

Word attack skills

Reading phonetically is a slow and laborious process. When good readers come across a new word, they don't use phonics unless they absolutely have to. Instead, they rapidly break it into syllables, like this:

e - le - quar - dest = elequardest

Phonetic analysis would be like this, a much slower process:

e - l - e = ele
qu - ar = quar
d - e - st = dest
ele - quar - dest = elequardest.

We're not saying that learning phonics is a waste of time, only that phonics is just one of many tools good readers use as necessary. Some children will never excel at phonics, so when we talk about children who struggle with reading, we should provide them with as many tools as possible to work with. That means phonics, but also sight vocabulary, syllabication, use of root words and endings (ex: **cook, cooks, cook**ed, **cook**ing), and intelligent use of context clues.

Sight vocabulary

Most educators say that a child should know 90% of the words in his instructional reading books. For a learning disabled child 95% would be a better number. These children often learn sight vocabulary more slowly than non-learning disabled children do, and in addition are probably struggling with the other skills we've listed.

Research shows that the average beginning reader—one with no learning problems—must see a new word about 35 times before he knows it on sight. A child with a reading problem will need even more. Parents or a tutor can provide that invaluable extra exposure. However, many reading specialists tend to discourage work on sight vocabulary. One of the common reasons given is that reading words by sight isn't much use if the child doesn't understand the words he's reading. In reality that happens quite rarely. Other specialists feel that phonics is such an effective and valuable tool for reading new words that memorizing sight words is a cumbersome method for learning. For some struggling children, however, it's phonics they find cumbersome.

Intensive phonics instruction should be done by people thoroughly trained as reading teachers, so this book will give only ways to review phonics *your child has already been taught*—to provide the extra practice he may need. This chapter will also provide a variety of ways you can work on instant recognition of words to take the pressure off your child just a little.

Comprehension

When you read the circus story on page 94, figuring out how to *pronounce* **elequardest** didn't tell you what an **elequardest** is. You used comprehension skills to determine that an **elequardest** could only be an elephant. Difficulty with comprehension is almost always a symptom, a clue about where the child's reading breaks down, and not a separate problem. Fix the underlying weakness that causes the child to struggle, and his comprehension will almost always improve.

For example, the child who reads slowly and laboriously—because of poor word attack skills and/or inadequate sight vocabulary—might be able to plow through the paragraph about the "elequardests." However, most of his energy would go to into reading the individual words. Since many of the words would be new or unknown ones they wouldn't stick in his memory, and he would get little or no meaning out of what he read.

Another child might have trouble comprehending because he doesn't always pay full attention to what he's reading. This inattention could happen in several ways:

- He might see the new word and impatiently skip over it instead of trying to figure it out. That interruption might be enough to diminish his attentional level for the rest of the paragraph, resulting in poor comprehension.
- He could impulsively substitute another word he already knew that started with *"ele"*—for instance, *"elevator."* Such a choice would destroy his comprehension:

"Billy watched the elevators parade around the circus ring. The elevator in front held his trunk high in the air..."

Worse, the interruption might diminish his attention so completely that he wouldn't notice that his substitution made no sense at all.

Other possible causes for poor concentration include overwhelming emotional, behavioral or personal problems, but the most common reason is that *the reading selection is just too hard for the child.*

Children with language disorders will be thrown by certain words and phrases in the story: perhaps ***"behind,"*** ***"forming a procession,"*** or ***"working together flawlessly."*** They won't be able to form a mental image of the story's events because words don't impart their full meaning to these children.

Such a child might figure out the story was about elephants and yet not know what the elephants did, where the elephants were, or what Billy thought about what he had witnessed. Or, he might have trouble with syntax—the additional meaning of words provided by the order in which they were written. Whether such students read the story themselves or someone reads it to them, they will miss important elements.

Finally, some children lack commonly-known basic knowledge they need to understand what they read. In the circus story given earlier, for instance, we assume the reader knows what elephants and circuses are, and we assume they know that elephants can be trained to do tricks. However, those children who are what we call *culturally deprived* may have never seen an elephant—even in a book. They haven't been to a circus. They can't understand the story because the story deals with events and things they've had no experience with. That's what culturally deprived means: because of lack of experiences, such a child doesn't have a common reference point about things that happen within his larger culture. He might as well be reading, or hearing, a story about life on another planet.

The tips and tricks in this chapter will help boost *minor to moderate* reading problems in all the areas we just discussed. If you try several and they don't seem to help, your child may need the services of a reading or learning disabilities specialist. Reading is the single most important skill your child will develop in school; all other subjects will depend to some degree on his ability to understand the written word. This chapter should be used in addition to remedial reading or expert tutoring—not instead of that help.

Tips and tricks: word attack

PROBLEM: Your first-grader isn't getting the hang of phonics.

INFORMATION: Although most of us know how to sound out words, good readers use that skill only rarely. After sounding out the same words a couple of times we know them by sight.

Strengths	Weaknesses

Sounding words out phonetically is hard work. It slows reading, and if done frequently, interferes with comprehension.

SOLUTION: *"More than one way to get there"*

Attention
Deficit

Your child should work on sight words as well as phonics. Try the suggestions titled "Stacking the Deck," "Keep it Up!" and "Loading the Dice" in the "Sight Words" section of this chapter.

INFORMATION: Concrete learners (see Chapter Three) learn phonics better after they've learned some sight words, particularly words that name familiar objects such as "cat" or "tree." Learning these concrete words helps printed words become less abstract and more "real" to them.

weak
memory

The author's experience is that a child who knows 200 words instantly will learn basic phonics adequately. That doesn't mean he will prefer phonics or master all the finer points, but he will develop usable word attack skills.

weak
basic skills

WARNING: Many children have difficulty mastering phonics at first. Don't give up on phonics until fourth grade. Your goals are first, to find ways to make phonics easier for your child, and second, to make sure your child has more than one reading strategy.

WARNING

PROBLEM: *Your child uses consonants when sounding out words but makes guesses about vowel sounds.*

WARNING: Use this method only if your child has learned the vowel sounds already and just doesn't *use* the skill. This method is *not* a good way to teach vowel sounds for the first time.

WARNING

SOLUTION: *"What's my cue?"*

Materials:
    3 X 5 cards
    colored markers

weak
auditory

Together, you and your child make "cue cards." Decide what picture will stand for each vowel sound, such as an elephant for short e. Draw the picture on the card—or cut one out from a comic strip and glue it on the card. He can use these cards to help him decide which vowel sound he needs. Here's one example of what the cards might look like:

weak
sequential

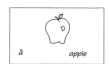

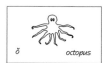

TIP: You'll find larger copies of these cards on page 117 if you don't want to make your own, but children with ADD should make their own.

WARNING: Don't make your child sound out all words, all the time. Sounding out words takes so much effort for some children it interferes with comprehension. When the reading goal is comprehension, put the emphasis on understanding, not learning phonics. If he's reading for recreation or to study, just tell him the words he doesn't know.

However, if the homework is a phonics assignment, then he should be using his phonics skills while completing it.

PROBLEM: Your child needs extra practice using phonics skills.

SOLUTION: "Mystery words"

Works with
most

Materials:
  Magnetic letters
  Reading Yellow Pages for Students and Teachers
  (sources for materials given at the end of the chapter)

Get a set of magnetic letters at a teacher supply store, toy store or via mail order (see page 91). Each day put a "mystery word" on the refrigerator for your child to sound out. Choose words you know he can figure out—or have one easier word and one harder one for a bonus word.

For variety, tell him that sometimes the word will make no sense (ex: *bome, nisk*). Your child may enjoy figuring out whether he's been tricked or not.

TIPS: If you're not sure which skills to practice, show his teacher the *Reading Yellow Pages for Students and Teachers* and let her select lists for you to work from.

If the words you put up seem too easy, put up one easier one and one harder one.

Strengths   Weaknesses

Use a simple sticker chart to keep track of the number of words he's figured out.

PROBLEM: *Your child needs more practice using vowel sounds.*

SOLUTION: *"Wheel of fortune!"*

Materials:
   Cue cards (see pages 98 and 117)
   Recommended: *Reading Yellow Pages for Students and Teachers* (see the end of the chapter).

STRONG
global learner

*weak
auditory*

For example, perhaps he's having trouble with the middle (sometimes called "median") vowel in three-letter words. To practice this skill, write out some three-letter words on a paper with the vowel missing, like this:

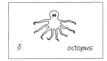

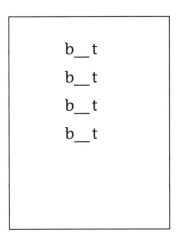

The *Yellow Pages* book can help you choose suitable words based on your child's needs.

Then, with the cue cards laid out above the paper, say either *"bit,"* or *"but,"* or *"bat."*

It will be enough that your child names the right vowel. He doesn't have to write it, but he should pronounce it. If he finds that too hard, you pronounce it and then have him repeat it. Eventually he should be able to put the sound in himself.

If you keep this paper, you can use the same words in review sessions. Just mix the order up.

Choose the word lists you use from *Reading Yellow Pages for Students and Teachers* based on recommendations from his classroom, reading or resource teacher.

If he finds choosing from all five vowels difficult, pick two vowels to concentrate on first and then gradually add the other vowel sounds.

WARNING: Be careful to keep your face neutral, so you don't give the right answer away. Children who have trouble with phonics get very good at reading facial clues to figure out which answer the adult wants. Also, encourage your child to answer with confidence: "Ah!" not "Ah?"

PROBLEM: Your child is intimidated by big words.

SOLUTION: "One step at a time"

STRONG
visual

weak
sequential

Materials

    2 Colored markers

    3 x 5 cards

    If needed: dictionary or spelling dictionary—see end of chapter for recommendation

Have your child choose two colors of markers. Then you write the word, syllable by syllable, like this:

re·mark·a·ble

Attention Deficit

Put the letters in one color and the dots separating them in the other.

Then the child can sound the word out section by section instead of all at once. If your child is ready to read more complex words he will usually recognize many of the separate syllables easily, especially the more common ones such as *re* and *ing*.

To make the invidivual syllables more clear, cut the card apart at the dots and separate the pieces, like this:

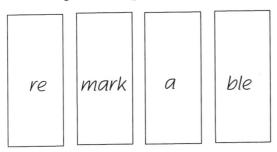

More on sight vocabulary

Tips for practicing sight words

- *Never* be the first person to teach new words to your child. Initial instruction should be done at school, and you should only review and reinforce that work.
- **Work on twelve words** at a time; no more.
- **Seven of the twelve words** should be ones your child already knows *very well*.
- When you choose the five newer words, **deliberately pick words that look a lot alike** and that can't be easily drawn or acted out. For instance, you can include *the, these, they, then,* and *them*. Later, when you include *there* as a new word you can use *these* as a known word.
- **Pick words he needs to know.** In older children the words might include specialized vocabulary from math, science or social studies.
- **Choose words** whose meaning isn't immediately clear to a new reader. Many common words, such as *with, and, the* and *on*, are quite difficult for children to learn. That's because they aren't concrete. Your child knows what a dog is, and he knows what "*jump*" means. But what's a "*the*?" He can't draw a picture of it or act it out. These are the words with which he will probably need the most help.
- **Keep your sessions short**—no more than five minutes at a time at first, building slowly to *ten minutes maximum*.
- **Use several activities** even in those very short sessions.
- **You want to increase memory,** not review phonics skills.

These games make it easy

Use these three games, in the order presented, to nail sight vocabulary down:

1. "Show Me"
2. "Flip It"
3. "Knock, Knock"

Do not proceed from "<u>Show Me</u>" to "<u>Flip It</u>" until your child can play "<u>Show Me</u>" *perfectly.* Do not proceed to "<u>Knock, Knock</u>" until your child can play "<u>Flip It</u>" with *100% accuracy.*

Materials:
3 x 5 cards
Record sheet found in the Chapter Nine Appendix
Colored marker
Lists of words—both the ones your child knows and the ones he's currently working on. Get these lists from your child's reading teacher.

FIRST GAME: "Show Me"
1. Double-check: ask him to read all the words he's supposed to know already, to make absolutely sure that he can read seven of those twelve words. Do not proceed until you have seven words he knows *well* in the stack.
2. Mix the cards and lay them all, face up, on a table or the floor, like this:

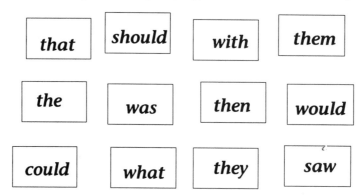

3. Say to your child, "Show me ...." and name one of the words. If your child finds the word he can turn it over.
4. Continue: "Show me ...." "Good! Show me ... ." Plan ahead so that the last card facing up is one he already knows, not one of the newer words.
5. If he's having difficulties with the new words, give clues. For instance, you can say "It's a three-letter word" or "The last letter is a *t.*"

6. For the last word left face-up, change what you say: "What does this word say?" Since you made sure one of his known words would be the last one facing up, he'll be able to read it.

7. When he can play "Show Me" and get all the words right with no clues or hesitation, he's ready to go to the next game.

SECOND GAME: "Flip It"

1. Lay out the cards just as you did at the beginning of "Show Me," face-up.

2. This time your child should scan the cards. Each time he spots one he can read he should read it and then flip it over. He continues reading until all the words have been flipped over. It doesn't matter what order he reads the cards in; just mix them up each time so he doesn't see them in the same place each time.

3. Write troublesome words three more times so he sees those words more often. In this example, the child had difficulty learning *with* and *they*, so now each of them are in the cards four times instead of only once.

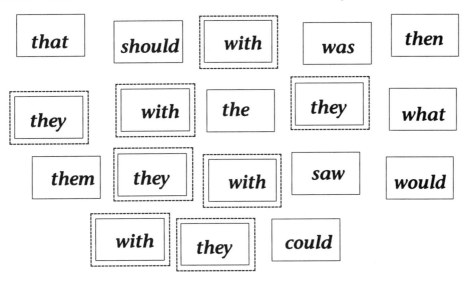

4. It's all right if he reads all the cards saying the same word at the same time. For instance, he can read *with* and flip it, and then read the other three copies of *with* one after the other: "*with... with... with... with!*"

5. When he can play "Flip It" and get all the words right with no clues and no hesitation, he's ready to go to the next game.

THIRD GAME: "Knock, Knock"

For some reason children just love this game. We suspect the reason is that they realize they're learning, and learning is a lot of fun when it works well. Follow the instructions to this game *precisely* because although they seem silly, they help the child focus his attention.

1. Place the cards mixed up and in a stack, face-down.
2. Your child should make a fist and rap twice (not once, and not three times) on the top card. He says "Knock, knock" as he raps. Don't allow any variation; the repetition of this pattern, done quite consistently, increases accuracy.
3. You turn the top card over and say "Who's there?"

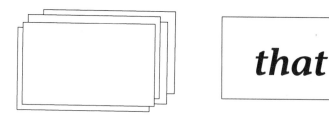

4. Your child reads the card.
5. If he gets it right, he sets it aside. If he misses it, you read the word correctly for him and put it back somewhere in the middle of the pile.
6. Continue until the stack is finished.

Other games

(Use these only after your child has mastered "Show Me," "Flip It" and "Knock, Knock.")

"Concentration"

1. Write each word (up to twelve words) twice on 3 x 5 cards, making 24 cards.
2. Shuffle the cards and lay them out face-down on table or floor.
3. Have your child turn two cards up and read them. If the words match, he keeps them and gets another turn. If they don't match, it's your turn to try. Whoever gets the most pairs wins.
Note: Be sure your child reads each word as he turns them up. It's quite possible for him to play this game—and win—using words he can't read.

"Tic Tac Toe"

Play Tic Tac Toe the standard way, but both parent and child should read a word before taking a turn. To have a little extra fun with the game, you can deliberately misread a word occasionally. If your child catches your mistake he gets an extra turn.

"Go Fish!"

Make a card deck by writing each word four times. Then you play "Go Fish" the standard way, except the child asks for words: "Do you have any cards that say 'with?'"

Strengths	Weaknesses

More Sight Vocabulary Activities

PROBLEM: Your child comes home with sight words to memorize.

SOLUTION: "Stacking the deck"

Works with
most

Materials:
    Sight word list
    3 x 5 cards
    Colored markers

*weak
memory*

When your child comes home with sight words to practice, take a moment to write up to twelve words (no more) on 3 x 5 cards. Do all the words in the same color. Then ask your child to read each word. The stack should contain at least seven words he already knows. He will rapidly become discouraged if he's faced repeatedly with words he doesn't know.

*weak
visual*

Set aside any words he misses. Make three more identical copies of those words, and scatter them throughout the stack. That way, the next time he goes through the stack he'll see the harder words four times as often as he sees the ones he knows. Leave in the ones he knows; a struggling student can't experience too much success.

TIP: Going through the stack three times at one sitting is plenty. If you want the child to have more practice, do the stack three times, set them aside for several hours (morning and evening works for many people) and do them again.

COMMENT: This method will have two effects:
– reduce impulsive guessing
– provide the needed extra practice on the tougher words.

WARNING: Any more than five minutes at one time on sight words is worse than a waste of time; it's counter-productive. It will cause problems but not solve any. Review Chapter Four on how children learn if you have any doubts of this.

TIP: Once your child is familiar with this method he should make his own study cards.

Strengths   Weaknesses

PROBLEM: You've used "Stacking the Deck." Now you have to make sure your child remembers all the words he's learned.

SOLUTION: "Keep it up!"

Works with
most

weak
memory

If you practice those sight words, eventually you'll have a larger stack of previously-learned words. These should be reviewed once a week or so. If he's forgotten any of them, return the forgotten word to the list of words to learn. See the end of this chapter for a record sheet you can use to keep track of the words.

For new words, stick to the plan of having no more than twelve words in the stack, and make sure he knows seven of them solidly.

PROBLEM: Your child learns new sight words slowly.

SOLUTION: "Loading the dice"

weak
memory

Ask your child's teachers to "load the dice" in favor of better learning for your child. It's easily done. Just ask his remedial reading or special teacher to pre-teach new sight vocabulary to your child before it's presented in his reading group. He can bring the new words home that night for another quick review with you (see "Stacking the deck" earlier in this section). This additional practice will improve his ability to learn during his reading instruction at school.

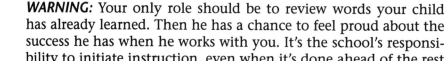

WARNING: Your only role should be to review words your child has already learned. Then he has a chance to feel proud about the success he has when he works with you. It's the school's responsibility to initiate instruction, even when it's done ahead of the rest of the class. You should not be introducing new sight words to your child for the first time.

Good
IEP
idea!

IEP IDEA: If your child's IEP lists reading as a weakness, the school must use methods known to help your child. So if "Loading the dice" helps your child he is entitled to this help—by the regular classroom teacher or someone she assigns it to, such as teacher assistant, remedial reading teacher or special teacher.

You can guarantee that "Loading the Dice" will be tried with your child by having a trial of pre-teaching sight vocabulary written into his IEP.

Tips and Tricks: Comprehension

PROBLEM: You need entertaining ways to work on reading comprehension.

SOLUTION: "Giggles 'n gags"

Look for books of jokes and riddles your child can read easily (meaning he can read 95 of 100 words without help).

STRONG
verbal

SOLUTION: "Now we're really cookin'!"

Thumb through a children's cookbook with your child and pick some yummy recipes to try together. Let the child choose what he wants to make. Don't take over too quickly: lead your child to read, then understand, then do.

Works with most

COMMENT: Pre-read the instructions in the cookbooks, model kits and other items that come with instructions before trying them with your child. Sometimes those directions are written badly or unclearly, and you'll want to find problem spots ahead of time.

STRONG
global learner

weak
verbal

TIP: We examined a variety of children's cookbooks and recommend *KidsCooking*, published by Klutz Press, as being well-written and well-suited for children. See page 116.

SOLUTION: "Read about 'hot topics'"

Use your child's interests to his advantage. Keeping his reading ability in mind, get him a book or two on his favorite hobby or sport. See "Five-Finger Exercise" elsewhere in this chapter on page 112 and use it to determine if the books you consider are too hard or not.

**Attention
Deficit**

INFORMATION: Some books tell humorous sports stories and can be a lot of fun to read. Humor encourages comprehension.

SOLUTION: "It's In the mail!"

If your child has a special interest, subscribe to a magazine that covers the topic. Some examples include *Cat Fancy, Sports Illustrated for Kids,* and *Kid City.* Also explore magazines aimed at children such as *Highlights for Children* and *Cricket.*

STRONG
nonverbal

Strengths   Weaknesses

TIP: Before spending money on a subscription, take a trip to the library. Examine some magazines and pick one or two your child particularly likes. Depending on how well your child reads you might look in the adult magazine area as well.

SOLUTION: "Simple science"

Attention
Deficit

Go to the library or bookstore and find a book of easy science experiments for children to do together. Again, supervise carefully for safety.

See Chapter Sixteen for inexpensive science kits you can buy or order.

SOLUTION: "That's a hoot!"

STRONG
nonverbal

weak
auditory

Read humorous poetry and act it out (you act it out too, Mom and Dad!) See poems by writers like Shel Silverstein and Jack Prelutsky. Some suggested books are listed at the end of the chapter.

INFORMATION: Reading humorous materials requires excellent comprehension while providing the motivation to work at it.

SOLUTION: "Time to tinker"

STRONG
nonverbal

weak
verbal

Get a simple model, or use directions to build a doghouse or birdhouse. Be ready to help, but always try to lead your child to figure out what the directions mean before explaining. Supervise the use of tools and glue carefully. If you can, tie the project into some special interest the child has. If your child asks for help with the reading too quickly, a good dodge is to say "I'll be there in a moment..." and give your child another 15 - 30 seconds to sort it out himself.

WARNING: Don't get too "teachy." This is supposed to be fun! Keep your child's strengths and weaknesses in mind. If he tends to be clumsy with his hands, be ready to assist (he can hold a part in place while you apply the glue, for instance), but let him do as much of the project—and the reading—as possible.

Strengths   Weaknesses

PROBLEM: *Your child doesn't always remember what he's read.*

SOLUTION: *"Just the facts, please."*

Have your child read a paragraph silently and then tell you the main points he read. If he finds this hard, photocopy what he's reading and have him highlight what he thinks the key words or phrases are. (These photocopies make excellent study materials when he has to prepare for a test.)

INFORMATION: Sometimes children better understand what they've read when they read it out loud. When reading silently they sometimes skip words, or lines, or just don't pay full attention. By reading out loud they catch many of those mistakes. In addition, the information enters their brains by three routes: eyes, ears and motor (as their mouths move).

STRONG
auditory

weak
verbal

weak
basic skills

PROBLEM: *Your child doesn't concentrate on what he's reading.*

SOLUTION: *"Centering thoughts"*

Before your child begins to read, he should consider all the supporting information provided.

If he's reading from a textbook, he should look at the pictures and read the captions under them. He should also scan for titles, subtitles, and words printed in bold—most likely that's new and important vocabulary.

If he's reading a story, he should examine any accompanying illustrations. He may need guiding questions from you while looking at the illustrations: which person do you think is the main character? How old is he or she? Can you tell from the pictures if the story could happen now, or does it take place in the past or future?

Ask just enough questions to get the child's interest in the reading raised, but if the pictures and illustrations provide valuable information make sure he notices those details.

Attention
Deficit

STRONG
global learner

weak
sequential

weak
verbal

PROBLEM: *Your child can read most of the words in his textbook, but it still doesn't make any sense to him.*

SOLUTION: *"Closing the gaps"*

Read the selection aloud to your child and discuss it with him. Search for necessary knowledge your child might lack: does he know there's a continent called "Europe" and another called "Asia?" Does he know that China is part of Asia? Get the globe

STRONG
verbal

weak
basic skills

out. Also see the tip called "Just the Facts, Please" elsewhere in this chapter.

TIP: If you don't have a globe, get one. Globes are much easier to understand than flat maps.

PROBLEM: Your child reads his textbooks but has trouble remembering the details of what he's read.

SOLUTION: *"Making connections"*

STRONG
verbal

weak
basic skills

Read assignments with your child and discuss new concepts as you go along. Example: "Europeans wanted goods from Asia—spices, silk, etc.—as badly as we want whatever is 'hot' and new at the mall. They couldn't go to a mall, though, because it was so far away, so trade routes developed...."

TIP: Providing this sort of background information might be a good task for a tutor. If you can afford it, get an encyclopedia so you and your child can look up information to expand his general knowledge about the topic.

SOLUTION: *"Rainbow reading"*

Attention
Deficit

weak
visual

Materials:
 Highlighters in several colors
 Photocopy of material to read

Your child should read the material one paragraph at a time. He should highlight new vocabulary in one color, important names in another, important dates in another, and important concepts in a fourth. This list may not suit all subjects, but he can devise his own system. The point is to use the highlighters as a way for him to begin to notice what kinds of information are buried in the material he reads for school. If this works, photocopy chapters from textbooks ahead of time.

Once marked, these photocopies make excellent study materials for tests.

Strengths	Weaknesses

Other Tips and Tricks

PROBLEM: *Child loses his place while reading.*

SOLUTION: *"Line by line"*

Materials:
    5 X 8 index card or other piece of cardboard

Attention
Deficit

Use a line marker. The child holds the marker under the line he's reading, and moves it down one line at a time. Markers are particularly useful when copying text from dictionaries or when using other books with small print, such as encyclopedias.

*weak
visual*

INFORMATION: Teachers often don't like line markers. They feel use of markers sometimes results in bad reading habits. However, the point of reading is comprehension, and if a child skips lines there's no way what he reads will make any sense.

IEP IDEA: If reading with a marker helps your child, you might want to have the method listed on his "Modifications and Adaptations" page. Otherwise some teachers may insist that he put the marker away.

*Good
IEP
idea!*

PROBLEM: *Your child feels foolish in front of his friends because he can't read the menu at popular restaurants, common street names in his town, etc.*

SOLUTION: *"One From column A..."*

Ask the restaurant manager for a menu to take home so he can practice reading it. Most will be glad to help when you tell them the reason.

Works with
most

Also practice reading greeting cards and street signs in your neighborhood. Encourage your child to combine skills when doing this. For instance, if he knows that he's at the intersection of Price and Cherry Streets, the initial consonant—P or C— will tell him what street he's on. Menus often include picture clues he can use to help him read.

PROBLEM: *Your child has trouble picking books he can read by himself.*

INFORMATION: Teachers have used the method given below informally for years when they didn't have test scores to guide them.

| Strengths | Weaknesses |

Works with
most

___

SOLUTION: "Five finger test"

Ask him to him read a page out loud from the book he wants. He should put up a finger for each word he doesn't know. If he puts up five fingers before he's finished the page, the book is probably too hard for him.

This assumes ten words to a line and ten lines to a page, or about 100 words, so adjust your estimates accordingly.

INFORMATION: To read a book easily or independently a child should know 95 of 100 words without any struggle.

ADDITIONAL INFORMATION: The "Five Finger Test" is most appropriate for fiction books and for *required* non-fiction reading.

Some highly curious children enjoy looking at non-fiction books even when they can't read all of the words. Even if they do little more than look at the pictures they may understand more than we would expect. They may combine many reading skills: context, picture clues, maybe even some phonics if you're lucky, so it's not wasted time.

TIP: If the teacher asks your child to fill out a sheet of books he's read, include these partially-read books. He should get credit for all attempts to read.

___

PROBLEM: Your child is learning to read but gets frustrated easily.

COMMENT: When your child is struggling to read, any reading is good reading.

___

STRONG
visual

weak
verbal

SOLUTION: "Read it all"

Allow your child to read comic books, and encourage him to read comics in the newspaper. Comics provide detailed pictures which often give valuable clues. This encourages both comprehension and independent reading.

___

PROBLEM: Your child wants to read the same book over and over.

___

SOLUTION: "One more time!"

Works with
most

Let him. This behavior is meeting some need. Perhaps he can't read many books yet, or perhaps he senses that he's memorizing new sight words by re-reading it. Maybe the book touches him emotionally, or is so funny that even after several readings he still enjoys it. Reading is always better than not reading.

Strengths   Weaknesses

INFORMATION: Young children enjoy—and benefit from—hearing the same stories and nursery rhymes over and over.

WARNING: There is one exception to this rule. The bright child with Attention Deficit Disorder may re-read books without paying full attention to what he's reading, thus forming extremely poor reading habits. These children may seem to always have their nose in a book. They can read a familiar, easy book while putting out remarkably little effort. Sometimes they have read the same book superficially several times and are still picking up major events or points for the first time.

The teacher should not allow your child with ADD to pull out books and read in the classroom instead of completing his work. If necessary, give the teacher permission to remove any books he reads instead of completing class work.

PROBLEM: *Your child needs more books to read at home.*

SOLUTION: *"Reading on the cheap"*

Encourage your child to participate in book clubs at schools. Flyers come home about eight times a year inviting children to order paperback books at extremely low prices, often one to two dollars. The books contain interesting, well-written stories.

Works with
most

Allow brothers and sisters to order from each others' book clubs. Your fourth grader may be quite willing to order from his second-grade sister's flyer because the books are so interesting at all levels. It's an inexpensive way to build a reading library at home.

PROBLEM: *Limited funds make it hard to buy books your child can read.*

SOLUTION: *"Keep a wish list"*

Ask librarians to recommend books your child might enjoy having. Gift-givers can use these titles for presents.

WARNING: Make sure the librarian understands your child's reading ability.

Strengths   Weaknesses

PROBLEM: Your child's reading skills have grown but he lacks confidence and hesitates—even when he's reading fairly well.

INFORMATION: Sometimes when children follow this pattern it's because they received many, many corrections from teachers and other adults while learning to read. Quite naturally they don't trust their skills.

STRONG
auditory

SOLUTION: "Supported reading"

Choose material he can read reasonably well. As he reads out loud, quietly read along with him. That way you provide the unknown words immediately so comprehension isn't interfered with. Don't stop to make corrections or explain why a word is spelled the way it is. The goal is to help him build his confidence, and corrections will interfere with that goal.

PROBLEM: The child tires easily when reading.

Works with
most

SOLUTION: "Taking turns"

Let him read a paragraph. Then you read a paragraph, and so on. If you're reading for fun, let your child decide when to stop. If you're doing required reading, break large assignments into chunks with short breaks between sessions.

PROBLEM: Your child can read short sentences but bogs down when sentences get longer.

INFORMATION: Sometimes when children have trouble learning to read, they read stories made of very short sentences for a rather long time. The child gets used to the rhythm of short sentences. Then when he gets to longer sentences the new rhythms of the sentences are different, and it throws him.

When this happens the children read longer sentences as if they expect every word to be the last one. So they might read like this:

"Often these children read.
Longer sentences.
As if.
They expect.
Every.
Word.

To be.
The.
Last.
One."

By the time they've reached the end with all those false starts and stops they've lost track of what the sentence was saying.

SOLUTION: *"Togetherness"*

TIP: Choose an easy book, one where the child knows 95 out of 100 words. It should be a book he's read before. That will help when he comes to longer sentences.

STRONG
global learner

weak
verbal

1. You and the child read a paragraph of the book out loud, together. Your child should set the pace, and your voice should be quieter than his.
2. Pick one or two longer sentences from the paragraph and the two of you practice them together several times. Each time your voice should get softer so your child depends more on himself. That's called "fading."
3. Tell your child why he's struggling with longer sentences so he understands why he's having difficulties. He's already struggled a lot while learning to read as well as he does now. If he starts having trouble again he may panic, fearing he's gone as far as he can in reading.
4. Ask your child to tell you what he's read in his own words. This encourages understanding

TIP: Do this once a day for a few minutes only, and gradually your child will get the sound of longer sentences in his ear.

INFORMATION: The opportunity to hear many kinds of sentences is one of several reasons why it's important to read to your child. Even if his reading progress is slow, he'll hear more advanced stories and won't be so startled by more complex sentences when he gets to them himself.

PROBLEM: *Your child resists reading at home.*

SOLUTION: *"Motivation"*

Works with
most

All children like to thumb through catalogs. As your child's birthday or a special holiday approaches, let him use catalogs to make lists of gifts he'd like. You'd be smart to get at least one or two things from this list once he's struggled to read the catalog.

Strengths   Weaknesses

PROBLEM: *He thinks reading is over-rated.*

SOLUTION: *"Be a role model"*

Works with
most

Children imitate their parents. Let your children see you reading, even if it's only some sections of the newspapers, or magazines, or even comics.

Materials you might consider purchasing:

Long and Short Vowels Tape:
This is printed tape that you place across the top of a child's desk. It shows each of the five vowels with pictures for each of the vowels' two basic sounds, long and short. The tapes are sold only in package of 35, so make some points at your child's school. Use one for your child's school desk, and one for his home desk, and donate the other 33 to the school. Manufactured by the Judy/Instructo company.

Reading Yellow Pages for Students and Teachers. Published by Incentive Publications, Inc., Nashville, TN. ISBN 0-86530-029-1.

Alphabet Magnets:
72 upper/lower case magnets (also includes numerals and math symbols). From Educational Insights, $7.95.

Scratch 'n Sniff Stickers:
96 for $1.69. Put on good work, or put on a chart. Some children prefer to keep them in a sticker album.

Recommended children's books

KidsCooking. 1994, Klutz Press. ISBN 09–32592–14–7, $12.95.
This was the best children's cookbook we could find. The instructions are easy to read and understand, and the recipes are appealing. KidsCooking comes with a set of "child-friendly" measuring spoons.

Prelutsky, Jack. *Something Big Has Been Here.* Morrow. ISBN 0-688064-34-5, $15.95.
and
Silverstein, Shel. *Where the Sidewalk Ends.* Harper-Row. ISBN 0-06026-67-2, $15.95.
Both these books contain delightful children's poetry. Buy them, or suggest them as gifts for your child, or check them out from the library regularly. If your child can't read them yet, read them to him—with lots of expression.

ă   apple

ě   elephant

ĭ   fish

ŏ   octopus

ŭ   umbrella

Tips and tricks:
spelling

It's a darned poor mind that can think of only one way to spell a word.

Andrew Jackson, edited

Structuring spelling progress

Your child will make the most gains in spelling when:

1. practice is carefully planned so she is likely to concentrate while working on the words,
2. she studies frequently and effectively, and
3. she has a variety of methods available to practice the words.

Children who struggle with spelling need carefully-planned study sessions. All of the suggestions we're going to make in this chapter fit into one of the three key elements just listed.

Here are some ideas on how to put these three keys to work for your child.

Step One: Structure practice

Work out an effective study schedule, and stick to it.
— Divide the list into three sections. Make sure each section has some easy words and some hard ones.
— Study the first section on Monday—including a review of any troublesome words; study the second section on Tuesday night; the third section on Wednesday. If your child has some conflict one night, such as sports practice, that prevents her from studying the words on that evening, start on Sunday night.
— On Thursday night review all words.

Step Two: Study effectively

Research shows that the average student—one with no particular learning problems—needs to spell a word eight times before she will learn it well. The actual spelling activity your child chooses doesn't matter much so long as she works with the word. Children who struggle with spelling need both more chances to practice their words and more ways to study them than other children. Your child should check the accuracy of her work herself when she practices her spelling words. Research shows that self-checking increases learning. In addition, it puts the responsibility for success where it belongs—on her.

Three tips are especially effective no matter what method your child uses to work on her words:
— After she looks at a word there should be a pause of several seconds before she spells it. This strategy of postponing a person's response is called "forced delay." For instance, she can look at the word, walk to the door and back and then write it down. This short delay requires your child to hold the spelling of the word in her head long enough to begin to learn it.
— If your child writes each word on a 3 x 5 card she will focus on each more deeply. These cards also make it easier for her to check her work carefully. Buy a file box and dividers to organize and store her cards.
— Your child should always practice her words using manuscript printing, not cursive. Children think more accurately about phonics, syllables and letter sequence when they print their spelling words than when they write them in cursive.

Step Three: Study in a variety of ways

Children are quite naturally bored by tasks they're not good at, and variety is the most effective tool against boredom. Many methods in this chapter have been included solely to provide your child with a variety of spelling activities to choose from.

Although she will develop strong preferences, often one method is no better than another. She should experiment with several methods that appeal to her and then choose the ones she enjoys the most. She'll appreciate the chance to have some control over her efforts.

So now we move on to the spelling activities. All methods address the issues of variety and delayed response. Some use visual approaches and some auditory; some involve movement (kinesthetic learning) and others combine two or more approaches. They all have the same goal: to improve your child's memory for spelling words.

Spelling tips and tricks

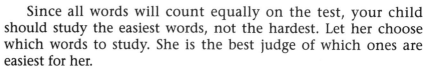

PROBLEM: Your child waited to study until the night before the test.

INFORMATION: On spelling tests, easy words count as much as hard ones do. Take advantage of this fact!

SOLUTION: "Damage control"

Works with most

weak memory

Since all words will count equally on the test, your child should study the easiest words, not the hardest. Let her choose which words to study. She is the best judge of which ones are easiest for her.

Attempting to study an entire list the night before a test seldom works well; trying to earn an A or a B at this late date may be counter-productive. Most struggling spellers need the repetition of studying for short periods of time on successive days. If she limits last-minute studying to selected words and raises her test score, say from 40% to 70%, she will still help her grade.

WARNING

WARNING: Consider the consequences of trying to do too much in a short period of time. If she's unsuccessful and "blows" the test, two things could happen:
- she may get a lower grade than she would have had she not studied at all, and
- she may conclude that studying does not pay off. In that regard she would be right, as it was done poorly. Bad studying is worse than none at all.

TIP: Look in this chapter for enjoyable but effective ways to study the words each night so that "Thursday Night Panic" doesn't happen any more in your home.

PROBLEM: Your child doesn't study her spelling words consistently, week after week.

INFORMATION: Sometimes students slack off after one or two good grades. They don't understand how teachers arrive at grades, and they think one or two good grades means that spelling is no longer a problem for them. They don't realize they can get good grades on half the tests and still end up with a D or an F.

SOLUTION: "Reality training"

Show your child how grades are averaged. Make up fictitious grades (perhaps 80%, 77%, 82%, 72% and 84%). Average these grades: add them together and divide by the number of grades—in this case, 5. The result is 79%, in many school districts a high C. That's a respectable grade for a child who struggles in spelling.

Works with most

Attention Deficit

$$
\begin{array}{r}
79 \\
76 \\
81 \\
75 \\
+84 \\
\hline
395
\end{array}
\qquad
\begin{array}{r}
79 \\
5\overline{\smash{)}395} \\
-35 \\
\hline
45 \\
-45 \\
\hline
0
\end{array}
$$

Then change two of the scores to low numbers—say, change both 81% to 51% and 84% to 44%. Now the average has dropped to 65%, a D or F in most schools.

Let your child experiment with the calculator, combining various possible grades. Once she understands the damage a few low grades can do she may be more willing to work regularly.

PROBLEM: Your child often forgets her spelling book.

SOLUTION: "Teamwork between school and home"

Ask the teacher for an extra copy of the spelling text for home use. If that's not possible, periodically copy upcoming lists of words from her textbook. Once you have the word lists, if she forgets her spelling book she can work with her words using one of the suggestions from this chapter instead. Then if she was leaving the book at school on purpose there will be no payoff: "forgetting" won't get her out of homework.

Attention Deficit

weak memory

IEP IDEA: If your child's learning difficulties include organizational difficulties, or if your child has an attentional problem, she may be entitled to a duplicate set of textbooks for home use. If she shows this need, write it into her IEP.

Good IEP idea!

Strengths   Weaknesses

PROBLEM: Your child has difficulty using phonics to spell words.

INFORMATION: We tend to think of phonics as the perfect tool to sound out words. However, in the English language some letters can have more than one sound, making phonics quite confusing for certain learning disabled students. President Abraham Lincoln supposedly demonstrated once how the letters *"ghoti"* spell "fish": *gh* for the sound of *f* as in *rough*; *o* for the short i sound as in *women*; *ti* for the *sh* sound as in *motion*. It's no wonder children find phonics confusing sometimes.

STRONG
global learner

weak
auditory

SOLUTION: "Sensible phonics"

She should use the phonics she knows (say, initial consonants) and then rely on memory for the rest of the word. Many of the methods listed in this chapter will help her memorize spelling words. As she masters more phonics skills, she will gradually learn to combine phonics and memory more and more efficiently.

In addition see the method that comes next, "Breaking up is (not) hard to do"—another good coping strategy when a child struggles with phonics.

PROBLEM: Your child has difficulty learning to spell longer words.

STRONG
visual

weak
sequential

SOLUTION: "Breaking up is (not) hard to do"

Break the words into syllables for study. Say the words for her syllable by syllable so she can concentrate on each one separately. The cards should look like this example:

re·mark·a·ble

To make the syllables more obvious, use two colored markers. Write the letters in one color and the dots that separate them in the other. Your child should make the cards herself with your

Strengths   Weaknesses

guidance as necessary. When you're not sure how to divide a word, check a spelling dictionary (see page 132).

SOLUTION: "Another way to break up"

Practice common prefixes and suffixes, such as "re" and "able" in the card on page 122.

After your child has learned some suffixes and prefixes she should practice adding them to root words. See the book *Reading Yellow Pages for Students and Teachers* listed at the end of the chapter. It contains carefully-selected lists of words you can use for this purpose.

STRONG
nonverbal

PROBLEM: Your child seems to know the words but doesn't do well on the class tests.

SOLUTION: "Printing power"

She should try printing the words while taking the test. If the teacher insists on cursive for spelling tests, she can print them first and then copy them into cursive after the test is over.

INFORMATION: Some children who have difficulty spelling begin to spell better just by printing words instead of using cursive.

Works with
most

SOLUTION: "Right place, right time"

She can take the spelling test in the resource room.

INFORMATION: Some children focus on the task better when in a quieter, less distracting setting. For others the resource room reduces pressure.

IEP IDEA: The point of the spelling test is to find out what words the student knows. Reducing stress and helping her think clearly by using strategies such as printing are reasonable. Write any suggestions that work into your child's IEP. If she takes the test in a special setting, the special teacher and classroom teacher should work out a plan for working her back into the classroom for spelling tests eventually.

Attention
Deficit

weak
sequential

*Good
IEP
idea!*

Strengths   Weaknesses

Attention Deficit

SOLUTION: "Time enough"

Your child can be given extra time to take the test. If she needs a lot of extra time, a teacher assistant or even another classmate can give her the test separately.

weak grapho-motor

INFORMATION: Some children's spelling scores improve dramatically when they're allowed to signal the teacher that they're ready to go on to the next word. The teacher waits for that signal from her slower-working students before proceeding to the next word on the test.

In some cases these students need more time to think, because even intelligent children recall learned information at varying rates. In other cases decreased stress seems to cause the improvement.

PROBLEM: Your child has to take a "pretest" every Monday to see which words she already knows. She doesn't do well on these pretests and finds them demoralizing.

WARNING: Repeated failures every Monday on unknown words can discourage your child so badly she will give up on spelling completely. Pre-tests don't count toward your child's final grade but can be terribly destructive to motivation.

weak memory

SOLUTION: "The best defense is a good offense"

She can start studying the next week's words the weekend before or even the Friday before. She may not score 100% on the pretests, but her scores will increase, and the extra time spent on the words will help raise her final test score.

Works with most

SOLUTION: "Sensible use of time"

Have your child scheduled into the Resource Room during the classroom's pre-test time. In the Resource Room she can do effective spelling practice. If your child has this difficulty and the classroom teacher resists excusing her from the pretest, write it into your child's IEP.

PROBLEM: The weekly word list is just too hard.

weak memory

SOLUTION: "Short and sweet"

Shorten the word list: have your child learn the first 50%, or first 75% of the list.

Strengths	Weaknesses

SOLUTION: "Simplify"

Eliminate the harder words. This is an easy way to modify standard classroom assignments to a child's real instructional level in the subject.

Works with most

SOLUTION: "More than one way to simplify"

If one of the words is "recreation," for example, a child needing simpler words could be given "create" instead. Later, when she has learned more complex word structure, she could then practice adding prefixes (such as "re" in recreation) and suffixes (such as "tion") to root words she's learned.

weak sequential

SOLUTION: "Keep a record"

Assign fewer words, with long-term retention the goal. Pick words that she uses often or that will help develop her spelling skills. Include frequent review of old words in nightly study sessions to ensure she'll remember the words she learns. Use the "Word Record Sheet" (see the Chapter Ten Appendix, pages 230–233) to list your child's weekly spelling words and keep track of their review. A tutor or support teacher can also use this form.

weak memory

IEP IDEA: These suggestions are curriculum modifications. The ones that help your child need to be written into your child's IEP; that will require her teachers to use them.

Good IEP idea!

WARNING: Curriculum modifications should be used only when necessary and only for as long as necessary. The goal must always to be to normalize your child's education whenever possible, not modify it whenever possible. Gradually increase either the number of words she studies or the complexity of the words. But don't rush her; you don't want her grades to drop or for her to feel discouraged again.

WARNING

More novel ways to practice spelling:

For all these methods, start with the spelling words legibly written on individual 3 x 5 cards. Your child should concentrate on the card as long as she thinks she needs to and then turn it over. After a short delay she should write the word down, using printing, in whatever method she's chosen, then flip the card back over to check her work. Soon she will see that she has more trouble with some words than others. She should put those words on cards two or three more times and add them to her stack. That way the troublesome words will get more practice.

Strengths   Weaknesses

TIP: Making study cards would be an excellent and productive way for her to use her time instead of taking a pre-test on Mondays.

SOLUTION: "Chalk it up"

weak grapho-motor

Get a small chalk board and colored chalk. Writing with chalk on a board gives a different feel through the fingers, and that different sensation helps some children learn.

SOLUTION: "Sand writing"

weak grapho-motor

Place sand in a 9 x 13 baking pan; trace the letters with fingers in sand.

SOLUTION: "Vertical spelling"

Attention Deficit

Have your child practice writing the words vertically—

v
e
r
t
i
c
a
l
l
y

—instead of horizontally. You can also do "vertical spelling" syllable by syllable like this:

ver
ti
cal
ly

SOLUTION: "Rainbow spelling"

Works with most

Pick two colors of fine-point magic markers. Write consonants in one color and vowels in the other, like this:

Strengths	Weaknesses

SOLUTION: *"Brush up on spelling"*

Paint the words in water on the driveway with a big brush. On a warm day the water evaporates quickly, keeping the child's attention focused on the word longer!

weak grapho-motor

PROBLEM: *No matter which method my child chooses she still finds some words troublesome.*

SOLUTION: *"Let the fingers do the walking"*

Type spelling words on the computer, using fancy fonts. Let your child be creative and playful so long as she works accurately. She will enjoy printing out the results of her font choices.

Works with most

weak grapho-motor

INFORMATION: Hunting for the letters creates that all-important "delayed response" as she hunts for the right keys on the keyboard, so she should look at the card and turn it over before typing—this isn't a copying exercise.

SOLUTION: *"Up against the wall"*

Turn out the lights and trace the letters of the word on the wall with a flashlight.

Works with most

SOLUTION: *"Round-robin spelling"*

You say (or write) the first letter, your child says the next (or writes); you say the third; she says the fourth, and so on. You can combine "Round-Robin Spelling" with sand-writing and the other methods here.

Attention Deficit

SOLUTION: *"Scrambled Spelling"*

INFORMATION: This suggestion is a little more time-consuming to set up than most of the other ones. We include it for two reasons:

STRONG nonverbal

weak grapho-motor

Strengths   Weaknesses

weak
memory

weak
sequential

— although it's a little time-consuming it completely bypasses letter formation during actual study, giving it a tremendous advantage for younger children with serious pencil-paper difficulties
— it *works*—sometimes when nothing else seems to. For older students we recommend you save this method for troublesome words.

Materials:
3 x 5 cards (or 5 x 8 for longer words), cut into strips
scissors
marker

1. Write the word on a strip cut from a 3 x 5 or 5 x 8 card. Leave a little space between each letter.

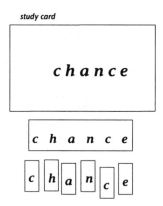

2. Cut between each letter on the strip, like the example above.
3. Then the student turns the study card over and mixes up the individual letters...

4. ...and combines all her spelling skills—phonics, memory, etc.—to reconstruct the word. It doesn't matter what order she selects her letters, and she can rearrange them as many times as she wishes until she thinks she has it right (see the next page for an example).
5. Finally, she checks her work by turning the study card back over.

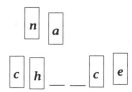

By using this method several times, most students will master at least some of the words they find difficult. Once your child has practiced a harder word using "Scrambled spelling," she can review it using other suggestions in this chapter that don't require quite so much work before the child actually studies the word.

TIP: If this method works get some magnetic letters (see the end of the chapter) to use with this suggestion.

PROBLEM: Your child needs a way to tap into her non-academic strengths to learn her words.

Solution: "Sing-along"

We all learned the alphabet by singing it. She can sing the spelling of words to her favorite popular songs. Singing involves both melody and rhythm and taps into parts of her brain that she doesn't typically use to learn. Sing along with her sometimes—it will enhance her concentration.

STRONG
auditory

Solution: "Karate kid"

Children who have learned some karate or other martial art method can spell out loud, punctuating each letter with a movement.

STRONG
nonverbal

PROBLEM: Your child has trouble spelling words she needs in her school assignments.

SOLUTION: "Look it up (efficiently)"

Get a spelling dictionary. Spelling dictionaries list the words but not the definitions and are easier to use than definition-based ones. See our recommended spelling dictionary at the end of this chapter.

weak
visual

SOLUTION: "Do-it-yourself dictionary"

Your child can make her own customized spelling dictionary of frequently-needed words, such as specialized school vocabulary.

STRONG
global learner

weak
visual

Strengths   Weaknesses

A steno tablet works well for this purpose—assign one or two pages to each letter. Some steno pads come with a printed list of often-misspelled words on the back cover as well.

PROBLEM: Your child doesn't always know what her spelling words mean.

weak
verbal

SOLUTION: "Defining the problem"

Discuss the meanings of the words with her.

TIP: If your child studies a reduced word list, whoever chooses her words should take the usefulness of the words into account. For instance, the author saw one fourth grade list that included the word "accord." This is not a word fourth graders are likely to need or use. For those students with adjusted spelling lists we eliminated that word and included words they were more likely to find useful.

PROBLEM: Your child can spell her words during practice but seems to "mis-hear" the teacher's pronunciation during tests.

weak
auditory

Solution: "Motorboat, motorboat, go so slow..."

She may need to hear the words said at different speeds before the test. At the beginning of the week say the words for your child slowly and distinctly, even exaggerating the differences between syllables. By Thursday night say them more rapidly.

INFORMATION: Children with auditory problems sometimes perceive words quite differently when they hear them at different tempos.

PROBLEM: Your child rushes through her spelling practice.

Attention
Deficit

SOLUTION: "Yes-no spelling"

You say the word and then have your child spell it, one letter at a time. As she says or writes each letter tell her immediately whether she's right or not by saying either "yes" or "no." Discourage conversation while partly through a word as it will interfere with learning.

Strengths   Weaknesses

PROBLEM: The teacher insists your child write each word she misses on the pre-test five times each (or ten times or whatever) "to practice them."

SOLUTION: "Don't do it!"

There is no worse way for a child with writing problems or Attention Deficit Disorder to work on spelling words. It's worse than ineffective; it actively interferes with learning.

Attention
Deficit

weak
grapho-motor

IEP IDEA: If necessary, write it into your child's IEP that she will not be required to write her spelling words repetitively. Also include that her grade is not to be lowered for skipping this activity. Some other, more effective, practice method should be substituted instead. For instance, she could use that time to put the week's words on 3 x 5 cards.

*Good
IEP
idea!*

PROBLEM: You and your child have busy lives. It's hard for you to find time to practice the words enough for her to learn them well.

SOLUTION: "Portable practice"

She doesn't have to study the whole list at one time. With the spelling words on 3 x 5 cards she can take them with her on errands. She can practice one or two words at a stop sign; in a restaurant where service is slow she may get through the whole list. Set up some sort of simple method on the back of the card to keep track of her progress on each word so you know which ones have been studied and which ones she finds most troublesome.

Works with
most

PROBLEM: Your child misspells common words that can't be sounded out such as "they," "people," etc.

SOLUTION: "Personalized spelling lists"

Each time she misspells a commonly-used word, have her teacher add it to her weekly spelling list as a substitute for another word on the list.

Attention
Deficit

Strengths   Weaknesses

weak
memory

COMMENT: Often inattention is part of the child's difficulty. Many times children can spell these common words correctly but have formed the habit of putting anything down when they write. Adding these words to the weekly list is a gentle "nuisance factor" that makes it worth it to a child to be a little more careful.

TIP: After years of spelling these words wrong it may take your child several weeks to learn some of them correctly. You should use the "Spelling Words Review List" form you'll find in the Chapter Ten Appendix to keep track of these added words.

Materials you might consider purchasing:

Books:

21st Century Misspeller's Dictionary, Princeton Language Institute. Dell Publishing Co., ISBN 0-440-21545-5. Paperback, $5.99.

This dictionary contains no definitions. It gives common misspellings of words in the left column and the correct spelling on the right, like this:

droped   dropped
ounse   ounce
sensetive   sensitive

The back of the book contains a section of commonly confused words (such as they're and their). It also gives lists containing the books of the Bible, the names of states, months of the year and other sets of words.

The only thing we didn't like about this book is that the print is small. Students with visual-perceptual difficulties will find it helpful to use an index card under the word they need.

Reading Yellow Pages for Students and Teachers. Incentive Publications, Inc., Nashville, TN. ISBN 0-86530-029-1.

Purchase this book if you need lists of words grouped together by phonetic or structural traits, such as words beginning with "bl," words ending in a "silent e," etc.

Materials

Rubber Stamps:

These stamps come in sets of upper or lower case (use lower case for most spelling). Using colored stamp pads you can use color with meaning: consonants blue and vowels red; or each syllable a different color. Color used with meaning enhances learning. Be sure to state whether you want upper case or lower case stamps. Manufactured by Educational Insights. Bradburn's catalog also includes stamp pads with washable ink.

Alphabet Cubes:

50 plastic cubes with letters on all six sides (upper and lower case). Use for building words, practicing spelling, etc. Manufactured by Language Arts.

Magnets:

72 colorful magnets in the shape of letters. The set includes both upper and lower cases as well as numerals and math symbols. Manufactured by Educational Insights for $7.95.

Chalkboard:

Large (slightly smaller than the top of a school desk), this board has a good-quality surface with lines painted on. Easy to clean. Manufactured by Ideal (#3435), $4.25. Get a box of colored chalk to go with it.

Wipeboard:

Smaller than the chalkboard above but children love them. Wide-pointed dry-erase pens may work better than the fine-pointed ones. Bradburn's and most office supply stores carry these boards in several sizes.

Tips and tricks: math

Mom: *"Well? How's your math homework coming along?"*
Calvin: *"I've almost started!"*

Bill Watterson, in a Calvin and Hobbes cartoon

Introduction

Too often people think only of reading when they think of learning problems. To many people, the term *learning disabilities* means *dyslexia*, or reading problems. The very real and sometimes severe difficulties struggling students can experience in math get overlooked in this too-narrow definition.

Math mastery is essential to a well-rounded education. The following suggestions won't fix a severe learning problem in the area of math, sometimes called *dyscalculia*, but they may help solve some serious problems in this all-important subject.

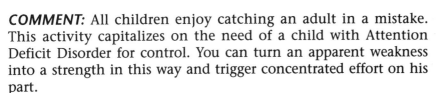

PROBLEM: *Your child works carelessly, making different errors in each problem. He seems to know what he's doing, but never does everything right in any one problem.*

SOLUTION: *"Nobody's perfect"*

You do three problems. Make mistakes in two of them. Have your child find which problems are wrong, and have him find the mistakes. Let him use a calculator for facts if necessary so he can concentrate on the steps involved.

COMMENT: All children enjoy catching an adult in a mistake. This activity capitalizes on the need of a child with Attention Deficit Disorder for control. You can turn an apparent weakness into a strength in this way and trigger concentrated effort on his part.

Attention
Deficit

SOLUTION: *"Double-checking"*

Have your child do the first three problems independently and then check with you to make sure he's doing the problems right. After that he can check with you at set intervals—say, at the end of each row. This way if he gets confused you'll know it before he's done the whole assignment wrong.

WARNING: Set reasonable standards for accuracy. If he brings home math papers with grades in the 60 - 70% range or lower, require him to get four out of five problems right to start. If his math grades are more in the 70 - 80% range, require 85 - 90% accuracy. If you insist that every single problem be done perfectly under all circumstances, no matter how hard he's worked or no matter how much improvement he's shown, he may not want to cooperate by bringing the work to you.

TIP: Let your child decide how many mistakes he should be allowed. This gives him some control, and you may be surprised when he sets his target for accuracy higher than you would have.

Attention
Deficit

Works with
most

WARNING

SOLUTION: *"Electronic checking"*

Let him check his work using a calculator.

*weak
grapho-motor*

Strengths   Weaknesses

PROBLEM: Your child can't write numerals well, or makes many reversals when writing them.

INFORMATION: Your child has probably been taught to write his numerals using only the small muscles of his fingers. Sometimes when the whole body gets involved a child learns the shapes of the numbers better. The following suggestions often eliminate reversals as well as poor memory for the numbers' shapes.

Materials:

  Finger paints
  1" trim brush (found at any hardware store)
  old clothes
  washable chalk
  large sheets of paper
  wipe board
  wipe board markers

Attention
Deficit

STRONG
global learner

weak
grapho-motor

weak
memory

weak
visual

SOLUTION: "One at a time"

Working on only one numeral per day, he should create it in a variety of ways. Using a 1" trim brush and finger paints, he can paint the "number of the day" many times, as large as possible on the driveway. Make sure he has a model of the numeral to refer to. Finger paint will wash off asphalt but the author isn't so certain about concrete, so choose where he paints carefully.

Make sure he forms the numeral correctly. For instance, "7" always starts at the upper left, moves to the right and then down at a slight angle. He should make the 7 all in one stroke, so the numbers should be as big as he can make them while still painting them with the movements he would use to write them. If you're not sure how he's being taught at school, check with his teacher. Most schools can provide a printed writing guide that shows how each letter and numeral should be formed.

He should use many colors, and the numerals can overlap. You can wash the driveway off easily afterwards with a hose.

If no suitable asphalt surface is available he can make the numbers as large as possible on large pieces of paper.

Other alternatives include washable chalk on driveway or chalkboard, or multi-colored markers on "wipe boards." If you get a wipe board make sure you get markers specifically designed to be used on them. Wherever he writes the numerals, the goal is to make them much larger so he uses the large muscles of his body instead of just the muscles of his hand and forearm.

Strengths   Weaknesses

PROBLEM: Your child has great difficulty counting.

Materials:

Small toys to count, such as a block, an airplane, an animal figure and a little car. Any small objects will do so long as he knows their names.

SOLUTION: "First things first"

Sometimes children have trouble with math because they don't understand the words the teacher uses as she explains the concepts. Make sure your child understands "before" and "after." Ask him to place objects, perhaps small toys, in a row. Then ask him which toy is "before the airplane" and "after the ball."

WARNING: Difficulty with basic language concepts interferes terribly with learning in all subjects. If you suspect your child has difficulty learning school-related language, report the problem to his teacher. Some children have subtle language delays, and remediation often helps tremendously. Sometimes a language problem shows itself in math first because the teacher uses new and complex vocabulary in precise ways during instruction.

SOLUTION: "Get concrete"

Materials:

Pennies

Perhaps your child can count but often does so inaccurately. If so, it may appear to your child's teacher that he has not yet mastered the skill.

Take a page where your child is supposed to count. Perhaps he's supposed to count five stars, like this:

weak
auditory

weak
verbal

WARNING

Attention
Deficit

STRONG
nonverbal

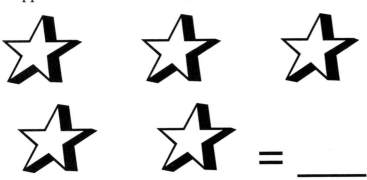

Strengths   Weaknesses

To make the task more concrete, cover each object on the page with a penny. Then have your child count out loud as he moves the coins off to the side. Actually moving an object focuses his abilities better and allows him to double-check. In addition he uses three senses—visual, auditory (as he listens to his counting) and motor, instead of only one—visual.

INFORMATION: If your child can count when he has physical objects to count, his counting abilities are all right. However, he should be able to count pictures of objects on a page nearly as well as he can count real objects. If having movable objects improves your child's counting significantly, keep an eye on his developing strengths and weaknesses. Difficulty with counting objects on a printed page is typical of children with visual perceptual weaknesses and/or Attention Deficit Disorder.

TIP: If moving objects helps him count he can use tangible counters at school such as small blocks.

PROBLEM: *Your child finds using a ruler confusing.*

Materials:
    Ruler, yardstick, tape measure

SOLUTION: *"Inchworm, inchworm"*

STRONG
nonverbal

weak
visual

First, ask your child to measure something simple, such as a 3" by 5" card. Suggest to your child, "I'd like to know how big this card is...." Pick objects that don't involve judging parts of inches first, and then gradually make the measuring more complex.

Once he's comfortable with the concepts of inches and feet, play guessing games: "How long do you think that table is?" Then measure to see how close your guesses were.

SOLUTION: *"Yummy math"*

Materials:
    Sharp, thin knife
    Some food your child likes that can be cut well with a
        knife. See the recipe for "Foolproof Fudge" at the end
        of the chapter.

Attention
Deficit

Works with
most

Help your child cut the chosen food into a one-inch portion. Then he should cut it in half (half-inch) and in half again (quarter-inch).

After that you can cut the food into some length including part of an inch: 2 1/2″, or 1 1/4.″ The measurement may be slightly off; the important thing is that your child learn to judge partial inches using a ruler.

INFORMATION: Edible lessons are as concrete as lessons get.

TIP: Cooking gives a child an excellent opportunity to work on measurement skills. See the end of the chapter for the title of a cookbook written for children. Make sure you have the right tools before beginning a recipe. If your child already has difficulty with measurement, having to combine two quarter-teaspoons to get a half-teaspoon will be counter-productive.

SOLUTION: *"It's a fine line..."*

Materials:
    Light-colored plastic ruler
    Indelible fine-point pen

Use the indelible marker to make inch marks more obvious on the ruler. When your child can measure to the inch easily, mark the half-inch as well. The half-inch mark should be shorter than the inch mark. When he can measure accurately to the half-inch, mark the quarter-inch marks.

weak
grapho-motor

weak
sequential

weak
visual

WARNING: Indelible pens make marks that won't wash out of clothes and can't be removed from furniture or carpets. Store that pen out of reach of small or curious hands.

TIP: Continue to give your child lots of opportunities to measure things around the house—his bed, his desk and the wall—to decide where to place furniture, etc. All these activities will make workbook measurement exercises more meaningful.

PROBLEM: *Your child has difficulty with story problems, sometimes called "word problems."*

SOLUTION: *"Now I see it!"*

Draw pictures to illustrate the story (see the next page). Once your child has the idea, he should draw pictures.

Attention
Deficit

*weak
verbal*

For example: "Bobby had three toy planes. Johnny gave him two more. How many does he have now?"

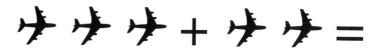

PROBLEM: Your child works slowly and has trouble completing assignments.

INFORMATION: Children don't just work slowly, they work slowly *for some reason.* Whatever that reason is, it needs to be respected. Possible causes for slow work are an attentional problem, poor fine-motor skills, slow recall of information, or not knowing the skill solidly.

SOLUTION: "Divide and conquer"

*Attention
Deficit*

If your child understands the problems he's working, shorten the assignment. The final goal is mastery, not number of problems completed.

If you can't shorten the assignment, divide it into four sections so he can see his progress more clearly.

*weak
grapho-motor*

IEP IDEA: Shortening long assignments is a common IEP modification. Before asking for this accommodation, though, be certain your child really needs it. You don't want to reduce his work load so much that he doesn't have a chance to master new skills solidly. Other ways to reduce his work load could include providing photocopies instead of requiring him to copy problems from the board or book. There may be many ways to help your child cope with an inability to work fast, and the solution you want is the one that helps the most while interfering with his academic progress the least.

*Good
IEP
idea!*

PROBLEM: Your child has trouble remembering which way the hands move on a clock.

Materials:
Cardboard clock to practice with (see end of chapter)

weak
visual

SOLUTION: "This-a-way!"

Using a marker, draw an arrow around the clock showing the direction the hands move. Directional confusion complicates learning to tell time.

STRONG
nonverbal

weak
sequential

SOLUTION: "Time flies (down the throat)"

Materials:

Soft cookies (Mrs. Alison's™ molasses cookies work well)

Use a thin, sharp knife to divide soft cookies into halves and quarters. Leave the pieces in the position they were in before the cookies were cut. Then let your child eat the first quarter hour, the second quarter hour, the third quarter hour, etc.

weak
visual

If your child gets confused about which way the hands move, draw a circle slightly larger than the cookie on a piece of paper. Around the outside, draw an arrow showing the direction the hands move. Then place the cookie pieces inside the circle.

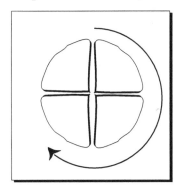

PROBLEM: Your child can tell time to the hour but finds the half-hour and quarter-hour confusing.

SOLUTION: "Minute by minute"

Teach him telling time to the hour and then to the minute. After he can tell time well by the minute, explain the quarter-

Strengths   Weaknesses

hours and half-hours as shortcuts. If your child understands money, use the example of an hour as a dollar. He'll be able to see the connection between quarters in money and quarters of hours. A half hour would be the equivalent of a half-dollar.

INFORMATION: Your child should be able to count by 5's to 60 before learning to tell time.

WARNING: If your child finds some of the language used in telling time confusing, such as "quarter to four" and "quarter past four," tell his teacher and ask if he finds other language concepts confusing.

PROBLEM: *Your child copies math from the board inaccurately.*

SOLUTION: *"Good use of time"*

**Attention
Deficit**

weak
grapho-motor

weak
visual

He should copy the first three problems for the practice and then be provided with a photocopy of the activity to do the work. This way he develops his ability to copy accurately, but any weaknesses don't interfere with his math progress.

If he has trouble copying because he works slowly, he simply should *not* have to copy the whole assignment—either from the board or from a book. He'll spend too much time on the part of the activity that teaches nothing.

If he copies inaccurately he may have a problem with visual perception or attention. Either way he needs to concentrate on the math, not the copying.

PROBLEM: *Your child adds when he should subtract, or vice-versa, because he doesn't notice the operational signs (+, −, x, ÷).*

INFORMATION: Make sure your child actually knows the differences between the signs. Young children with visual perceptual difficulties often have difficulty learning the difference between +, − and =. Children with Attention Deficit Disorder understand the differences but don't take notice of them.

Materials:
Highlighter or highlighters

Strengths	Weaknesses

SOLUTION: *"Watch for the sign"*

1. Your child can use a highlighter to make operational signs more noticeable. One option is to color + signs in one color and − signs in another.
2. He can use a highlighter to circle all the addition problems or all the subtraction problems.

INFORMATION: Using a highlighter in this way draws the child's attention to the operational signs. For children with attentional problems the process of highlighting the signs will help them include the depth with which they focus on the problems.

Attention
Deficit

weak
visual

PROBLEM: *Your child can't seem to get the hang of "regrouping" in subtraction.*

INFORMATION: Regrouping is sometimes called "borrowing," but regrouping is the more accurate word for it. We have to regroup when one of the numerals in the top number is smaller than the numeral under it.

$$\begin{array}{r} 63 \\ \underline{-27} \end{array}$$

In order to solve this problem we'll have to subtract seven from three, a seemingly impossible thing to do.

SOLUTION: *"Understanding is power"*

The numerals **63** stand for the words "sixty-three." When **63** is written in what we call *expanded notation*, the **6** becomes **60**. **63** is actually a kind of abbreviation for **60 + 3**.

Using expanded notation it's easy to see that the number **63** can be written in more than one way. When we regroup, all we do is we take **60 + 3** and re-write it as **50 + 13**. Since **50** and **13** add up to **63**, we can use the number in that form and still get the right answer when we subtract.

PRACTICE: Have your child re-write several two-digit numbers such as **63** in expanded notation: **60 + 3**.

57 becomes	**50 + 7**	
83 becomes	**80 + 3**	
46 becomes	**40 + 6**	

Attention
Deficit

STRONG
nonverbal

weak
sequential

weak
visual

Strengths   Weaknesses

Then have him write the number as it would be if regrouped for subtraction:

57 becomes	50 + 7 becomes	40 + 17
83 becomes	80 + 3 becomes	70 + 13
46 becomes	40 + 6 becomes	30 + 16

After he's expanded ten to twenty two-digit numbers he'll understand why he re-writes the top numbers in subtraction problems before subtracting.

Later in his math instruction, when he begins subtracting three-digit numbers, he can practice "expanding" larger numbers in this way:

| 564 | becomes | 500 + 60 + 4 |
| 500 + 60 + 4 | becomes | 500 + 50 + 14 |

if he has to regroup in the ones' place, or

400 + 160 + 4

if he has to regroup in the tens' place, or

400 + 150 + 14

if he has to regroup twice.

Attention
Deficit

STRONG
nonverbal

weak
sequential

weak
visual

SOLUTION: "Graph it!"

Materials:
Graph paper with lines at least 1/4″ apart
Colored fine-line pens

Step 1: Write the problem in one color, perhaps blue. Draw the subtraction symbol (–) and the line separating the problem from the answer in a second color, perhaps purple.

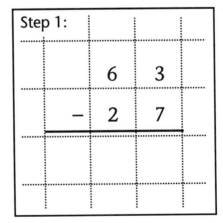

Step 2: Use a third color, perhaps red, to write in the changes that have to be made to the top number, so the problem can be completed. The author recommends turning the 3 into "13" instead of just adding a "1" to the side of it because it uses the expanded notation he learned earlier and makes the mathematical process clearer: the child really is adding ten to the 3 to make 13.

Step 2:

```
          5   13
          6́   3́
      −   2    7
```

Step 3: Complete the problem by writing the answer in with the red pen.

He should use the red pen only as a tool to learn where to place the numbers. Once he understands and is able to place the numbers easily and accurately he should start using a pencil again.

INFORMATION: The combination of color and graph lines helps the child "organize his visual field." That is, it allows him to recognize the meaning communicated by the placement of elements in the problem.

TIP: If this suggestion helps your child he can soon do his problems using notebook paper. However, rotating the paper so the holes go across the top instead of down the side will give him vertical lines that make effective guides.

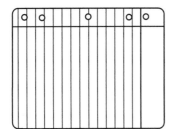

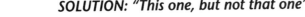

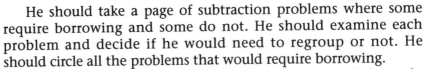

PROBLEM: Your child can only regroup when he has to use the skill on all problems. He doesn't seem to judge well when he needs to regroup and when he doesn't.

Materials:
   Fine-pointed marker
   Photocopy of one appropriate page from your child's math book

Attention
Deficit

SOLUTION: "This one, but not that one"

He should take a page of subtraction problems where some require borrowing and some do not. He should examine each problem and decide if he would need to regroup or not. He should circle all the problems that would require borrowing.

The first time he uses this method he should do all the problems he circled and then do the other ones. After he's used this method several times he should start doing the problems in the order they appear on the page.

Works with
most

If this strategy works there's no reason he can't use it when doing school work.

PROBLEM: Your child hasn't memorized his addition facts. He needs a fast and accurate way to figure the answer to facts so he can continue to work in math while he learns them.

weak
memory

SOLUTION: "Finger-addition"

Counting on fingers is easy until the answer is bigger than ten. Finger-adding is the most efficient and reliable way to figure out the answer to unknown facts.

To begin he says the first number, in this example *7*. Then he puts up fingers for the bottom number, in this case four, always starting with the thumb. He says the number that follows the first one (seven), and counts across the fingers he's put up: "eight, nine, ten, *eleven*." Using this method—and both hands for larger numbers—he won't run out of fingers.

$7 + 4 = \underline{\quad}$

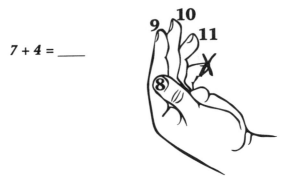

INFORMATION: This is the best way for him to add on his fingers even when the answer is smaller than ten because it's so fast once he gets used to it.

PROBLEM: *He doesn't know his subtraction facts and needs a way to count on his fingers easily for subtraction.*

SOLUTION: *"Finger subtraction"*

weak
memory

Finger subtraction is very much like finger addition except that when he uses his fingers to subtract he won't know ahead of time how many fingers he's going to use. It works like this:

$9 - 5 =$ ___

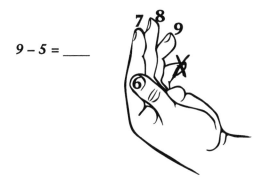

The missing number is the space from **5** to **9**. So this time your child raises his thumb and counts it as "six," and keeps raising fingers and counting "six, seven, eight..." until he gets to nine. In this example, when he gets to nine he's raised four fingers, and that's his answer: $9 - 5 = \underline{4}$.

This method works on all facts your child will be expected to learn.

INFORMATION: Of course you want your child to learn his math facts, but some children, especially those with memory problems or Attention Deficit Disorder, will learn their math facts slowly. Counting on their fingers will allow them to continue to learn concepts even though they don't know their facts perfectly yet. Some, but not all children, will learn many facts just by using their fingers over and over.

| Strengths | | Weaknesses |

Foolproof fudge

This recipe makes about three pounds of fudge.

First: Grease the bottom and sides of a 9 X 13" pan (have your child measure several pans to find the right one).

Second: Pick a heavy three-quart sauce pan. Three quarts equals 12 cups, so the right sauce pan should hold 12 cups of water and have at least two inches left between the surface of the water and the top of the pot. Your child can use a measuring cup, water and a ruler to judge whether a pot is suitable or not.

Third: Combine the first ingredients in the sauce pan:

> 3 cups sugar
> 3/4 cup margarine (usually 1 1/2 sticks)
> 2/3 cup evaporated milk

Fourth: Bring to a full boil and boil for five minutes, stirring constantly.

Fifth: Remove the pot from the heat and add:

> 7 oz. marshmallow creme (one small jar)
> 12 oz. chocolate chips (semi-sweet, mint-chocolate or raspberry-chocolate).

Stir until the marshmallow is completely blended in and the chips are melted.

Sixth: Pour into the 9 X 13" pan. Cool on the counter or in the refrigerator. Don't cut the fudge until it's completely cooled.

Materials you might consider purchasing:

Mini-clock:
> Small, with movable hands. To add instructional value, use peel-off stickers to mark 5 or 15-minute intervals around the clock face, depending on what part of telling time your child is working on. You can change the stickers as needed. Manufactured by Judy/Instructo for only $1.60.

Two-Faced Clock Dial:
> One side of this larger clock is already divided into quarter hours and 5-minute segments, and is labeled and color-coded. The other side is a standard clock face with no clues, so your child can practice what he's learned. We recommend this learning tool. Manufactured by Ideal, $12.95.

Number Line:
> You can order these from Bradburn, but you can easily make one yourself. Just write the numbers out clearly from 1 to 20 on a strip of paper. Your child can use

it to add and subtract instead of counting on his fingers. To make the strip more durable, cover it with clear plastic Contac™ Paper. The manufactured ones are self-adhesive.

Recommended books:

Helping Your Child with Mathematics by Riley, Eberts and Gisler. HarperCollins, ISBN 0-590-49140-7. $12.95.

KidsCooking. 1994, Klutz Press. ISBN 09–32592–14–7. $12.95. Comes packaged with easy-to-use measuring spoons.

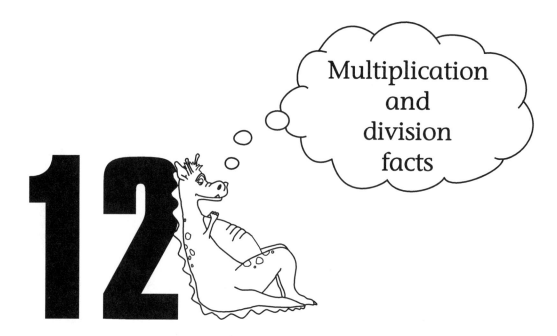

Multiplication
and
division
facts

"I was gratified to be able to answer promptly, and I did. I said I didn't know."

Mark Twain, in <u>Life on the Mississippi</u>

Multiplication and division facts are easier to memorize than the addition and subtraction facts—if your child is ready to learn them. A couple of reasons account for this. First, by the time she begins to learn multiplication and division facts she's had several years of experience with math. She understands how numbers work together better than she did in first grade. More importantly, unlike addition and subtraction facts, the multiplication and division facts follow predictable patterns that can be understood as well as learned.

When is a child ready for multiplication and division facts? Most children are capable of this task when they meet these simple tests:

- she understands that multiplication is a shortcut to fast addition—that is, *3 x 5* means *5 + 5 + 5*.
- she can skip-count well. In other words, she can count by 2's, 3's, 5's and 10's.

- she can do the 1's facts in her head when mixed up (*1 x 4 = 4*, *1 x 7 = 7*, *1 x 1 = 1*, etc.).

If she doesn't know these things, she's not yet ready for multiplication facts. Double-check with her resource or other special teacher if you have any doubts about her readiness for this job.

If you think your child is seriously behind in math skills but she isn't eligible for special help at school, hire a tutor to get her caught up. Of course you want your child to master the basic skills, but skipping preparatory skills to get to more advanced ones sooner will hurt her progress in the long run. It sets her up for tremendous levels of frustration and failure.

Guidelines for success:

If you don't follow any other suggestions from this chapter, follow these three:

1. *Don't work more than five minutes at a time*, two or three times a day. Space those short sessions as far apart as possible. Your child has probably tried already to learn these facts. She undoubtedly feels quite discouraged, and just ten minutes of work on them will seem like an eternity to her. Longer practice sessions will actually interfere with progress and cause more failure, not more progress. In addition we know from research that short sessions are far more effective for forming memories than long ones are.

2. *Make sure she has solidly mastered* each set of facts before going on to the next. This over-learning allows her to feel competent and smart and will tremendously improve her ability to use what she's learned in the more stressful and confusing classroom assignment. Re-read the section in Chapter Four about the "Four Stages of Learning."

3. *When in doubt—slow down.*

It's hard to think of any knowledge we teach more badly than multiplication and division facts. Teachers and parents alike seem to make the same mistakes, over and over:

- We present them in an overwhelming format—a box containing dozens of flash cards, all in one giant pile, a huge and intimidating task waiting to be mastered.
- We completely ignore opportunities to capitalize on skills the child already possesses. We could use previously-learned skills—such as skip-counting (ex: 2-4-6-8-etc.) to make facts much easier to learn, but most of the time we don't do it.
- We assume that the child can concentrate for long periods of time on tasks that are extremely difficult for her.
- We rigidly present the tables in numerical order instead of ordering the task for maximum success.

- We move to a new set of facts before previous ones have been solidly learned.
- We end review too soon.
- Instead of helping the child make the obvious connections between multiplication and division facts, we separate the two skills as much as possible. By doing this we make the division facts appear to be far harder than they really are, and perpetuate our pattern of not capitalizing on previously-mastered skills and information.

Improved teaching leads to improved learning

Three changes can dramatically improve most children's ability to learn math facts:

- throwing out those commercially-produced flash cards,
- learning the sets of facts out of order in a way that will make learning them easier, and
- allowing the child's progress to set the pace.

1. Stash those flash cards!

You know those flash cards you bought—the nicely-printed ones that contain all the multiplication and division facts? If your child is having trouble learning her facts, those flash cards are part of the problem, not part of the solution. They're the worst thing to use with such a child.

Commercial flash cards create two problems for your struggling child. First, boxed flash cards prompt teachers, tutors and even frustrated students to work ineffectively. We all think we know just how to use them, but in reality most people simply plow through the whole stack at one sitting without any logical plan. By doing so we present her brain with an overwhelming task. Worse, we tend to use the flash cards badly for long periods of time without breaks. If anyone has tried to teach your child multiplication facts using printed flash cards, just the sight of them could trigger feelings of frustration of panic and derail her best efforts to learn.

Pre-printed flash cards become an emotional hot-button for the child. To you the flash cards represent an important step in math progress, but to your child they represent physical proof of her inadequacy. Instead of using commercially-prepared flash cards, you and your child will make cards to practice with as she needs them. When she looks at the slowly-growing stack of cards she's made, she'll see tangible proof of success.

Discard any commercially-manufactured flash cards you may own, and never replace them.

2. Point of order, please!

We shouldn't insist the child learn facts in numerical order; learning them out of order makes the task much easier. She already can count by 2's, 3's and 5's or she's not ready to learn multiplication facts yet. We learn those sets first and use her skip-counting skills. We do the 9's next because—for reasons you'll see a little later in this chapter—the 9's are quite easy.

Once those four sets of facts have been learned—2's, 3's, 5's and 9's—your child will know 80 of the 100 facts and will have done little or no memorizing! In addition, since she will learn the related division facts as she goes along, she'll also know 80 of the 100 division facts.

3. Let the child set the pace

By following the steps mapped out below you will guarantee that your child learns the new facts solidly. You'll know she's retaining what she's previously learned as she moves on to the next set, because you'll be checking all the way. The speed at which individual children move through these steps may vary widely, but these steps, carefully followed, do lead to mastery.

How to do it

Your child may feel she already knows the 2's facts. We strongly recommend that you start with the 2's anyway. First of all she may not know them as well as she thinks she does. She probably doesn't realize how very well she has to know multiplication facts before they become useful to her. Second, even if she does know them extremely well, she probably doesn't know their corresponding division facts well.

The method detailed in this chapter results in solid mastery of both multiplication and division facts. We urge you to take no shortcuts. Skipping steps will slow your child down in the long run. In addition, do not let her teachers rush her. It is quite possible her teacher isn't fully aware of just how well a student, especially a struggling student, needs to know those facts.

Use the "Multiplication and Division Record Sheet" at the end of the chapter to record your child's progress on these facts. It will help you remember where you are; it will prevent you from accidentally skipping steps; and it will make her success quite visible to your child.

Step 1: Skip-counting forward

Your child already knows how to skip-count by 2's, 3's, 5's and 10's. When learning math facts, she uses skip-counting a little differently. She stops after she's counted by the interval—2, 3, 5, etc.—nine times. So if she's learning to multiply by 2, she should practice skip-counting from 2 to 18, like this: *2 - 4 - 6 - 8 - 10 - 12 14 - 16 - 18*. Counting by 3's she stops at *27*; counting by 5's she stops at *45*.

It's extremely important that she always stop on the correct number, and it helps to say the final number with more emphasis: "*14 - 16 - 18*!" when counting by 2, "*21 - 24 - 27*!" when counting by 3, etc.

Practicing in this way automatically teaches her the answer to the numeral times nine. We want to eliminate rote memorization whenever possible because it's the slowest and most undependable way to learn the facts.

Ways to practice skip-counting:

Scrambled Numbers: Cut a 3 x 5 card into nine sections and write each number on a card.

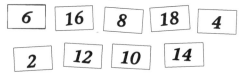

Then your child can just mix them up...

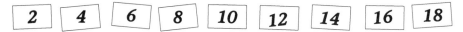

...and put them back in order.

2   4   6   8   10   12   14   16   18

The bouncing ball: She can say a number ("four!") and then bounce a ball and catch it. She should say the next number ("six!") and then bounce the ball again. She doesn't want to be rhythmic about this; she wants to stop and think before saying the next number.

A variety on this game is to play catch with a parent. Before each person throws the ball he or she says the next number, so the parent would say "eight!" and then throw the ball to the child. The child then catches the ball, and says "ten!" before throwing it back.

If the child makes a mistake, for instance, saying "nine!" instead of "ten!" the parent says "no" in a kindly way (no need to be stern or harsh) and throws the ball back for her to try again. The parent should not tell her the right answer; she learns by coming up with the answer herself. We often mistakenly think that telling her will be a help, but actually it's a hindrance.

If your child has difficulty with one part of the number sequence she should practice just that part for a while instead of going back to the beginning. For instance, if she struggles with "12 - 14 - 16" she should practice just those three numbers in order, not go back and start with "2."

When she can do the whole sequence from 2 to 18 without any hesitation whatsoever, she has mastered it. Then she can mark that step done on page 164's chart (by putting in the date she accomplished it) and go to the second step.

Don't work for more than five minutes at a time—even if your child wants to go on. Instead, work several times a day for very short times.

Step 2: Skip-counting backwards

This is where she learns to skip-count in a new way, a way that will help her learn her facts. She practices just as she did in Step 1, except that she counts backwards: "*18 - 16 - 14 - 12 - 10 - 8 - 6 - 4 - 2.*" Use the same methods you did in Step 1 to practice counting backwards. When she can count this way with ease she should mark that box on the chart with the date.

Step 3: Make effective flash cards—2's only for now.

You'll make the other sets as you need them.

Each set of facts should be written in different colors on 3 x 5 cards—red for 2's, blue for 3's, green for 5's, etc.

Since multiplication facts can be written in two orders, present the facts both ways—2 x 6 and 6 x 2, for 17 cards—there's no point to including 2 x 2 twice.

2 x 1	*1 x 2*
2 x 2	(skip 2 x 2; it can't be reversed)
2 x 3	*3 x 2*
2 x 4	*4 x 2*
2 x 5	*5 x 2*
2 x 6	*6 x 2*
2 x 7	*7 x 2*
2 x 8	*8 x 2*
2 x 9	*9 x 2*

You can write the facts on the cards for the first set, but your child should put the answers on the back. It doesn't matter how she gets the answer: she can count on her fingers or use a calculator.

Double-check to make sure she put the right answers down, and make sure she can't see the answers through the fronts of the cards.

Then make a "helping card." Using the same color you used for the flash cards, take an eighteenth card and write out the numbers in sequence, just as she counted them:

2-4-6-8-10-12-14-16-18

This step is on the chart; mark it with the date, like this:

multiplication and division record sheet	2's	3's	2's, 3's	5's
Step 1: Skip-counting forward	¹⁰/₁		✗	
Step 2: Skip-counting backward	¹⁰/₃		✗	
Step 3: Make mult. flash cards and helping card	¹⁰/₅		✗	
Step 4: Practice multiplication facts				
Step 5:				

Step 4a: Practice the facts

Mix up the flash cards you just made. Spread them out on a table or on the rug answer-side down, with the "helping card" above—like this:

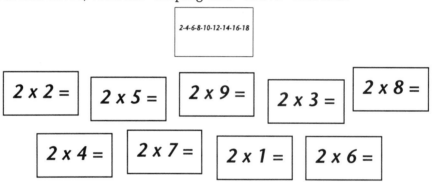

Your child should answer them out of order, just as you laid them out, one at a time. After she answers each one she should flip it over to see if she was right or not. If she's not sure of the answer, she can use the "helping card" to help her find the answer.

If you find that she has more difficulty with some facts than others, make three duplicates of those cards and add them to the deck. In the next example, the child struggles with "2 x 7:"

Since she's now actively studying these facts, she should mark her chart off at "Step 4."

Step 4b: Facts flipped around

She also needs to practice these cards in their alternate form.

$$
\begin{array}{r}
7 \\
\times 2 \\
\hline
14
\end{array}
$$

Use the practice methods you used in Step 4a.

Step 5: Judge if your child has mastered this set of facts.

1. Remove any duplicate cards. For instance, if she had trouble with "7 x 2" and you made extra cards, remove the extras, but make sure one copy of the fact remains.

2. Mix all the cards up.

3. Show her the cards, one at a time, and have her say the answer. If she's in third grade allow her five seconds to answer, but if she's in fourth grade or higher allow only three seconds to answer. When she can answer each fact rapidly, she knows them well enough to move on to Step 6. She should record her progress on the chart.

Step 6: Extra practice if needed

Sometimes you'll be able to skip this step, but if she wasn't able to answer all the facts rapidly, provide extra practice. Play tic-tac-toe or other games, but require her to answer a fact before taking a turn. She should answer the troublesome facts more often than the ones she knows well.

Remember: keep work sessions short, and take the time to make sure she learns each set of facts thoroughly before moving on. Do not rush past steps five and six.

Step 7: Turning this knowledge easily into division facts

Don't make any flash cards yet. First, show your child how the facts are related. For instance, the numbers *2*, *6* and *12* generate four different facts: *2 x 6* and *6 X 2* but also *12 ÷ 2* and *12 ÷ 6*.

Now you're ready to make cards for the division facts. You write the facts this first time, and have your child put the answers on the backs of them. After this set your child should make them.

You need special cards designed to show your child how division facts relate to multiplication facts, and then you use those special cards to help her master that concept. One set will have the numeral she's been skip-counting by as the first number (in this case, 2). In the second set, that number will be the answer she'll come up with for the blank space. See these examples:

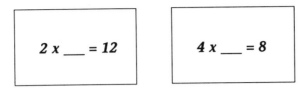

Use the methods from Step 4 to practice these new facts. Again, mastery occurs when she can answer each one within five seconds in third grade or within three seconds in fourth or fifth.

Don't work for more than five minutes at a time—even if your child wants to go on. Instead, work several times a day for very short times.

If your child has difficulty understanding how multiplication facts turn into division facts, put the cards you just made and the ones you made at Step 3 side by side, like this:

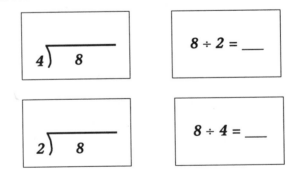

If she doesn't see how they relate, she may not be ready to learn multiplication and division facts yet. Check with her classroom teacher, special teacher or tutor to see what math skills she needs to work on next instead of multiplication facts.

If she understands how division facts relate to multiplication facts but still has trouble with the division facts, she doesn't know the multiplication facts well enough yet. Back up to Step 6 or before; it's too soon to move on.

Step 8: Make division flash cards...

...with each fact in four formats:

$4\overline{)8}$

$8 \div 2 = \underline{}$

$2\overline{)8}$

$8 \div 4 = \underline{}$

Step 9: Practice the division facts, using Step 4's methods.

Step 10: Check for progress.

Use the same mastery standards you used for Step 8.

Doing it all again

Once your child has been through the ten steps learning the 2's she'll move through them more quickly for the 3's and 5's.

Steps 1–10, Repeated for the 3's:

Next your child learns the threes, following the same ten steps you used for the 2's above.

Mixed practice

Mix the 2's and the 3's together, like the example below. Your child has to be able to answer multiplication facts easily even when not in organized sets. Use the same mastery standards throughout—answering within 5 seconds for third grade, but within three seconds for fourth or fifth grade. Be sure you keep her record chart up-to-date.

2 x 2 =	3 x 5 =	3 x 8 =	2 x 7 =
3 x 2 =	2 x 1 =	3 x 7 =	2 x 3 =
2 x 8 =	2 x 4 =	3 x 6 =	3 x 1 =
3 x 4 =	2 x 5 =	2 x 9 =	2 x 6 =
	3 x 9 =	3 x 3 =	

Moving on to the 5's

Next your child learns the 5's, repeating the ten steps. She should move through the steps somewhat faster this time.

Next: mixed practice

Mix the flash cards for the 2's, 3's, and 5's.

Practice them, then test and record on the chart. Don't work for more than five minutes at a time—even if your child wants to go on.

Now the fun begins: the nines

Most teachers don't know the information you're going to learn next about the 9's facts. We do the 9's next because, as you will see, they are easy. They are so easy that your child does not have to learn to "skip-count" by nine but can go straight to learning the facts.

We also do the 9's next because she will feel quite smart when she's learned them. The 9's are cool because they are so predictable.

Look at the table of the nines facts below.

The first thing you'll probably notice when you look at the answers vertically is that they appear in numerical order. You can start with the zero in "09" and count down the tens column to 9. Then you can jump to the zero in "90" and do it all over again going back up through the ones column.

If you write this chart out for your child using six colors like the example above, the pattern will be even more clear.

Your child might enjoy showing her "9's in Color" chart to her teacher and thus get some teacher recognition for her growing skills.

The nines are also cool because they can talk. They will tell the answer to anyone who knows how to listen. It's not cheating, either! For instance, look at the fact on the next page:

$$9 \times \mathbf{7} = 6\,3$$

If the fact is **9 x 7** the answer will start with a **6** in the tens' place. For **9 x 3** the answer starts with a **2** in the tens' place; and for **9 x 5** the answer starts with a **4** in the tens' place.

But that's not all the nines have to say. If you listen longer, they'll tell you the whole answer to the fact, because any time you multiply by nine the digits in the answer will add up to nine. Look at the answers in the chart:

18:   **1 + 8 = 9**
54:   **5 + 4 = 9**
72:   **7 + 2 = 9**

So in our example **9 x 7** we know the first number will be a six, because the fact is nine times seven. Since we also know that **6 + 3 = 9**, and we know that the answer has to add up to nine, the answer can only be **63**. This works with any number times nine.

Testing what we've just said:

Let your child get out a calculator. Have her make up any random number, say **7063**, and multiply it by **9**.

$$\begin{array}{r} 7063 \\ \times\ \ 9 \\ \hline 63{,}567 \end{array} \qquad \begin{array}{r} 6 + 3 + 5 + 6 + 7 = 27 \\ 2 + 7 = 9 \end{array}$$

One other interesting fact about the 9's may help your child remember the answers: if you'll look at the curved arrows on the previous page's chart, you'll see that half the answers are mirror images of the other half: **09** becomes **90**, **18** becomes **81**, etc.

Now you're ready to make flash cards for the 9's. Be sure to make them in both number orders—that is, include both 9 x 7 and 7 x 9.

When your child says the answers for these cards, encourage her to let the facts tell her the answer: have her say the tens' number by itself first to help her learn this helping pattern. So if you show her "**9 x 8**" she should say: "seven...seventy-two."

Mapping out her progress

Take the Math Facts Chart on page 163 and have your child x out every fact she knows. It will look like the example on the next page, and she will be both amazed and proud.

Count the number of facts she's leaned so far: 0's, 1's, 2's, 3's, 5's, 9's, and 10's. That's seven sets, each containing nine facts, or 9 x 7 = *63* facts learned! However, since she's also learned the facts both ways (6 x 2 = 2 x 6) she's really learned 126 facts. And since she's also learned the division facts, she has learned up to 252 math facts so far. Looking at the chart, you can see that not many are left:

1	2	3	4	5	6	7	8	9	
2	X	X	X	X	X	X	X	X	
3	X	X	X	X	X	X	X	X	
4	X	X	16	X	24	28	32	X	
5	X	X	X	X	X	X	X	X	
6	X	X	24	X	36	42	48	X	
7	X	X	28	X	42	49	56	X	
8	X	X	32	X	48	56	64	X	
9	X	X	X	X	X	X	X	X	

What's left?

Your child should practice division facts involving the numbers zero and one. Although they are easy in multiplication, the numbers one and zero make division more confusing.

She has to learn the 4's, the 6's, the 7's and the 8's going through the eleven steps outlined earlier. However, by the time she gets to the 8's there will only be one completely unfamiliar fact left: 8 x 8.

Common questions about multiplication facts

Should my child have to take timed facts tests?

Some children have great difficulty passing timed facts tests even when they know the facts very well. This is especially true of those with grapho-motor deficits or attentional problems. Since the only purpose for timed tests is to make sure the child learns the facts well, these children should be tested orally.

My child doesn't know the math facts. What can she do to keep learning math skills while she gets caught up on her facts?

Make two photocopies of the Multiplication Facts Chart at the end of the book (you have the publisher's and author's permission). Block off facts she's already learned solidly with stickers, or cover them with opaque tape. That way she'll use the facts she's mastered and yet have help when she needs it for the ones she doesn't know well yet. Make charts for both school and home.

Each time she gets past Step 7 for a group of facts, cover those answers up, like the example on the next page:

1	2	3	4	5	6	7	8	9	
2									
3									
4			16		24	28	32	36		
5									
6			24		36	42	48	54		
7			28		42	49	56	63		
8			32		48	56	64	72		
9			36		54	63	72	81		

When should my child have the math facts mastered?

Most schools start teaching multiplication facts in third grade and expect children to know them well by the end of first semester, fourth grade. Since division facts are usually taught separately, mastery for them comes a little later. Full mastery of multiplication facts, where the child can recall the answers with ease and when under stress, is necessary to succeed at long division and computation with fractions. Both these skills are taught in fourth grade.

My child's teacher keeps a chart on the bulletin board that shows who has passed the timed tests and who has not. My child feels humiliated because she's behind most of the other children.

Insist that your child's name be removed from the chart. It's no one's business but hers, her teacher's and her parents' whether she has learned all her facts or not. It is not appropriate to display her struggles with school work for classmates and others to examine.

What's the hardest fact to learn?

7 x 8 is the fact most adults have trouble recalling, so we assume that's the hardest fact. However, there's an interesting detail about that math fact: **7 x 8 = 56**, and if you re-arrange the numerals in counting sequence you get **5 - 6 - 7 - 8**. Take out the two you're multiplying (**7** and **8**) and you have the answer: **56**.

Multiplication Facts Chart

1	2	3	4	5	6	7	8	9	
2	4	6	8	10	12	14	16	18	
3	6	9	12	15	18	21	24	27	
4	8	12	16	20	24	28	32	36	
5	10	15	20	25	30	35	40	45	
6	12	18	24	30	36	42	48	54	
7	14	21	28	35	42	49	56	63	
8	16	24	32	40	48	56	64	72	
9	18	27	36	45	54	63	72	81	

multiplication and division record sheet

	Step 1: Skip-counting forward	Step 2: Skip-counting backward	Step 3: Make mult. flash cards and helping card	Step 4: Practice multiplication facts	Step 5: check for mastery	Step 6: extra review if needed	Step 7: Convert multiplication facts to division facts	Step 8: Make division flash cards	Step 9: practice division facts	Step 10: Test for division facts mastery
2's										
3's										
2's, 3's	✗	✗	✗				✗			
5's										
2's, 3's, 5's	✗	✗	✗				✗			
9's										
2's, 3's, 5's, 9's	✗	✗	✗				✗			
4's										
2's, 3's,4's, 5's, 9's	✗	✗	✗				✗			
6's										
2's, 3's, 4's, 5's, 6's, 9's	✗	✗	✗				✗			
7's										
2's, 3's, 4's, 5's, 6's, 7's, 9's	✗	✗	✗				✗			
8's										
2's, 3's, 4's, 5's, 6's, 7's, 8's, 9's	✗	✗	✗				✗			

*"Do not concern yourself with your difficulties in mathematics.
I assure you that mine are still greater."*

Albert Einstein, in a letter to a student

Problems in math stem from multiple causes, but certain learning styles cause predictable difficulties.

- Some children have trouble sequencing the steps to complex problems, or can't seem to memorize math facts, or get easily confused during instruction.
- A child with weak *active working memory* struggles with initial instruction. Such a child does better with one-on-one instruction from his special teacher before he covers the same skills in his regular class. A plan like that helps him understand the lesson in the regular classroom. Children with *attention deficit disorder* are especially likely to have this kind of memory problem.
- The child with *short-term memory* difficulties will initially seem to follow the contents of the lesson, but when he's required to work on his own he won't be able to recall what to do accurately.
- The child with a *visual-perceptual* deficit may struggle when instruction is given from the blackboard. The child with an *auditory-perceptual* deficit won't fully benefit from the teacher's instruction, and a child with a *grapho-motor*

deficit may expend so much energy copying a problem and setting it up on his paper that he has little brain power left to think about how to do the problem.

- Wandering or superficial *attention* will especially affect math problems involving multiple steps, such as regrouping in subtraction, long division, and multiplying by more than one number.

The single most effective solution for all these difficulties is over-learning—that is, repeated, frequent review. The tips and tricks in this chapter all provide ways to provide this kind of support for your child. If your child has a lot of difficulty mastering new kinds of math problems, look through his textbook to see if he lacks basic skills he needs to learn them. For instance, to master long division a student must have mastered these skills well:

- can write numbers easily and accurately—some children write them upside down or backwords, or reverse the order, such as writing *71* when they mean *17*.
- has mastered rapid, accurate recall of subtraction, multiplication and division facts
- can regroup in his head while subtracting
- can sustain well-focused concentration for at least five minutes—children work long division problems very slowly at first
- can keep columns of numbers lined up
- can keep long division's complex form organized on paper.

A weakness in any of the skills listed above will make long division extremely hard for your child. Sometimes a student has learned the necessary skills well enough to perform them in isolation but can't use them within the long division problem. This type of student needs to over-learn any weak areas before tackling more advanced ones.

Smart support for your child

Children who have difficulty learning need a variety of strategies, but these suggestions will help most of them most of the time:

- **Use summer break** to give your child a chance to shine in the next grade by reviewing basic computation skills with him. The next year's math instruction will begin with review, and if your child can already do the problems he will start out far more successfully. See the suggestion titled "Practice makes perfect" on page 173 for a way to organize short, simple review.
- **rushing your child's progress:** don't add new types of computation skills until the child has mastered previous skills.
- **Allow him to use helping tools** such as the Multiplication Facts Chart on page 163 for unknown facts. Or, he can use a calculator for math facts, and do the rest of the problem with pencil and paper.

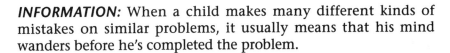

- **Extra time on tests** will give your child a chance to compensate for his difficulties. The point of a test is to find out what the child knows. For some children, rigid time limits hide what they know instead of showing their knowledge.

More math tips and tricks

PROBLEM: Your distractible child's mind wanders when he works on math assignments, resulting in work that contains too many avoidable errors.

SOLUTION: "Enough is enough"

Attention
Deficit

Sometimes it's appropriate to reduce the number of problems in the assignment. Your child may learn more by doing ten problems to the best of his ability than by doing twenty of them—many of them incorrectly and carelessly. The number of problems required might be tied to accuracy: if he does half the problems and gets four out of five right, for example, perhaps he should be allowed to stop. He has, after all, demonstrated that he knows how to do them, and he's gotten valuable review and practice done.

weak
grapho-motor

INFORMATION: When a child makes many different kinds of mistakes on similar problems, it usually means that his mind wanders before he's completed the problem.

TIP: Let your child decide what accuracy level he wants to strive for. You may be surprised at how high he sets his standards.

SOLUTION: "Now hear this!"

He should do his work out loud. The addition of auditory and motor activity (as his mouth moves) may help keep attention focused.

STRONG
auditory

weak
visual

SOLUTION: "Earth and sky"

Your child works to maintain his concentration up until he finishes a problem. He checks it immediately with a calculator, and then makes the choice to daydream for a moment or two before continuing.

This break between problems seems to helps the child focus when he starts the next problem. Children who can control their tendency to daydream to this extent may develop the ability to

Attention
Deficit

weak
basic skills

Strengths   Weaknesses

work for longer periods of time, so it's worth a try. The author has explained this to students using the following illustration:

$$847 \times 36 \qquad 439 \times 52 \qquad 438 \times 49 \qquad 724 \times 28$$

She asks the child to try very hard to maintain good concentration until the problem is completed, and that the cloud before the next problem is his reminder that it's OK if he relaxes a little between each problem.

PROBLEM: Your child knows how to do the problems, but he doesn't complete the assignments.

Attention Deficit

weak basic skills

SOLUTION: "Good management"

- Help your child break the assignment into smaller sections. He should do a section and then take a short break.
- Talk to his teacher about reducing the size of assignments as a reward for improved accuracy.
- Your child can do fewer problems, but check each one with a calculator. If he typically gets about 70% of his problems right, don't require 100% accuracy. Aim for, perhaps, 85% accuracy at first.

WARNING: Children who tend to make random errors won't change their nature completely. Setting a goal of perfection or near-perfection will only frustrate both you and your child.

SOLUTION: "Time off for good behavior"

Attention Deficit

Materials:
Stopwatch, kitchen timer

Give your child a stopwatch. You and he can use it to determine how long he is able to work accurately without a break. Then use a timer. If he can work for ten minutes reasonably well, then he should take a short break every eight minutes or so. Since his mind will take breaks anyway, it's better to structure those interruptions and gain some control over them. That means choosing to take a break before his mind wanders against his will.

PROBLEM: *Your child's work is messy.*

SOLUTION: *"Now I see!"*

Keep a model of work he's completed relatively neatly for comparison. See other suggestions from this chapter: "Enough is enough" (page 167), "Visual organization" (page 169), "Compensate" (page 171), "Another way to compensate" (page 171), and "Nothing like a good secretary" (page 172).

Attention
Deficit

weak
grapho-motor

weak
visual

PROBLEM: *Your child's difficulty with learning by looking interferes with his math progress.*

SOLUTION: *"Visual organization"*

Materials:
Highlighter, ruler

First, your child should rotate his notebook papers so the holes go across the top instead of down the side. The lines will be more helpful to him when they're vertical than when they're horizontal.

Then he should use a highlighter and ruler to divide his paper into sections, like this:

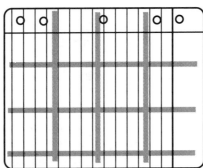

Each problem gets done in one section of paper. He may need help estimating how much space he'll need for each problem. Forget about wasting paper; he should worry about wasting his efforts to learn.

weak
grapho-motor

weak
visual

Attention
Deficit

weak
memory

weak
visual

SOLUTION: "Traffic light"

INFORMATION: Children with visual-perceptual weaknesses some-times look at a math problem and can't remember where to begin. If they do enough problems correctly without this initial confusion, eventually most will learn to start the problem in the right place automatically. So the trick is to provide help and struc-ture until they have gotten to that point. Place a green spot over the side of the problem where they're supposed to begin. Children are familiar with traffic lights and know that green means "go." See the example below:

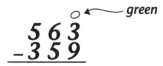

Once he understands, try placing the green spot in the upper right-hand corner of his paper instead of marking each problem.

SOLUTION: "Done with you!"

Visual structure also makes complicated multiplication prob-lems more clear. The child x's out the first number after he's multiplied with it, like this:

$$
\begin{array}{r}
8\,6\,3 \\
\times\ 5\,2 \\
\hline
1\,7\,2\,6
\end{array}
$$

Attention
Deficit

weak
visual

PROBLEM: *Your child uses a pencil slowly and awkwardly.*

SOLUTION: "Wise use of time"

Reduce the size of assignments based on his ability to produce written work. Look for ways to minimize the amount of copying required: he should spend his time learning. When he has to copy math problems from his textbook, for instance, he could copy the first three and someone else could copy the rest.

Of course, he should be required to copy those three as care-fully as he can, getting the numbers on the line and the columns straight. This way he gets the practice he needs to further develop his ability to copy but can still spend the bulk of his homework time learning.

Attention
Deficit

weak
grapho-motor

Strengths   Weaknesses

WARNING

WARNING: These children should always do their math assignments on lined paper—no exceptions!

weak
grapho-motor

SOLUTION: "Compensate"

Your child should develop calculator and computer skills. Adults don't often do their math with pencil and paper any more. A certain amount of pencil-and-paper work helps a child master calculation, of course, but once he's learned the skill well he can do a few problems with pencil (to demonstrate that he really does know what he's doing) and then complete the rest electronically.

weak
sequential

Attention
Deficit

SOLUTION: "Enough time"

Provide extra time on tests to allow for his slower production rate.

INFORMATION: Having memory difficulties isn't the same as not knowing the information asked for on a test. Some children retrieve information from their brains inefficiently. For those children, extra time on a test gives them a chance to display what they really know. Of course, if the child has hasn't learned the skills asked for solidly to begin with, the extra time won't help him.

weak
grapho-motor

weak
memory

SOLUTION: "Another way to compensate"

Sometimes children with grapho-motor problems benefit from enlarging their assignments on a photocopying machine. This makes room for their larger numbers and makes the page easier to understand when they look at it. Since the photocopying helps compensate for a disability and isn't done simply to avoid buying the book, making such copies does not violate copyright law.

weak
grapho-motor

weak
visual

PROBLEM: Your child doesn't think well with a pencil in his hand.

INFORMATION: When a child has grapho-motor problems, using a pencil takes up huge amounts of his brain power, leaving less to learn with. Good solutions either reduce the amount of pencil work, especially while still learning the skill, or make using a pencil easier for him.

SOLUTION: "Bypass that pencil"

Attention Deficit

STRONG
nonverbal

weak
grapho-motor

If you have a computer, look for software your child can use to practice math skills from the keyboard. Ask the computer specialist at your child's school for software recommendations.

SOLUTION: "Nothing like a good secretary"

Attention Deficit

weak
grapho-motor

When he's just learning a skill, let your child do the thinking, but you write down his calculations for him. Don't assume he knows precisely where a number should be written, though. Have him point to the spot where each number should go.

Be very careful not to give any clues at all; keep your face and voice neutral. Sometimes it will be better teaching to just do as he says and write the number down in the wrong place if that's what he told you. When it's down on paper he'll have a chance to look at his work and see what his mistake was.

TIP: Eventually he should complete some of them completely on his own, including the writing. Save this suggestion for new skills.

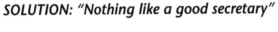

PROBLEM: Your child ignores the operational signs (+, −, x, ÷).

SOLUTION: "Plus or minus?"

Attention Deficit

weak
visual

Your child can use a highlighter—for instance, on a page of mixed addition and subtraction problems—to highlight the subtraction signs. He should mark them himself, as that will help remind him that the page contains more than one kind of problem.

Strengths | Weaknesses

PROBLEM: Your child learns new math skills but then rapidly forgets them.

INFORMATION: He needs extra practice on old skills to hang on to them.

Materials:
> 5 x 8 cards, box to store them in
> Review cards on 5 x 8 cards

SOLUTION: "Practice makes perfect"

Attention
Deficit

Make up sets of 5 x 8 cards with samples of problems your child has learned to solve. Choose problems from his textbook after consulting with his teacher about what skills he's mastered.

You'll use these cards more than once, so the first time your child does the problems from a card, have him write the correct answers on the back so he can check his accuracy easily.

Limit each card to four or five problems. If he's learned ten new skills you can put five of one kind on one card and the other five on the next card.

Mix skills: don't put all fraction problems on one card and all multiplication on another. See this example:

weak
memory

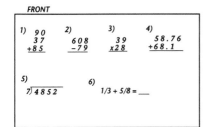

weak
sequential

Make up seven or eight cards to begin with, including one or two kinds of problems. Gradually add each kind of problem he learns to selected cards. Again, check with his teacher periodically about what kinds of problems to include.

Store the cards in a 5 x 8 card box and have him do one of the cards at least three times a week. Soon you'll have a collection, and you can reuse them without fear that he'll remember the answers. If he has a severe problem with long-term memory, do one card each day.

Place the most recently-completed card in the back of the card box, and take from the front. This guarantees he'll review a variety of skills over time. Add cards as necessary, and remove cards that seem to be out of date.

weak
basic skills

TIP: If he has a lot of homework, negotiate with his teacher to reduce his math homework load and include review cards as part of it instead.

WARNING: If he's forgotten how to do a problem, try reviewing the skill with him quickly. If that doesn't get him going, send a note to the teacher or specialist and let her know: "Tim seems to have forgotten how to divide with fractions. Would you please review it with him?"

PROBLEM: Your child has trouble reading large numbers.

SOLUTION: "Follow the pattern"

weak sequential

weak visual

Materials:
    Colored fine-point pens
    Ruler
    Graph paper

Using graph paper, take the black marker and put in a vertical line after every third column as shown below. Label each column. If your child isn't working with numbers in the millions yet, just make the hundreds and thousands columns to begin with (although once he understands how very large numbers are built he may enjoy experimenting with some).

Then have your child make up a number to read by calling out random digits to you—"Eight! Two! Six! Three!" etc.

You write these digits as one number. Put the hundreds in one color—say red, thousands in a second color—say blue, and millions in a third color. It should look something like the example below:

millions			thousands			hundreds		
8	2	6	3	1	9	7	0	5

He should read the number out loud: "Eight hundred twenty-six millions, three hundred nineteen thousands, seven hundred five." You may have to help him think of each group separately the first few times.

Strengths	Weaknesses

Then have your child make up a second string of digits. This time have him put the commas in, and then write it on the chart in the three colors.

Make sure you include numbers of various sizes—four, five, six, or seven digits if his math book goes that high—not just even sets of three.

PROBLEM: Your child hasn't learned all his multiplication facts yet, making it hard for him to learn how to use them in problems.

SOLUTION: "Focus on the most important skill"

If he's supposed to multiply by **78** but he hasn't learned the 7's or 8's yet, use correction fluid to change the bottom number so he can use facts he's more comfortable with—perhaps the 2's and the 5's—like this:

weak memory

weak basic skills

$$568 \times 84 \qquad 568 \times \bigcirc\bigcirc \qquad 568 \times 52$$

Then he can concentrate his brain power on learning how to do the problem instead of coming up with math facts.

PROBLEM: Your child has trouble counting money.

SOLUTION: "Skip it!"

No, don't skip learning about money—use skip-counting to help him learn. Children learn to skip-count by 5's and 10's, making nickels and dimes fairly easy for them to count, but then they have trouble with quarters. So teach your child to skip-count by 25's to 100. The best way to do this is to put four quarters in a row and practice counting real money.

STRONG auditory

weak memory

weak sequential

weak basic skills

Strengths   Weaknesses

**Attention
Deficit**

*weak
sequential*

*weak
visual*

*weak
basic skills*

PROBLEM: *Your child gets confused when he has to count pictures of mixed coins on a printed page.*

SOLUTION: *"Real money"*

Keep a small jar of change handy, and put real coins over their pictures. Then your child can push the coins to the side and count them.

TIPS: Encourage your child to start with the largest coins and work down to the smallest. So in this example he should say "Twenty-five, thirty-five, forty, forty-one, forty-two...forty-two cents."

If the assignment is too hard for him, eliminate the bigger ones—say, the quarter—and have him count the coins he can. Then he can write that amount down on scratch paper and add 25 cents to it. Practicing what he knows and doing the rest with pencil is better than stopping all progress on such an important skill.

PROBLEM: *Your child understands the concept of adding columns of figures but has difficulty completing the problems.*

INFORMATION: Several things interfere with this skill including inadequate mastery of addition facts, attentional problems and being a poor visual learner

---

SOLUTION: *"Simplify the problem"*

**Attention
Deficit**

*weak
sequential*

*weak
visual*

Do the problem in several steps, like this:

$$\begin{array}{r} 75 \\ +\ 43 \\ \hline 118 \end{array} \qquad \begin{array}{r} 58 \\ +\ 35 \\ \hline 93 \end{array} \qquad \begin{array}{r} 75 \\ 43 \end{array}\Big\rangle\ 118 \qquad \begin{array}{r} 58 \\ +\ 35 \end{array}\Big\rangle\ \begin{array}{r} +\ 93 \\ \hline 211 \end{array}$$

There's no need for him to do more math in his head than he's ready to.

TIP: This is a slower way to work, but some children simply can't add columns of numbers well in their head. Once he's demonstrated that he knows what he's doing, strike some sort of compromise with the teacher—perhaps doing half of the problems with pencil and paper, and half with a calculator.

Strengths	Weaknesses

PROBLEM: *Your child can multiply or divide by one number but not two.*

SOLUTION: *"Instant adjustment"*

Until he's ready to multiply by two numbers, use a bottle of error-correction fluid to cover up one numeral, like this:

*weak
basic skills*

$$568$$
$$\underline{x\,\heartsuit\,4}$$

Then he can do the same assignment as the rest of the class modified to meet his needs. We like to use Pentel™ brand correction pens because they contain no harmful vapors and they place the liquid on the paper exactly where it's wanted.

Taming Long Division

We don't recommend that you try to teach your child how to do long division. However, once your child has practiced this skill at school, here are some tricks he can use to help him keep all the steps straight.

PROBLEM: *Your child isn't sure where to write the numbers in his answer.*

SOLUTION: *"X Marks the spot"*

Some children have great difficulty figuring out where to put the first number in a division problem. They should place an x where the first number should go before beginning the problem, like this:

*Attention
Deficit*

$$\frac{\quad x\quad}{7\overline{)4\,8\,5\,2}}$$

Then they can begin the problem confident that when they have a number to write down they'll put it in the right spot.

*weak
sequential*

*weak
visual*

Strengths   Weaknesses

PROBLEM: Your child gets the order of the steps mixed up.

SOLUTION: "Helper card"

Works with
most

Make your child two 3 x 5 cards like the example in figure 1 on the next page. If he forgets what the letters and symbols on the card stand for, make his card like the example in figure 2. The words to the right of the card, "Does McDonald's Sell CHeeseburgers DOWNtown?" are a mnemonic device—a phrase used to help him remember the steps.

Once he's memorized the contents of the card he can put it away.

PROBLEM: When your child looks at a division problem he gets mixed up. He can't remember where to place the numbers.

SOLUTION: "Technicolor division"

Attention
Deficit

STRONG
nonverbal

weak
sequential

weak
visual

See figures 3 and 4 on the next page. First, your child uses one of his fine-pointed colored markers to put in the structure of the problem: subtract signs (–) to the left of the number and a long division bar (figure 3) below it whenever he subtracts.

The subtraction sign reminds him to subtract, and the long division bar provides crucial information—this is the point in the problem at which the steps repeat, so he divides the number inside the long division bar.

The arrows below the **3** and the **8** help your child bring those numbers down in the right column.

PROBLEM: Your child can't keep the columns straight.

SOLUTION: "Rotated paper"

weak
visual

Your child should turn his paper so the holes go across the top instead of down the side (see figure 5 on page 179). Then he can use the lines on the paper to keep his columns straight. Computer data-processing paper with alternating green and white stripes can work well also when turned so the bars run up and down.

figure 1

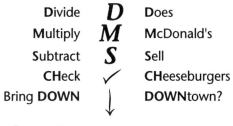

Divide	***D***	**Does**
Multiply	***M***	**McDonald's**
Subtract	***S***	**Sell**
CHeck	✓	**CH**eeseburgers
Bring **DOWN**	↓	**DOWN**town?

figure 2

(draw in color)

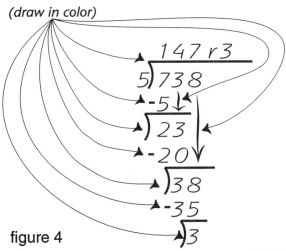

figure 4

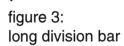

figure 3:
long division bar

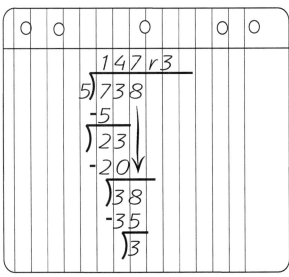

figure 5

PROBLEM: *Your child gets confused when he gets to the subtraction steps because he can't subtract easily in his head.*

SOLUTION: *"Focus on the goal"*

Attention
Deficit

weak
sequential

    Let him use a calculator for the subtraction steps. The more he can focus on the very complicated process of long division, the better. After he thoroughly knows how to do long division, he can do the subtraction parts of the problems with a pencil off to the side or on scratch paper.

PROBLEM: *Your child seems to understand how to do long division problems, but in a few days he forgets.*

SOLUTION: *"Use those review cards!"*

Attention
Deficit

    Add long division problems to his review cards (see "Practice makes perfect," page 173.) If you're not sure what kinds of problems should be on them, ask his teacher.

PROBLEM: *Your child finds zeroes confusing, as in 705 ÷ 5.*

SOLUTION: *"Money talks"*

STRONG
auditory

STRONG
global learner

weak
visual

    Have your child read the confusing number out loud, pretending it's money: "Seven hundred five dollars." If he says $75 instead of $705, simply ask him which amount of money he would rather have. Thinking about numbers in terms of money often makes the importance of zeroes clear to children.

Other math skills

PROBLEM: *Your child has trouble figuring out the area of an object.*

SOLUTION: *"Recycled SCRABBLE® pieces"*

Attention
Deficit

    Use the tiles from a SCRABBLE® game. Suppose, for instance, he needs to find the area to the rectangle on the next page.

Strengths

Weaknesses

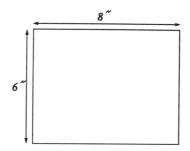

8″

6″

STRONG
global learner

weak
memory

He would lay out six rows of tiles, with eight tiles in each row:

STRONG
nonverbal

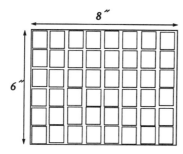

8″

6″

Then he can count the tiles. He should then multiply the two measurements (*6* and *8*) to see that he gets the same answer either way: *48 sq. in.*

PROBLEM: *Your child has difficulty calculating the volume of objects.*

SOLUTION: *"Recycled building blocks"*

Construct the figure to be measured using 1″ building blocks. If, for instance, he's measuring the volume of a box that measures 4″ by 2″ by 3″, he would first lay out two rows of four blocks, and then add two more layers. When he counted the blocks he would find he had used *24* blocks.

After he's counted them, he should multiply the *4* and the *2* to get *8* (the number of blocks in each layer) and multiply the *8* by the number of layers (*3*) for the answer: *24* cu. in.

Attention
Deficit

STRONG
global learner

weak
memory

STRONG
nonverbal

Strengths   Weaknesses

Those frustrating fractions

First Tip: Your child must know his multiplication facts extremely well to learn fractions easily.

Second Tip: Your child should also understand what factors are and be able to figure out a number's factors easily before beginning calculation with fractions.

$$2 \times \underline{\quad} = 12 \qquad 6 \times 2 = \underline{\quad}$$

A number's factors are all the numbers that can divide into it evenly. So, the factors for the number *12* include *1* and *12*; *2* and *6*; *3* and *4*, but not *5*, *7*, *10*, or *11*.

If you and your child used Chapter Twelve to help him learn his multiplication facts, he has already worked with factors. When he used multiplication facts in Step 7 (page 157 and the example below) to help him learn division facts, he has already used factors.

Often (but not always) larger numbers will have more factors than smaller numbers. Any number that has only two factors—itself and *1*—is called a prime number. *7* is a prime number, because its only factors are *7* and *1*.

PROBLEM: Your child finds only a few factors for each number.

SOLUTION: "Practice and more practice"

Works with most

Factoring is one of those skills that improves tremendously with practice. To encourage him to think of as many factors as possible for a number, give him a point for each factor he comes up with. A certain number of points—say, 50—can be traded for some reward, such as a five-minute break from homework.

WARNING: If he understands factoring but has difficulty with it, a multiplication chart like the one on page 163 should help. If he can't determine factors even with a multiplication chart, he doesn't understand the concept well enough to proceed. Ask his teacher to reteach the concept to him.

TIP: He should always try dividing big numbers by *2* and by *3*. For example, if he has to find factors for *78*, dividing by *2* will get him *39*, and dividing by *3* will get him *26*, numbers he probably would have missed otherwise. Add factoring to his review cards (see page 173).

Strengths	Weaknesses

PROBLEM: Your child can find the factors but has trouble making use of them.

Attention
Deficit

SOLUTION: "Do the two-step"

First, he should find all the factors for the number, in any order that occurs to him. For 36 he might write:

36—1, 6—6, 12—3, 4—9.... Then he would check for **2** and **3**; since he had found **3** already he would divide by **2**, and get **18**.

Next he should write the factors in numerical order. The easiest way to do that is to x out each number as he writes it, like this:

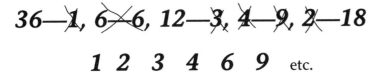

1 2 3 4 6 9 etc.

weak
sequential

PROBLEM: Your child finds initial fraction concepts confusing.

INFORMATION: Many children have trouble with the initial concepts involved with fractions. Looks can be deceiving: in fractions, larger at first appears to be smaller.

Example:

1/3 is *larger* than *1/4*

How can this be? We all know that four is bigger than three.

SOLUTION: "Candy bar math"

Attention
Deficit

Take two candy bars. Divide one into three equal pieces, and one into four equal pieces. Then tell him he can eat only one piece. Would he rather share the candy bar with two other people (three pieces) or three other people (four pieces)?

Naturally, he'll choose the largest piece—which, when written, is the one with the smallest number on the bottom. The bottom number always shows how many people have to share the "goodies." So if he eats 1/3, the candy bar was divided into three pieces, and he's getting one piece from that division.

This is a good time to let him play with his food. He should physically move the candy around, finding 3/4, 2/3, etc., and comparing their sizes. To really nail the lesson down, let him eat some of the candy, stating how much he's going to eat as a fraction first: "I'm going to eat 1/3."

STRONG
global learner

weak
sequential

STRONG
nonverbal

weak
verbal

Strengths ☐ ☐ Weaknesses

COMMENT: This exercise won't teach him everything there is to know about fractions. It doesn't translate the physical facts of dividing candy bars into numeric symbols (fractions). But when the teacher starts teaching in those symbols, your child will be able to remember the pieces of candy and relate them to the symbols, which will now have more meaning to him.

Word problems

PROBLEM: Your child has difficulty with word problems, sometimes called story problems.

TIP: A child can't work a story problem he can't read. Make sure your child reads well enough to do the problem. If he can't read the problem with great ease, you read it to him and help him note the important numbers, etc.

weak
sequential

SOLUTION: "Hit the highlight(ers)"

Use two colors of highlighting pens. With the first one, your child should highlight all the numbers in the problem. With the second highlighter, he should highlight all the words that might tell him what to do, such as "How many were left?" or "How many in all?"

Next, he should reason whether his answer will be bigger than the numbers given or smaller. For instance, if items are being combined the answer should be bigger ("Jimmy has two blocks and Bobby has three. How many do they have altogether?") If the items are being shared (as when things are divided among friends) or reduced, the answer should be smaller. ("Jimmy had three toy cars, but he broke one and threw it away. How many does he have now?")

TIP: If your child has a lot of difficulty with story problems most of the time, ask her teacher to teach her specific strategies for solving them. Often, children who have trouble with these problems benefit from studying a list of key words and learning whether those words tell them to add, subtract, multiply or divide. "How many in all" tells the child to add, but "How many were left" tells the child to subtract.

Recommended book:

Helping Your Child with Mathematics by Riley, Eberts and Gisler. HarperCollins, ISBN 0-590-49140-7, $12.95.

Tips and tricks: printing and cursive

"It doesn't matter what he does. He'll never amount to anything."

One of Albert Einstein's teachers

Introduction

Few things bring struggling students more criticism (both at home and at school) than messy work. Rightly or wrongly, teachers tend to believe a student has made little effort when work is torn and smudged, with letters scrawled, seemingly placed without regard for the lines on the paper.

This chapter contains specific, simple things parents can do with their child to improve the quality of her pencil-and-paper work.

Specific learning problems cause difficulty producing neat, legible work. For example, look at the letter formation on the next page, typical of first graders who are later diagnosed with either a learning disability or an attentional problem.

Many kinds of problems

This letter is typical of the efforts of a very young child just learning how to form letters, say early in Kindergarten. When a child halfway through first grade still has this much difficulty it indicates significant difficulty learning how to write.

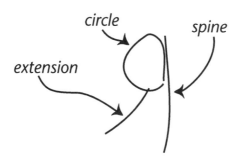

Besides the obvious reversal, other problems are evident: the spine of the R isn't straight; the circle is neither round nor closed; the circle doesn't touch the spine of the letter; the line extension is bent, goes off at an awkward angle, pierces the circle and doesn't descend as far as the spine does. That's nine separate problems with one letter out of 52 (both upper and lower case must be learned). And this example doesn't even demonstrate problems with size, spacing, whether a capital was called for, whether the child's pencil grip helps or gets in her way, whether she presses too hard, too lightly, or inconsistently, whether the parts of the letter were made in the right order and with her pencil moving in the right direction, and whether or not she can form the letter with adequate speed.

What causes writing problems?

Just by looking at the letter we don't really know why the child writes with difficulty. She might have a problem with visual perception or with grapho-motor skills (which might be either a problem with fine-motor control of her fingers, difficulty making her fingers mimic what she sees, or a combination of both). In addition, children who have attention deficit disorder often show fine-motor coordination problems. By their very nature they won't take as much care with written work as other children would, won't attend as well to instruction, and will be prone to think up their own creative-but-incorrect ways to form the letters. Sometimes problems with auditory perception keep the child from understanding the teacher's directions, and memory difficulties may interfere with retaining either how the letter forms should look or the right way to make them.

The suggestions in this chapter won't tell you how to fix each of the many little things that can go wrong when children learn to write. Instead it will provide simple solutions which may help your child to spontaneously self-correct without a lot of laborious instruction.

Strengths	Weaknesses

PROBLEM: Your child has trouble writing her name legibly.

Materials:

Ask the teacher for a chart showing how children are taught to form their letters in your child's school. Most writing methods used by schools include examples of the letters on an 8 1/2 by 11 master so teachers can provide parents with a copy.

- If the sheet your child's teacher provides is too hard to read (too light or duplicated poorly), ask for a more legible one.
- If the letters on the chart are very small, take it to a photocopying center and have it enlarged so your child can see the letters clearly.

SOLUTION: "Practice makes perfect"

If your child is having a lot of trouble, have her practice one letter at a time. She should make five only, but make them the best she can.

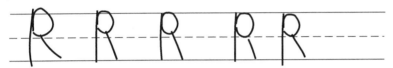

Then she should pick the one she thinks looks best and put a smile face on that one with a highlighting pen.

TIP: It's a good idea to practice both upper case (capitals) and lower case of each letter during the same session. It will help her learn that they are not interchangeable.

Attention
Deficit

STRONG
global learner

weak
grapho-motor

weak
visual

PROBLEM: The teacher says your child uses an awkward pencil grip.

SOLUTION: "The right tool for the job"

Once a child has formed the habit of using an inadequate pencil grip it's quite difficult to change it. Some children benefit

Works with
most

Strengths   Weaknesses

weak grapho-motor

by using pencil grips, which help the student hold the pencil correctly. Pencil grips come in various shapes, but all have a hole in the middle through which the pencil slides. Place the grip where your child should hold the pencil. Some are triangular, like this one:

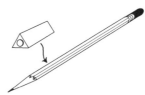

Another kind is shorter and more like a molded, rounded square. Get one of each type and let your child choose the kind she prefers. Then buy several; they get lost easily.

PROBLEM: *Your child has trouble remembering how to form the letters.*

SOLUTION: *"a is for apple"*

STRONG
auditory

weak
memory

You and your child evaluate the shape of each letter and choose some object it resembles. Try to use initial consonant sounds to aid memory. For instance:

SOLUTION: *"Out Loud, Please"*

Attention
Deficit

Have your child state what she's doing as she forms her letters. For instance, when practicing upper case B, she might say, "Top to bottom...pick up pencil...top bubble...bottom bubble."

STRONG
verbal

SOLUTION: "From top to bottom"

Have her practice writing her name not on the top line but on the second line. This way, she'll have a boundary line at the top of her letters as well as at the bottom. If this works well for her, you might suggest it to her teacher as well.

WRONG:

Bobby

RIGHT:

Bobby

Attention
Deficit

weak
visual

SOLUTION: "Computer paper"

Computer paper—the kind with alternating green and white lines—can help a child make the constant judgments she has to make to keep her letters the right height. If using computer paper helps her, you can use a paper cutter to trim it to the size of standard notebook paper (8 1/2" by 11") and use a paper punch to turn it into notebook paper.

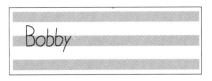

weak
grapho-motor

weak
visual

SOLUTION: "The whole thing"

Have her practice writing her whole name several times. Ask her to choose the one she thinks looks best, and put a smile face on that one.

INFORMATION: Forced choices (like choosing the one she thinks is best) raises her awareness of what the work looks like when well done.

Attention
Deficit

Strengths   Weaknesses

Attention
Deficit

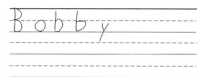

STRONG
global learner

weak
visual

PROBLEM: Your child can write her name, but it sprawls across the top of the page, with letters uneven in size, and with too-big spaces between them.

SOLUTION: "Scrunched writing"

Ask her to write the letters of her name so closely together they look silly to her. Encourage her to scrunch them closer and closer together until the spacing looks right to you.

WRONG:

Then tell her: "That's really the way you're supposed to do it." She'll probably be surprised. Then have her practice it four or five times this new way, and put a smile face on the one she thinks is best.

RIGHT:

Bobby

If she has trouble staying within the top and bottom lines, highlight those two lines, and—you guessed it—have her pick the one she feels stays within the lines best, and put a smile face on it.

PROBLEM: Your child's writing has poor spacing between words.

SOLUTION: "Finger spacing"

Works with
most

Have her say out loud what she will do: "I'll leave a space between each word."

Have her say how she'll do it: finger spacing. She finger-spaces by using the width of one finger of her non-writing hand to measure the space between words. She knows how to finger-space; she's been taught in school.

Strengths   Weaknesses

Special problems of left-handed children:

Finger-spacing is harder for left-handed than right-handed writers, because it's more awkward: their left hand has to cross over their right.

An alternative to using a finger is to use a tongue depressor. The child can place it between words instead of using a finger or two. (Don't let the child decorate the depressor as that can be very distracting. Get two from your pediatrician so she can play with one as she wishes.) If the tongue depressor works, get one for her to use at school.

SOLUTION: "I think I can..."

When she shows improvement, photocopy a good page and save it. The next time her spacing is poor, say "I'd like you to try to make the page you're doing now look as nice as the spacing on this page..." (pull out the photocopies).

Attention
Deficit

STRONG
global learner

PROBLEM: Your child's paper often tears.

INFORMATION: Children with writing problems press too hard with their pencil and tear it. They also tend to tear their paper while erasing, and they erase more than most other kids.

SOLUTION: "Only the best for My child!"

Standard first grade writing paper is made of a very fragile and poor-quality paper, often called "newsprint" quality. Besides its tendency to tear you can spot it easily by its yellowish color. Green-and-white striped computer paper doesn't tear easily and will tolerate erasures well.

There's no reason your child can't do her school work on computer paper trimmed to 8 1/2″ x 11″ size although you may have to make it for her. At the very least, have it on hand for home use.

weak
grapho-motor

weak
nonverbal

SOLUTION: "Armed and ready"

Stock her school desk with transparent tape (the kind that can be written on), and teach her how to repair tears herself. This may take some practice if she's not good with her hands.

weak
grapho-motor

Strengths   Weaknesses

If your child has an IEP, you can stipulate that she be given heavier-grade paper to use.

PROBLEM: Your child makes reversals when writing.

Attention
Deficit

weak
visual

SOLUTION: "Backwards on purpose"

Have your child write the letters the right way and the wrong way on purpose. For instance, have her practice upper case R like this:

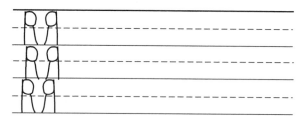

INFORMATION: The goal is for your child to notice when a letter is reversed. Then she'll be able to gain some control over reversals while writing. To write a letter backwards *on purpose* forces her to notice which way it faces.

PROBLEM: Your child has had a lot of difficulty learning manuscript printing, and you're afraid she'll have similar difficulty with cursive.

Attention
Deficit

weak
grapho-motor

SOLUTION: "Don't delay!"

If your child has an IEP, make sure that one of her goals is that she be instructed one-on-one in cursive writing before it's begun in her classroom. Children who have difficulty learning to write don't learn it well in large-group instruction.

If your child doesn't have an IEP, hire a tutor. Ideally, the tutor or teacher should start cursive instruction *before* it's begun in her classroom. The tutor should contact your child's classroom teacher and then teach the letters using the same letter formations that will be used in school, in the same order.

PROBLEM: Your child tries hard but still can't seem to master forming cursive letters with pencil and paper.

Works with
most

SOLUTION: "Recycled tips and tricks"

Go back through the suggestions given in this chapter for manuscript writing. The following ones also work well with

| Strengths | Weaknesses |

cursive: "Computer paper," "The whole thing," "Scrunched writing," and "Only the best for my child!"

SOLUTION: "A Picture's worth a thousand words"

The writing instruction programs schools use to teach manuscript and cursive usually come with guides. The teachers are encouraged to distribute them to parents, so ask for one. Then photocopy it, enlarged, several times. Cut the letters apart and glue them on individual 3 x 5 cards. Larger models often help learning disabled children, and separating the letters so the child sees only one at a time often helps those with either visual-perceptual problems or attention deficit disorder.

Attention
Deficit

STRONG
global learner

weak
visual

SOLUTION: "Giant writing"

Hang a large piece of kraft wrapping paper on the wall. Your child should use a thick-pointed colored marker to write the letters, in cursive, as large as she can and still write the letter in one movement. Make sure she has a model to work from; see the suggestion before this one ("A picture's worth a thousand words"). Such larger models will work better than smaller ones.

STRONG
global learner

weak
grapho-motor

INFORMATION: Sometimes a child learns fine-motor skills best by doing them with larger muscles first.

WARNING: Check before beginning to make sure the markers don't bleed through to the paint behind the paper. Put up extra sheets of paper for protection if necessary.

WARNING

PROBLEM: Your child can write individual letters in cursive but has trouble writing words with ease.

SOLUTION: "Many ways to connect"

Your child probably needs as much practice connecting the letters as she did learning to form them. Different letter combinations connect differently, and the child who has trouble learning the individual letters will also have difficulty mastering the many ways they combine when used together.

Attention
Deficit

Strengths		Weaknesses

weak
grapho-motor

weak
memory

These letter combinations can be particularly troublesome:

ac	*ce*
ag	*cr*
av	*f* with any other letter before
aw	it or after it
ax	*gu*
ay	*gh*
az	*gl*
b with every possible combi-	*gr*
nation, but especially:	*o* with any other letter before
ba	it or after it
be	*r* after *o* or *w*
bi	*any* combination with *u, v, w*
bo	or *x*
bu	*y* any time it's in the middle
bl	of a word
br	*z* in any combination

She should practice the combinations individually and then use the book we've recommended before, *Reading Yellow Pages for Students and Teachers*, to find shorter, and then longer, words containing the troublesome letter combinations.

WARNING: Teachers almost always move children with grapho-motor problems along too fast in cursive skills. If your child has difficulty learning to write, someone needs to be responsible for making sure she is completely learning, and retaining, these skills.

weak
memory

SOLUTION: "Gift of time"

Concentrate on lower case letters first. Her teacher should allow her to print those upper case letters she hasn't yet learned in cursive until she's mastered them.

PROBLEM: You need to make sure your child's writing skills are progressing.

SOLUTION: "Progress checks"

Works with
most

Once a month have your child write all the letters, upper and lower case, to the best of her ability. These monthly checks will give you some idea of her progress. If she shows no progress, alert her teacher, tutor or specialist. You can do similar checks of her ability to write words and sentences by asking her to copy a short paragraph. Stop her after two minutes; there's no need to copy the whole thing. If she's progressing she should be able to copy more in two minutes a couple of months after she's started working on her writing than she could at the beginning.

Materials you might consider purchasing:

Handwriting Instruction Guides:
These stiff plastic cut-out templates come in three forms: traditional manuscript, cursive, and D'Nelian-style, sometimes called "transitional." The child places her pencil in the cut-out and traces the shape of the letter.
Benefit: This multi-sensory practice provides a different type of experience forming the letters correctly. The templates will be most effective when used with supervision. Manufactured by School-Rite, $8.95 each.

Alphabet Desk Cards, manufactured by Ideal.
The alphabet is printed in both upper and lower case on flexible rubber so it won't slide off the student's desk easily. They're easy to carry from classroom to classroom if your child changes classrooms during the school day.
Model #2284 has traditional printing on one side and cursive on the other.
Model #2283 shows what they call "modern" manuscript, something much like D'Nelian for those whose schools use that printing style.

Reading Yellow Pages for Students and Teachers. Incentive Publications, Inc., Nashville, TN. ISBN 0-86530-029-1. $12.95.

Make some fancy letters!

Your child can string beads on pipe cleaners and then bend it into the shapes of letters or numbers. Twist part of the pipe cleaner over the first and last beads so they won't fall off, and leave a little extra space on the pipe cleaner that's not covered with beads or you won't be able to bend it. *Benefit:* Multi-sensory approach; motivating.

Beads you can use for this activity:

Sorting Beads, manufactured by Ideal #4237, $6.95.

Jelly Beads, manufactured by Bemiss-Jason, $7.35.

Tips and tricks:
written expression

*Treat people as if they were what they ought to be and you
help them to become what they are capable of being.*

Goethe

Introduction

Putting thoughts on paper is the hardest task we ask of students. They must first organize their ideas in their head, then keep the spelling straight, form letters and stay on topic—all at the same time.

Some children can do each of these things separately but can't coordinate them smoothly. When we evaluate these children, we find that they know to use capitals and periods and that they understand basic grammar. When they try to write down their thoughts, however, they have trouble using what they know. More instruction on grammar, punctuation, etc. won't help these students: when a child already understands, more teaching becomes part of the problem, not part of the solution.

If more teaching won't help, what will?

1. Improve early instruction in printing and cursive.

Children who have trouble learning to use manuscript and cursive easily need extra, carefully-guided practice before writing will become fully automatic and effortless. For some of these students, writing never becomes completely automatic. For them—all through school—any time they have to write they simply can't think as well.

2. Teach written expression well.

Find out how your child's school teaches written expression.

In some schools, first graders complete workbook pages on difficult concepts such as parts of speech with little or no time left to actually write. The problem with the workbook approach is that it's not concrete, and first graders still respond best to concrete approaches. If children are going to learn to write they need to write, not analyze whether a word is a noun or a verb. Once they've learned to love writing, they'll want to know more about words, and will be ready to learn technical details about them in a later grade when parts of speech are a more appropriate topic.

A child needs to start writing at an early age while his thoughts are still simple and while he'll be satisfied with simple structure and shorter sentences. Then he can gradually develop his writing abilities over many years—just as he does with reading and math. His spelling and punctuation don't have to be perfect to begin with—any more than we would expect him to sing perfectly in tune the first time he sings a song.

3. Consider the child's temperament and learning style.

Often when a student has a learning or attentional problem, written expression taps into many of his weaknesses at the same time—grapho-motor difficulties, poor planning abilities, problems keeping track of details within a larger framework, spelling, and attention to multiple finer points such as use of capitals and periods.

4. Use his educational time wisely.

A child with difficulties in written expression should not spend his school time copying—either from the board or from a book. He should not be required to copy an entire sentence from the book, say, just to put punctuation at the end. He can simply number his page and then write only the missing punctuation. If the sentences contain multiple mistakes, the page can be photocopied so he can make the corrections on it. This is a legal use of photocopying—to compensate for a learning problem—and does not violate copyright laws, since it's done to compensate for a disability and not to avoid buying the book.

If he has tremendous difficulty with writing he should be allowed to form his capitals in manuscript and write the rest of the word in cursive. Since the lower case letters are used far more often than the upper case, this allows him to use writing automatically, which frees his brain to think more about what he intends to write.

Since such a child will produce written work slowly, it might be smart to require shortened written assignments in his IEP.

5. Usher your child into the computer age.

Children who struggle with written expression need to begin developing computer skills at as young an age as possible. This doesn't mean to teach him touch-typing, now called keyboarding, at an early age, though. Just give him a chance to develop basic computer understanding by providing programs he thoroughly enjoys. Your goal when the child is younger should be to let him use the computer in any way possible, including games, so that when he finally gets to keyboarding he's already familiar with both computers and keyboards.

In addition you can specify that he be enrolled in keyboarding on a trial basis and allowed to drop out and try later if he can't seem to do it. Schools teach keyboarding in classes, and if he fails in front of his classmates he may resist using the one tool most likely to help him with his writing.

Strengths	Weaknesses

Tips and tricks: written expression

PROBLEM: Your child has good ideas but can't organize them.

SOLUTION: "Six steps to better writing"

Works with
most

Materials:
    3 x 5 card
    Pencil (not pen)

INFORMATION: This method helps so many children so much that you should try it first. It often results in rapid and significant improvement. For younger children, start with two- or three-sentence stories.

> **Step 1.** Instead of starting out with a sheet of paper, give your child a stack of 3 x 5 cards. He writes one idea to a card, and one only. He doesn't worry about the order of his ideas, and he doesn't worry about spelling, or grammar, or punctuation. He just gets his ideas down one at a time, one to a card, as many as he thinks of.
>
> If your child's ideas come quickly and rapidly he can just jot down key words, and if your child's spelling interferes with this step you can write down key words for him.
>
> Note: spelling and written expression are separate skills. When focusing on written expression, provide spelling support. If your child has serious spelling problems, attempting to improve his spelling skills as he tries to write will actively interfere with the development of both skills.

Strengths   Weaknesses

Step 2. After has everything down he thinks he wants to say, he spreads the cards out and chooses the order he thinks he wants them in. He may set some aside and add more at this point.

Step 3. He numbers the cards in case they get mixed up.

Step 4. One card at a time, he polishes each sentence to the best of his ability. If you see numerous mistakes in his sentences, pick one to focus on—say using capitals and periods. Don't require adult perfection of his first efforts, but at this point he should make any necessary spelling corrections.

Exception: if he's going to produce his final story on a computer and he uses the spell-checker, he can type it in and then check the spelling. However, he should still look each card over and circle any words he thinks might be misspelled. Some people never become good spellers, but if they learn to spot misspelled words they can use a spelling dictionary or other spelling aid and compensate for their difficulty to a great degree.

Children who spell poorly should learn to look for the words, even if they can't fix them, from an early age, so it becomes a "habit of mind."

Step 5. He spreads the cards out and reads what he's written in order. He has another opportunity to rearrange his thoughts, throw some out or add more.

Step 6. He copies each sentence, one by one, onto his page in paragraph format (not as a list). If his teacher requires that he write in ink, he should switch to ink at this point. Get him a bottle of error-correction fluid such as Pentel Correction Pen™.

Can you keep a secret? Don't tell your child, but he just wrote a rough draft. Students hate rough drafts because they're too much work for what they accomplish. This method makes his work load easier and more manageable.

TIP: If your child's teacher requires a rough draft he can staple the cards to note paper and turn it in.

MORE INFORMATION: This is one of the few methods in this book that work well with both global and sequential learners.

Strengths   Weaknesses

Sequential learners like it because of its step-by-step approach. Global learners like it because they don't have to work sequentially: they can add new ideas and reorganize them at any point.

Other tips and tricks for written expression

PROBLEM: Your child is having trouble learning the parts of speech.

SOLUTION: "Everything has a name"

Works with most

Attention Deficit

STRONG nonverbal

Step 1. Tell your child you're going to play a game with him. Tell him that you've hidden something in the room, an object that has no name, and that his challenge is to find that item and bring it to you.

He'll bring you all sorts of things, but they'll all have names. If, for instance, he brings you a paperweight and says, "This has no name! I found it!" you say, "No. That's not it. This thing is called a paperweight. Keep trying."

After he's brought you a variety of items, tell him the truth: everything has a name, and that's what nouns are—the names of objects.

Step 2. Play another game. This time you name an action, and he does it. If you say "Hop!" he hops. If you say "Jump!" he jumps. To add to the entertainment, let him tell you some things to do. Then tell him that verbs are the names of actions—things we do.

Step 3: You mix the two up. Tell the child, "Now I'll say a word. If it's an object, bring it to me. If it's an action, do it. Then we'll decide if it's a noun (something you can bring to me) or a verb (something you can do)."

INFORMATION: This won't cover all nouns and all verbs, but it will raise his grade considerably, and give him information on the parts of speech he can use later to learn more about them. For instance, there are some nouns that aren't objects. They're called abstract nouns and include concepts such as freedom and honesty. Some verbs can't be acted out: in the sentence "I am finished with my dinner," the verb is am, a word not easily acted out. Nevertheless, this method will give him a start on the parts of speech.

Strengths		Weaknesses

PROBLEM: *Your child writes in short sentences and uses the same words over and over.*

INFORMATION: One reason children write using only small words is because they're so frustrated by trying to spell bigger, more interesting ones. The author once had a student who wrote:

"I went into the woods. And I went up a tree."

What he told her was:

"I sneaked into the woods because my mother didn't want me to go there. But it was really cool, because I climbed this big old sycamore tree on a hill and I could see for miles!"

Obviously his spoken story was much more interesting and advanced than his written one. When we gave him the correct spelling for the larger words, his third attempt—written—was even better than the one he told us.

SOLUTION: "3 x 5 dictionary"

Attention Deficit

Materials:
 3 x 5 cards
 3 x 5 file box
 3 x 5 alphabet dividers

weak **sequential**

Have your child tell you what he wants to say first. As he talks, you make a list of the words he's likely to have trouble spelling. Write each word on a 3 x 5 card, near the top. He should spread them out on the table so he can spot them easily as he writes.

After he's done his writing assignment, file the cards in his file box alphabetically. This file box then becomes a spelling dictionary he can add to day by day. It's much easier to use than a standard dictionary.

weak **basic skills**

TIP: If your child understands alphabetization, he can alphabetize them by spreading them out on a table and putting them in order. This way of alphabetizing requires no writing and allows him to learn that skill as easily as possible, and is also a good way to handle assignments that require him to alphabetize a list of words.

Strengths   Weaknesses

Attention
Deficit

STRONG
global learner

SOLUTION: "Details, please!"

Go back to the first suggestion in this book, "Six steps to better writing," on page 198. Ask your child to pick his two best ideas and add at least four details on separate cards. You might have to ask him some leading questions, such as "How long were you in the woods? Did you see anything interesting?"

Try not to plant ideas in his head or change the direction of his story. Your goal is to get him thinking more deeply about his story, not change it to something you think might be better.

Finally, ask him to pick the most interesting details from his new cards.

For instance, his first cards might say:

"I went into the woods" and *"I went up a tree."*

He might add details like this:

The woods were dark.
They smelled funny.
Mom said not to go but I sneaked in anyway.
I found an open place with a big tree.
It was a real big sycamore.
There's a sycamore on our street, too.
I climbed way up and I could see all over.
I can't see that far from my bedroom window.

Now he's in a position to begin learning what to include with his story and what to discard as off-topic, one of the most important things to learn about writing.

PROBLEM: Your child's ideas garble when he begins to write.

SOLUTION: "Back to the basics"

weak
grapho-motor

See the first suggestion on page 198, "Six steps to better Writing." In addition, make sure your child begins to develop computer skills. Typing is controlled by a different part of the brain than writing with a pencil is. Often children who have difficulty using pencil and paper to write find writing on a computer much easier.

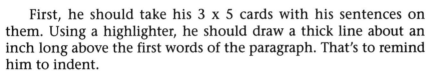

PROBLEM: Your child organizes his writing poorly on the page, ignoring things like margins and paragraph indents.

SOLUTION: "Structure"

Materials:
3 x 5 cards from "Six steps to better writing" (page 198)
Ruler
Thick black marker

weak
visual

First, he should take his 3 x 5 cards with his sentences on them. Using a highlighter, he should draw a thick line about an inch long above the first words of the paragraph. That's to remind him to indent.

To remember margins, he should take his ruler and draw a line down each side of the page. If he doesn't want to turn his paper in with lines drawn on it (they look "babyish"), he can make a "guide sheet." To do this he takes another piece of paper and draws the margins on that one with a thick black line. Then he puts the one with lines under the one he's going to write on, and paper clips them together.

If he still has trouble using the margin he should fold his paper on the margin line so the margins stick up. Then tell your child to pretend that his pencil is a car, and if he doesn't stop before he hits the "wall" of folded paper sticking up, he's going to have a wreck.

PROBLEM: Your child has good ideas but doesn't spot missing capitals, periods and other basic errors.

SOLUTION: "Checklist"

Photocopy the "Writing Checklist" at the end of the chapter. Use error-correction fluid to cover up the skills he hasn't learned yet, and then recopy it several times. He can use this list to systematically check his writing before turning it in.

Attention
Deficit

weak
visual

PROBLEM: Your child simply can't produce much written work.

INFORMATION: When he's older he may be able to write better on paper. If he doesn't, he can develop computer skills for writing.

| Strengths | | Weaknesses |

However, if he hasn't learned to develop ideas and put them in order, these skills won't help him—because his ability to think about writing will be way below the level of the things he'd like to say.

weak
grapho-motor

SOLUTION: "Other ways to learn"

Go back to the method on page 198, "Six steps to better writing"—but this time you do all the writing for him. If he needs practice with capitals and periods, leave them out when you write. He can make those simple corrections even if writing everything would be overwhelming. He can also choose the order of his ideas, add details (with your writing support as necessary), and eliminate ideas that he decides don't fit in.

For the final copy, use your best judgment. Perhaps he can copy the first sentence, or the first two sentences. Perhaps he can use "hunt and peck" to put the first sentence or two into the computer and then you can finish it. Although he won't do all the physical writing, he'll begin to learn how to organize and order his ideas. Then when he does have the capacity to write in some way he'll know how to do it.

Good IEP idea!

IEP IDEA: Some teachers will object to this much help, so write it into his IEP if it's what he truly needs, but make sure he has opportunities to gradually develop what writing skills he can. You need to make sure that other difficulties, such as organizational problems or frustration with spelling, aren't the main source of his problem, because those difficulties can be helped using the suggestions titled "Six steps to better writing" on page 198 and "3 x 5 dictionary" on page 201.

STRONG
verbal

weak
grapho-motor

SOLUTION: "Taped writing"

Tape recorded reports can work well, but you want your child to learn to organize and refine his ideas before recording his thoughts in any form—spoken or written. So use the 3 x 5 cards as mapped out in "Six steps to better writing," with you writing the cards if necessary. Then he can dictate his report into a tape recorder.

He should still attempt to write at least the beginning of the report to develop whatever skills he can that way.

IEP IDEA: If this suggestion helps, write the use of a tape recorder for reports into his IEP.

Good IEP idea!

PROBLEM: *Your child finds fixing his mistakes difficult.*

SOLUTION: *"One a day"*

Have your child fix one simple sentence each day, such as these examples:

the dog chased after the car. (no capital)
The two boys walked to the store (no ending punctuation)

Check with his teacher to see what proofreading skills he should work on, based on what he's learned so far and what he's being taught about correct writing in school.

Make sure you've tried the method on page 198, "Six steps to better writing," as it makes fixing mistakes fairly easy.

Attention
Deficit

weak
basic skills

PROBLEM: *Your child complains that he can't think of anything to write about.*

SOLUTION: *"Fantastic photos"*

Materials:
Old magazines with interesting photographs

STRONG
global learner

Have your child write about one of the photographs. Many of these photographs have special appeal to children, such as the one we found in *LIFE Magazine* of a mother hen sheltering one kitten under each wing. Another photo from LIFE shows a fawn and a kitten sharing a saucer of milk.

LIFE Magazine and *National Geographic* are two good sources to find intriguing pictures. *LIFE* in particular often ends each issue with humorous photographs. Many of the photographs accompanying their articles will serve well also.

TIP: If your child has great difficulty writing, ask the teacher to accept one sentence about a picture or photograph to begin with, and then increase expectations gradually.

Strengths | Weaknesses

**Attention
Deficit**

**STRONG
global learner**

SOLUTION: "Idea clusters"

Noted writing teacher Gabriele Lusser Rico describes this approach well in her book, *Writing the Natural Way: Using Right-Brain Techniques to Release your Expressive Powers*.

To use this method, your child simply writes key words or phrases any place on a piece of unlined paper, circles them and then draws lines between related ideas. Those connections form his paragraphs.

For instance, perhaps the child is working from the picture described before of the hen who adopted two kittens. His page of idea clusters might look like this:

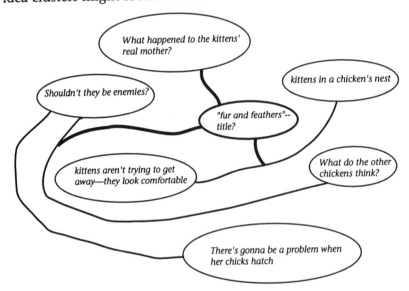

He could X out each balloon as he used it, as shown below:

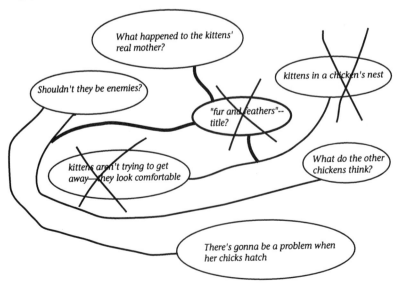

If your child has great difficulty writing, you can be a note-taker. Allows his ideas to flow without interference from spelling or pencil/paper problems. Again, he gradually should take over all parts of the task he can so long as they don't interfere with his ability to think up ideas or organize them.

SOLUTION: "One skill at a time"

Works with most

Encourage your child to write first and fix mistakes later. Sometimes people (adults as well as children) think all writing has to be perfect. The need to have everything perfect on the first try interferes with ideas, because we judge too harshly—our ideas might not be good enough, or we might think we've said them badly, or have misspelled a word, or have made a grammatical mistake—or any number of other errors. Again, the method on page 198, "Six steps to better writing," combats this problem well.

SAMPLE PROOFREADING CHECKLIST

❑ Do all sentences begin with capitals?

❑ Do all sentences end with periods?

❑ Are all paragraphs indented?

❑ Did I use margins?

❑ Did I start sentences with "and" or "or" more than once?

❑ Are there any words that might be mis-spelled?

Note: this checklist should be individualized. There's no point including errors your child rarely makes; and if the list is too long, too detailed, or too complicated, it will be overwhelming.

Other
tips and tricks

"A child becomes what he experiences."

Haim Ginott

Introduction

This final chapter of tips and tricks covers knowledge and skills across a variety of abilities and subjects.

Sometimes the way we work with learning problems in the schools leads to misunderstandings. For instance, your child's IEP may say "learning disabled in the area of reading." That may be true, but her difficulties probably affect other subjects in one way or another also. The law requires her IEP to name a specific core subject such as reading, but that doesn't mean that she will have problems *only* in reading. Her school records may never say "learning disabled in the area of science." To complicate things further, she may do some things in science, or social studies, or some other subject easily—and yet struggle with other parts of the same subject.

This chapter also includes specific suggestions for coping with some of the learning styles we've talked about throughout the book.

Strengths		Weaknesses

Tips and Tricks: General

PROBLEM: Your older student hasn't learned to read well, so she reads books with great difficulty.

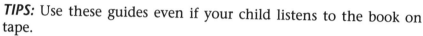

SOLUTION: "Study guides"

Publishers such as Cliff Notes have produced study guides for great works of literature—*Julius Caesar, Silas Marner,* etc. Although these study guides cannot and should not substitute for the real thing, they have two good uses:

Attention Deficit

- reading the summary first will help her understand the book
- the guides explain new words and give background information that help the book make more sense.

STRONG auditory

weak basic skills

TIPS: Use these guides even if your child listens to the book on tape.

A student who has this much difficulty reading will also have great difficulty writing. Be sure you read Chapter Fifteen, particularly "Six steps to better writing" starting on page 198 and "Taped writing" starting on page 204.

SOLUTION: "Videos"

Many great novels have been made into movies. Movies cannot substitute for reading the original book, of course, but watching the movie version of a book first may help your child understand what she later reads.

Attention Deficit

weak memory

weak basic skills

TIP: If your child has great trouble reading, she can listen to a tape of the book. Some children have trouble with comprehension and memory even when they hear the book on tape instead of reading it. Such a child might benefit from seeing the movie version before listening to the tape.

Strengths   Weaknesses

weak
basic skills

SOLUTION: "Talking tapes"

People who read with difficulty because of a learning problem may be eligible to use books prepared on tape for people with visual handicaps. See the end of the chapter for details.

TIP: Your child should try to read along with the tapes just a little bit each day. She should concentrate on one paragraph only but read that paragraph along with the tape four or five times, which won't take more than five minutes. We don't think any student should give up completely on reading. See "Supported reading" on pages 114–115 of Chapter Nine.

WARNING: Do not require your child to read along with more than one paragraph of the book a day. The tape may make reading possible for short spurts, but only with tremendous effort. Push your child too hard and you'll burn her out. Even worse, she'll resent the tapes and not want to use them any more, and she will have lost a valuable learning aid. When she's able to do more, she will on her own.

PROBLEM: Your child finds taking notes from books and articles frustrating and difficult.

INFORMATION: Often these students don't learn well by looking. The repeated need to look from book to paper, then back to book to find their place again, takes up too much of their mental energy.

Sometimes when an adult thinks a student hasn't tried, the adult has over-estimated the student's ability to complete the work well. Other times the student's standards are actually higher than the adult's, and if the student can't truly master something she'll resist merely going through the motions. Such a student needs a more appropriate task and lots of encouragement, not criticism for her high standards.

SOLUTION: "Finding your place"

Attention
Deficit

Materials:
   5 x 8 cards with lines
   Post-it® notes
   Photocopier
   highlighter

1. She can place a Post-it® note under the paragraph, chart, etc. she's taking notes from.

Strengths	Weaknesses

2. She can photocopy the text and highlight the information she wants to use before making notes.

3. If the print is extremely small, enlarging it on a photocopier may help. Kinko's and other copying centers often have these kinds of machines.

4. She should use lined note cards. If she writes with difficulty, she may find larger cards easier to use, but make sure she keeps one fact to each card. Larger cards shouldn't mean more information on each card, as that will make it much harder for her to organize her ideas later on.

weak
grapho-motor

weak
visual

TIPS: If she has a computer, she can take her notes on the computer. One easy way to do this is to set her word processing program to very short pages. Then she can type in one idea per page, just as she would on a note card, print them out and trim them to a smaller size.

See "Six steps to better writing" beginning on page 198 in Chapter Fifteen.

PROBLEM: *Your child seems to learn material but soon forgets it.*

SOLUTION: *"Organized review"*

Keep a list of skills and important material your child needs to remember, and review these skills periodically. See "Practice makes perfect" on page 173 of Chapter Thirteen for ways to use review cards.

Attention
Deficit

INFORMATION: Just because your child has passed a test doesn't mean she's learned the information it covered forever.

weak
memory

IEP IDEA: Sometimes these students can recall what they need to know when they have enough time. If this describes your child, write extended time limits for tests into her IEP.

Good IEP idea!

TIPS: By the time your child is in junior high or senior high she may need a tutor to organize repeated review of important information. Even if your child receives special help, the specialists will usually focus on new material. They may not have time to do any kind of systematic review even when they know she needs it.

Reread Chapter Four so you're thoroughly familiar with how students learn.

| Strengths | | Weaknesses |

Also see the section in this chapter beginning on page 218 called "Tips and tricks: study skills."

Tips and tricks: organization

PROBLEM: Your child has trouble getting ready for school.

Attention
Deficit

SOLUTION: "Checklist"

Help your child make a checklist. It should be quite specific and include all requirements—brush teeth, brush hair, wash face, eat breakfast, put breakfast dishes away, make bed, make sure homework is in backpack, put lunch by backpack, etc.

TIP: If your child doesn't read well yet, draw pictures for each task—a toothbrush, a hair brush, etc.

PROBLEM: Your child's teacher reports that your child doesn't follow class routines well.

Materials:
   3 x 5 card
   Clear plastic CONTAC® paper

Attention
Deficit

SOLUTION: "Classroom checklist"

Ask your child what she's supposed to do each day when she first gets to school. Some things might be to put away her coat, put away her lunch, sharpen two pencils, and check the blackboard for the first assignment.

Write these tasks on a 3 x 5 card and send it to school with a piece of clear plastic CONTAC® paper. Ask her teacher to look it over and make any needed changes. Then your child or the teacher can cover it with the plastic. Your child should tape this card to the top of her desk. The teacher may still have to help your child form the habit of referring to the card.

PROBLEM: Your child often forgets her lunch.

SOLUTION: "Personal involvement"

Involve your child at every step you can. Take her with you to the grocery store, and respect her food preferences when possible. Teach her to make her lunch herself. The more involved she is, the less likely she is to forget it.

INFORMATION: Any time you increase your child's involvement in her day-to-day life you help her build skills she can use later on to become more independent and responsible.

TIP: Teach her from the beginning that cleaning up is part of using the kitchen.

SOLUTION: *"Have a backup plan"*

Give her teacher a supply of peanut butter and crackers. They don't spoil, and she can eat them if she has nothing else for lunch.

Attention
Deficit

TIP: Your child would probably rather not have peanut butter and crackers for lunch day after day, so this solution may help her remember her lunch more often.

PROBLEM: *Your child doesn't bring home everything she needs.*

SOLUTION: *"An ounce of prevention"*

Sometimes a child's backpack or notebook is so messy she has what she needs but can't find it. Once a week your child should clean out her notebook, backpack and locker—with your help if necessary.

Attention
Deficit

SOLUTION: *"More help when needed"*

Judge realistically how much help your child really needs. Some children, especially those with attentional problems, really do have severe difficulty with basic organization. While it may make sense at first to insist they remember what they need or take the consequences, you can't force a child to do something she simply isn't capable of doing yet. Some schools, for instance, have band instruction every other day, making it harder for students to remember their instruments. Other events, such as holidays, unexpected family trips or field trips at school, will throw these children off more than their classmates. Lead your child to independence, but recognize the realities of what she's able to do reliably so far.

Attention
Deficit

SOLUTION: *"Color-coding"*

Help her color-code her school materials, including textbooks, workbooks, spiral notebooks, etc.—perhaps red for all her reading

Attention
Deficit

weak
visual

materials, blue for all her spelling, etc. You can help your child put plain book covers on all her textbooks and then she can write the name of the subject on the cover in color.

Then when she's gathering up what she needs for the day's homework, she'll know that if she has science homework, she should take everything home that has science's color code.

SOLUTION: "Double-checking"

Attention
Deficit

As soon as your child comes home from school she should compare her assignment book to the contents of her backpack. An adult (or responsible teenager if you can't be home) may have to help her judge whether she has everything she needs or not.

SOLUTION: "Well-stocked desk"

Attention
Deficit

Keep duplicates of supplies at home: hole reinforcers, tape, scissors, ruler, crayons, markers, poster board, pens, pencils, calculator, 3-hole punch, construction paper, and at sixth grade and beyond, compass and protractor.

Some children, particularly those with ADD, should have an extra set of textbooks supplied by the school to keep at home.

WARNING: Making photocopies of entire textbooks or workbooks for home use violates copyright law. There are times it's legal to photocopy parts of a textbook or workbook, but this isn't one of them.

Good
IEP
idea!

IEP IDEA: If your child needs an extra set of textbooks to have at home, write it into her IEP to make sure the school provides them.

TIP: While an extra set of books at home will help your child in the short-term, you still want her to learn to get supplies from home to school and back to the best of her ability. You might consider setting up a reward system for bringing things back and forth from school reliably. If you do this, however, double-check her backpack before she leaves each day (after she has checked) to make sure you don't end up with both sets of textbooks at home. Rewards have to be highly attractive to a child with ADD before they will overcome her innate and biological tendency to forget. Although some parents will dislike the idea, sometimes small amounts of money used in a well-planned behavior modification program gets good results.

Strengths		Weaknesses

PROBLEM: *Your child forgets to return things to school the next day.*

Materials:
    A small table

SOLUTION: *"Take-it table"*

Attention
Deficit

Put a table by the door your child leaves for school through each day. If there isn't room for a table there, then change the door she leaves by and put a table by that door. She places things that must go to school on that table, and stores her backpack under it. When she's done with her homework, she should place her backpack under the table immediately.

You can use the top for lunch (to keep it away from pets) and for things you need her to take, such as field trip permission forms.

TIP: Save this table for your child's school use only. Put the mail and other non-school things elsewhere.

SOLUTION: *"Mirror, mirror, on the wall..."*

Materials:
    Post-it® notes

Your child can write reminders on Post-it® notes, and place them on the bathroom mirror at nose level before she goes to bed. In the morning, she should do whatever she needs to do immediately, as soon as she sees the note, so she doesn't forget.

PROBLEM: *Your child forgets to bring home her gym clothes—week after week.*

Materials:
    Extra set of gym clothes

SOLUTION: *"Double up"*

Attention
Deficit

Get your child two complete sets of gym clothes. Seal one set in a zippered plastic bag so it stays fresh. Each Monday your child can open the new package and put her dirty clothes in the plastic bag. If she forgets to bring the used ones home on Monday, she has the whole week to remember to do it. She should launder the old gym clothes as soon as she brings them home, and take them

| Strengths | Weaknesses |

back (sealed in a plastic bag) as soon as possible. This plan won't cost any extra money in the long run because the clothes will last longer.

Tips and tricks: listening skills

PROBLEM: *Your child often doesn't remember what people tell her.*

INFORMATION: Such students have a tremendous disadvantage. If we don't understand something we see, we can simply look at it longer. Sounds vanish quickly, unavailable for review.

SOLUTION: "K.I.S.S." (Keep it simple, sweetie)

Attention
Deficit

weak
auditory

weak
verbal

Speak in short sentences, and avoid long, detailed explanations. If you must explain something in detail, do it in the form of a conversation, and double-check along the way to make sure your child understands what you're saying.

SOLUTION: "Whisper"

Attention
Deficit

Try saying what you want very softly, which will force the child to listen more carefully. Then have your child repeat back what you want.

SOLUTION: "Repeat after me..."

Attention
Deficit

weak
auditory

Have her repeat instructions. It will help her remember, and you can double-check to make sure she understood.

SOLUTION: *"Be precise"*

Be as exact as you can about what you want your child to do: "Put your books on the shelf," not "Put your books away;" "Put the socks in the hamper," not "Take care of your socks" or "Clean up your room."

Attention
Deficit

*weak
verbal*

SOLUTION: *"Taking notes"*

Your child should try to write down key words to help her remember what to do. Her teacher can help her build this skill by writing key words on the board as she teaches.

She should combine this tip with the next suggestion, "Note taker," so she'll still have good notes to study from.

Attention
Deficit

*weak
verbal*

TIP: If your child doesn't read well yet, draw pictures. If you want her to put her laundry away, draw a laundry basket and her dresser.

SOLUTION: *"Note-taker"*

Materials:
Carbonless paper

Attention
Deficit

INFORMATION: Many children with learning disabilities or attentional problems have great difficulty taking detailed, organized notes, and some never do learn to do it well.

However, you don't want your child to give up on this vital skill easily or quickly. Instead, have a good note-taker make automatic copies of her notes using carbonless paper, and give your child the copy.

Meanwhile your child should also take notes—if it doesn't interfere with her ability to listen and learn. At first, her notes may be sparse and nearly useless, but as she sees her classmate's copies she may gradually develop better note-taking skills.

*weak
auditory*

*weak
grapho-motor*

Strengths   Weaknesses

weak
memory

weak
verbal

TIP: When students enter college, most pay a small fee to the people who take notes for them.

Attention
Deficit

SOLUTION: "Taped notes"

Materials:

Tape recorder

Your child can tape class lectures. If this helps, write it into her IEP.

STRONG
auditory

weak
memory

weak
verbal

Good
IEP
idea!

Tips and tricks: study skills

PROBLEM: Your child has trouble figuring out what to study for tests.

Materials:

Class materials—textbooks, worksheets, etc.
3 x 5 cards

SOLUTION: "Study cards"

Attention
Deficit

She should look over her textbook, notes, etc., each night. She should then write questions the teacher might ask on 3 x 5 cards and put the answer on the back. She can carry these cards with her and use odd moments to study.

weak
memory

TIPS: If she has a lot of trouble writing, do the writing for her. If she has trouble deciding what is important, you can help her with that, but don't take it over completely.

SOLUTION: "Marked copies"

Attention
Deficit

Materials:
    Highlighters in several colors
    Photocopy of material to study

Using a photocopy, she should highlight new vocabulary in one color, important names in another, important dates in another, and important concepts in a fourth—she can devise her own system. Once marked, these photocopies make excellent study materials for tests.

STRONG
global learner

weak
verbal

Then she can either study directly from the highlighted copy or make study cards.

weak
visual

TIP: Since you're photocopying the material to make necessary educational modifications and not to avoid buying the book, this tip does not violate copyright law.

PROBLEM: Your child forgets to study for tests.

SOLUTION: "Money motivates"

Attention
Deficit

Try rewarding your child for studying for least two nights in advance of tests. Require cooperation if she needs help with either studying or study skills.

INFORMATION: This may seem like bribery to some parents—especially when the most effective reward, money, is used. However, it may also raise her grades quite a bit. At the same time she'll be learning better study skills that may stay with her for the rest of her life. Such an important skill may be worth using very attractive rewards.

Strengths	Weaknesses

TIP: This book discusses behavior modification briefly on pages 74–75. See pages 77–78 for books that explain behavior modification in more detail.

Tips and tricks: special problems of social studies

PROBLEM: Your child has trouble with map skills.

TIP: If your child doesn't learn well visually, call the school and find out when map skills are emphasized. Often they are taught early in fourth grade so the children can use and understand maps as they study about European explorers such as Magellan and Columbus. You should help your child with map skills *before* she studies them at school; this will make it much easier for her to follow the teacher's lessons.

Materials:
Large map of the United States or the world
Small, colored peel-and-stick colored dots

SOLUTION: "Been there, done that"

Works with most

Hang a map on the wall. You and your family discuss together trips you've taken, and then help your child spot the places you've visited on the map. Place a colored dot on each place you've been to. Be specific. Don't just say "We drove through Utah," say "We drove through Salt Lake City," then locate it and mark that specific place.

Use another color to mark where out-of-town friends and relatives live.

If your child reads a magazine that contains articles about other places, such as *National Geographic*, she can use another color of sticker to mark places she's read about.

STRONG
grapho-motor

STRONG
nonverbal

weak
visual

SOLUTION: "Pieces of the world"

Materials:
Map of the United States
Map of the world
Scissors
Black marker
Clear CONTAC® paper

First, use the marker to trace state or country borders, the outlines of continents, and major rivers.

Then use the scissors to cut the map into sections—states, countries, or continents.

TIPS: Covering the map with plastic will make it easier to cut, and then your child can use the cut-up map as a puzzle. If your child doesn't use scissors easily, you cut the map into smaller, easier-to-handle sections for her.

SOLUTION: "Edible social studies"

STRONG
nonverbal

weak
visual

Materials:
    Non-toxic marking pen
    Two oranges
    Four toothpicks
    Sharp knife
    Globe

First, put toothpicks in the top and bottom of each orange. They mark the North and South Poles.

Next, take the first orange, and help your child draw a line around the middle. That's the equator, and when you cut the orange in half along that line you'll have divided the orange into Northern and Southern Hemispheres. Show her the equator on the globe also.

Take the second orange, but this time draw down the side of the orange from one toothpick to the other and then back up the other side. This divides the orange into Eastern and Western Hemispheres.

Then your child should say what part of the world she's going to eat: "I think I'll eat the entire Western Hemisphere!" She should find the Western Hemisphere on the globe and notice

| Strengths | | Weaknesses |

which continents and countries will be gone after she's gobbled them up.

Works with
most

SOLUTION: "Maps are useful"

Materials:
 Road map
 Map of the United States or the world
 Globe
 Highlighter

Include your child when planning the route you'll drive on family trips. Show your child on both a flat map of the world and a globe where you'll be traveling. Compare your road map to a map of the United States and to the globe.
 As you travel, your child can use a highlighting pen to mark the roads you travel on. Use a mileage counter on the speedometer to record how many miles you travel on each road.

PROBLEM: Your child doesn't get good grades in social studies.

INFORMATION: The difficulties most likely to interfere with social studies are poor reading skills, difficulty learning by looking, and attentional problems.

Works with
most

SOLUTION: "Recycled tips and tricks"

Look in other chapters of this book for suggestions that help your child's kinds of difficulties, and think about how you can modify those ideas to help her in social studies.

Tips and tricks: science

NOTE: Science often requires a lot of study. See the tips and tricks above for developing organizational and study skills.

PROBLEM: Your child learns best with hands-on activities.

Materials:
 Magnifying glass

STRONG
nonverbal

SOLUTION: "Science fun at home"

You and your child go out into your yard and neighborhood, and look for things to examine. If you live near cliffs, watch for sedimentary rock (rock formed in layers)—you can hunt for fossils. Also look at leaves (including buds and fallen ones in Autumn), bugs, different kinds of dirt and sand and anything else you can think of. Take seeds and flowers apart to examine what parts make them up.

TIP: See the end of the chapter for inexpensive science materials you can buy for home use.

SOLUTION: "Science fun in the community"

Attend science-based events offered in your community. Check the newspaper's section on upcoming events. For instance, many communities have rock and mineral shows, and sometimes they let children select free samples. Get on the mailing lists of local science museums.

Works with most

Materials you might consider purchasing:

Geography

Map of the United States puzzle
   Benefit: helps children, particularly those with weak visual-perceptual skills, learn the shape and placement of states. Manufactured by Milton Bradley, $2.95.
      or
Magnetic Puzzle Map
   Benefit: easier to handle for children who don't use their hands well; motivating. Manufactured by GoMagnet, $19.

Note: Shop around for puzzle maps. Prices ranged from $3 to $25 in one store the author visited.

Science

Home Science Kits
   The various kits contain most materials for 21 experiments (you provide consumable materials such as batteries or common kitchen supplies). Kits include "Magnetism," "The Human Body," and things designed to grab a child's attention such as "Science Magic Tricks," "Spy Science," and "Ecology."
   The electricity kit is an example of how you can explore and support school education at the same time. Many science programs teach beginning electricity concepts in fourth grade. By using this kit before the classroom gets to electricity you can eliminate some problems. The child who has trouble learning new vocabulary can begin to learn it at her own pace. The child with clumsy fingers will get extra hands-on practice manipulating electrical clips and wires so she won't feel foolish and stupid at school. The child with ADD will be able to pay better attention

to the teacher because she'll understand where the teacher is heading with her instruction.

Benefit: many, but the most important may be opportunities to create increased interest in science. Manufactured by Educational Insights for $9.95 each.

Organization

Classroom Helper Daily Planner.
This tablet of sheets includes sections for "Things to do before school," "Things to do at school," and "Things to do after school." We suggest you punch them with a three-hole punch so your child can keep the list in her binder. These sheets make a good companion for an assignment book by providing a place to list those crucial but non-homework things that must be done. Printed by Creative Teaching Press, #CTP 6024.

Books on tape

Note: please read the comments at the bottom of page 59 and the top of page 227. Taped versions of books and texts hold the power to help your child progress in school even when she has severe reading problems. Some people have completed college and even graduate school using taped books and texts. The danger is that your child will move to books on tape either too soon or too completely. They are best used as a temporary measure, giving her more time to learn to read on her own.

Sources

National Library Service
Library of Congress
Washington, D. C.
202-707-5100
or your local library
The National Library Service requires a statement of need from a physician or psychiatrist.

Talking Tapes for the Blind
3015 South Brentwood Boulevard
St. Louis, MO 63144
314-968-2557
They provide popular reading materials not available from the National Library Service. Their eligibility requirements match those of the National Library Service.

Recordings for the Blind
Princeton, New Jersey
609-452-0606
They specialize in textbooks. Plan about six months ahead; if they don't already have the text recorded on tape, they will need time to prepare it. Eligibility requirements include a statement from psychologist, physician, learning disabilities teacher or other specialist.

Conclusion

Not everything that is faced can be changed, but nothing can be changed until it is faced.

James Baldwin

Remember Bobby, the young boy at the beginning of the book who asked to repeat kindergarten and who struggled through grade school?

Bobby is one of the success stories. After eight years of frustration, including trips to several experts and one retention, he was finally diagnosed as having Attention Deficit Disorder. Within eight weeks of beginning appropriate treatment, Bobby raised his grades from C's and D's to A's and B's. He found himself achieving up to his true potential for the first time (and on the honor roll) in eighth grade.

Not all children will experience Bobby's spectacular successes. Some readers of this book will travel a tremendous adventure of self-discovery. They will find that as they suspected, their child is smart, and capable of learning.

Some will find that their child was already just where he should have been.

And some will find that all their anger at the system, the teachers, the books, the methods, the schools, was misdirected—-that their child's learning problems are real, perhaps more serious than they realized, and that the people they railed against were actually doing the very best they could to help. The author realizes this book provides few answers for these parents, and can only hope that the information and sources which have been given will help guide them to the path they need to follow, because the only real defeat is in giving up.

A teacher at a private school for learning disabled children tells the story of a man who walked the beaches after every storm. He would pick up starfish stranded on the sand by the pounding surf and fling them back into the ocean. He knew the starfish could not make the journey on their own, that without his help they would die.

"Why bother?" a passerby asked. "You are only one person, and there are millions of stranded starfish. You can do so little. What does it matter?"

"I do what I can," he replied. "It matters a great deal to this starfish." And he threw another one back into the sea.

Chapter Seven Appendix

Things that help children with ADD cope in the classroom

(Note: this doesn't mean your child is entitled to all of these modifications. It might not even be a good idea. What you want to do is to give your child enough help that he can grow but not so much that growth is stifled. Be prepared; you and the classroom teacher may disagree often on just that issue.)

Low-level interventions:

- Use untimed tests (including standardized tests). One easy way to do this is to allow the child to start the test before school.
- Provide preferential seating (near the front, away from distractions such as classroom pets, aquariums and open doors).
- Provide testing in a quiet place.
- Allow breaks during testing.
- Allow the child to begin an assignment (say, do the first three problems in math) and then come to the teacher for confirmation that he's doing it right and to get a pat on the back.
- Allow the child to repeat directions back to the teacher.
- Set up a non-verbal "return to task, please" signal—catching his eye, touching him on the shoulder, etc.
- Allow the child to time how long it takes him to complete each segment of an assignment and write it down on the paper (watch out for impulsive answers just to improve his time).
- Give any needed reprimands in private.
- Actively seek opportunities to praise the child (the teacher can keep a 3 x 5 card taped to her desk as a reminder, and put a check mark for each positive comment). Children with ADD can't hear too much appropriate praise. If you doubt that, think of all the times they hear criticism.
- Allow the child to review directions with the teacher before he begins.
- Provide an extra set of textbooks to be kept permanently at home.
- Encourage the child to tape-record lectures to provide another method for review.
- Provide the amount of support and structure the child needs to succeed, not the amount of support and structure traditional for that grade level or that classroom.
- Allow adequate time for students to answer questions to allow the student to form a thoughtful answer.
- Have a study carrel in the room that students can choose to use if they feel particularly distracted.
- Provide a few minutes at the end of the day for students to get their homework materials together (discourage visiting and other distractions during this time).
- Write assignments on the board as they are given.
- Make sure the duplicated materials are clear, dark and easy to read.

More supportive interventions:

- Encourage use of a note-taker (done simply by providing a good note-taker with carbonized paper. The student with ADD should take notes as well to the best of his ability.)
- Divide assignments into three or four segments and allow the child to check in with the teacher after each segment is completed.
- Allow use of a calculator to check accuracy of math completed with pencil and paper.

Provide support while encouraging growth with these strategies:

- For children with strong computer skills, encourage use of word processing programs for all writing assignments.
- Encourage use of computer spell-checkers, thesaurus and grammar checkers.
- Allow a reduced course load.
- Provide extended time to complete courses of study.
- Provide photocopies of overlays, lecture notes, etc.
- For children who work slowly, reduce the size of required assignments.
- Invite an older student to come in and help the child get organized for the day (work this out with another teacher in the building who has a student needing a self-esteem builder). This will require some supervision and coaching at first. The child with ADD should have the same helper every day.
- Encourage "study buddies." The child with ADD checks with his study buddy to make sure he has assignments written down correctly, is taking home everything he needs, etc.
- When you give several assignments or multiple-step instructions, allow the child to write them down. Then provide him with a written list so he can double-check what you said.
- Allow the use of a calculator to get math facts not yet memorized.
- As you talk, write key words on the board to aid in note-taking.
- Help students with ADD plan how they will break larger assignments into smaller, more manageable tasks. They should create a checklist to keep track of their progress on the project.

Strong interventions; should be used only when other methods have failed:

- Use modified test formats (such as multiple-choice instead of essay). The older the child, the more potential this intervention this has to hold your child back. It's more serious when a tenth grader can't write an essay answer than when a third grader can't.
- Waive any foreign language requirement.
- Allow use of a calculator for all math under all circumstances.

Recommend these books to your child's school:

CH.A.D.D. *Educator's Manual.* CH.A.D.D., 499 NW 70th Ave., Suite 109, Plantation, FL 33317. $10.00 plus shipping/handling.

Hawthorne Educational Services Inc. *The Attention Deficit Disorders Intervention Manual.* For information, call 314-874-1710. For orders only, call 1-800-542-1673.

Rief, Sandra F. *How to Reach and Teach ADD/ADHD Children: Practical Techniques, Strategies, and interventions for Helping Children with Attention Problems and Hyperactivity.* 1993, The Center for Applied Research in Education. ISBN: 0-87628-413-6.

Chapters Nine and Ten Appendix

How to use the "Reading Words Review List"

Not all children will need this chart, so don't make extra work for yourself. You need to use this chart if your child has difficulty learning and remembering sight words. You'll use it to keep track of what words he's learned, what words he's retained, and what words need to be reviewed again.

If your child has great difficulty learning and remembering sight words, this chart becomes an easy way to keep reviewing the words he needs to learn. The chart will also keep you from giving new words to your child faster than he can learn them. If you find that he misses more than 10% of his review words, you are giving new words too fast. If the teacher is the one sending the new words home, take the chart to her and show her the difficulty your child has retaining the words he's studied.

Using the chart

1. List your child's new words in the "Words to learn" column. Include all words from his stack of cards—the ones he already knows as well as the new ones. For demonstration purposes we used *again* and *they* for the first week's words. Your child may have up to 12 new words.

2. Practice the words for a week using suggestions from this chapter.

3. At the end of the week, check to see which words he knows. Have him read the words from the list, not from his cards, in case he's using tiny smudges or other extraneous clues to help him when he reads the cards. In the "Week 1" column put "smiley faces" by any words he knows. Also put the day's date by the first word in that set so you know when they've been checked. In this example the child knew both of his new words at the end of the first week.

4. For the second week he'll have more words; list those below the first week's words. For demonstration purposes we listed only one new word— *where*. Your child would have multiple new words, but again, any words repeated from the previous week plus his new words should total no more than twelve words altogether.

5. At the end of the second week, you check all his words—last week's and this week's. In our example, the child has gotten the word *again* right two weeks in a row, but he missed *they* on 9/23. *They* was included with the next week's words.

In looking at the sample chart on the next page, we see that on 10/1, the end of the third week, this child got the word *they* right but missed *again*. The pattern of

READING WORD REVIEW LIST					
Words to learn	**Week 1**	**Week 2**	**Week 3**	**Week 4**	
again 9/8	9/15 ☺	9/23 ☺	10/1	10/8 ☺	
they	☺		☺	☺	
where 9/15	9/23 ☺	10/1 ☺	10/8 ☺		
they 9/23	☺	☺			

getting them right one week but not the next happens frequently and is why you need to keep checking. Any words he misses in this way can be added to the next week's words and listed again in the "Words to learn" column. Remember, one week's list of words should never contain more than twelve words. If he begins to learn them more quickly, add new lists more than once a week. Doing more than one list a week is far better than making the weekly list longer.

After a few weeks you may have a lot of words to check. You'll want to break these vocabulary checks into smaller sections at some point. There are two reasons you shouldn't skip checking that chart.

First, assuming your child hasn't been rushed through the words and knows them, it's a marvelous opportunity for him to succeed, and succeed well in your presence. Each "smiley" is tangible praise from you that can't be denied. Our experience is that children enjoy having their word lists checked because of all the "smileys" they get. They often enjoy counting all the "smileys" as well.

Second, if he isn't retaining the words he studies, you need to know as soon as possible. If you find he forgets more than 10% of the words from week to week, you need to alert his teachers so you and they can modify what you're all doing.

To use the Spelling Words Review List, follow the same steps just described for sight vocabulary.

The Sight Words Review List Form follows on page 232, and the form for keeping track of spelling words is on page 233. Except for their titles, they are identical. Feel free to photocopy these forms for your use.

READING WORD REVIEW LIST

	Week 1	Week 2	Week 3	Week 4	Week 6	Week 8

SPELLING WORDS REVIEW LIST						
	Week 1	Week 2	Week 3	Week 4	Week 6	Week 8

Taming the Dragon
by Nancy Eggleston

I peered through the crack in my son's bedroom door
and discovered a bundle asleep on the floor.

He was tangled in toys that he's played with all day.
I saw spaceships and monsters he'd made out of clay.

There were books about planets, comets and stars...
and models of rockets, and flashy race cars.

He was all twisted up in one glorious heap!
He'd played past his bedtime, then fell off to sleep.

But snug in the bed where my son ought to be
were two dragon eyes staring right back at me.

He was making some plans! I could see it again
from his playful, mischievous, imaginative grin.

With an authoritative look of motherly might
I bid this invisible dragon good night.

Then his breathing slowed down as he rested his head
and propped up his tail on the end of the bed.

So I tiptoed inside to the bed, where I sat
while the dragon and I had a heart-to-heart chat.

"You took my alarm clock apart once again
to see how the gears work," is where I begin.

"The concoction you made in my blender today
was a Pulitzer-prize winning potion," I say.

"But the homework you 'borrowed' for your paper airplanes
belonged to your sister, who's calling you names!

"And the haircut you gave yourself wasn't your best!
I can see in the dark that you've trimmed off the rest.

"It's hard to keep up with a dragon your size;
it's the havoc you play and the plans you devise!

"I'm confused!" I explode. "What's a mother to do
with a curious, frustrating dragon like you?"

Then the dragon shared secrets—most which I've kept
since the night that we talked while my little boy slept.

He talked about children who struggle to cope
and imparted some wisdom, and knowledge, and hope.

He told about taming the dragons within
and asked for some patience before I begin.

Then I hugged my dear dragon, and smiled at my son...
all tangled in hopes and in a life just begun.

Index